Spanning Time

A Diary Keeper Becomes a Writer
by Elizabeth Yates

Foreword by Barbara Elleman

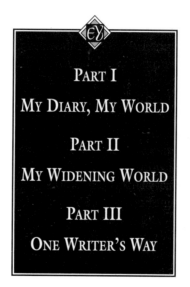

PART I
MY DIARY, MY WORLD

PART II
MY WIDENING WORLD

PART III
ONE WRITER'S WAY

COBBLESTONE PUBLISHING, INC.
7 School Street
Peterborough, New Hampshire 03458

Remembering my father and my mother,
who gave me great gifts—security, discipline, and their love.

Manufactured in the United States of America

Library of Congress Cataloging-in-Publication Data

Yates, Elizabeth, 1905–
    Spanning time : a diary keeper becomes a writer / by Elizabeth
Yates.
      p.   cm.
    Contents: pt. 1. My diary, my world — pt. 2. My widening world —
pt. 3. One writer's way.
    Originally published: Philadelphia : Westminster Press, 1981-1984.
    Summary: A collection of diary entries from 1917 to 1950 portray
the life of an aspiring writer.
    ISBN 0-942389-13-1
    1. Yates, Elizabeth, 1905- —Biography—Juvenile literature.
    2. Authors, American—20th century—Biography—Juvenile literature.
    3. Children's literature—Authorship—Juvenile literature.
    [1. Yates, Elizabeth, 1905- . 2. Authors, American.
    3. Authorship.] I. Title.
    PS3547.A745Z476 1996
    818'.5203—dc20
    [B]__
                      96-14192
                      CIP
                      AC

Excerpt from "Glad Day" in SELECTED POEMS AND PARODIES by Louis Untermeyer, copyright 1935 by Harcourt Brace & Company and renewed 1963 by Louis Untermeyer, reprinted by permission of the publisher.

Picture Credits

Elizabeth Yates Collection: front cover, 10, 27, 39, 53, 63, 75, 87, 105, 121, 137, 149, 171, 191, 205, 215, 219, 227, 236, 250, 259, 270, 281, 289, back cover; Museum of the City of New York, The Gottscho-Schleisner Collection: 127; Eunice Stephenson: 159; The Elizabeth Yates Collection, Boston University Libraries: 298, 312; Cover illustration by Nora Unwin from *Amos Fortune, Free Man* by Elizabeth Yates © 1950. Permission granted by Dutton Children's Books, a division of Penguin Books USA, New York: 305.

ABOUT THE COVER
Elizabeth Yates, about the time she began writing in her diary (front),
and in school at 15 (back).

Contents

Foreword

"Often it seems that writing is mostly thinking. Sometimes not a single word [gets] put down on paper, but they're all in my head, getting themselves ready." These words, written when Elizabeth Yates was 14, exemplify her deep belief in herself as a writer. And committed she was: In thinking about Maurice Maeterlinck's *The Blue Bird,* where Father Time says that each child brings something to the world, she writes— "I think I came with a pencil in my hand."

Despite parental objections, although not without their love, Yates persevered in her writing endeavors and, in 1951, her book *Amos Fortune, Free Man* won the prestigious Newbery Award, given by the American Library Association for a distinguished contribution to writing.

The diary of her early life, *My Diary, My World,* as well as its sequels, *My Widening World* and *One Writer's Way — The Creative Years,* are inspiring portraits of Yates' dedication to her craft. They present an appealing picture of a young girl growing up in the early part of the century who made books and reading an integral part of her life. The stimulation and comfort she found in the works of Austen, Keats, and Kipling helped mold her own poems and works of fiction. And while she carefully honed her skills, she also learned to deal with rejection as she attempted to get her works published.

Today's would-be writers will find Yates' story profound. While some readers will see her diary as a path to beginning their autobiographies, others will be motivated to study their own family history; still others will simply find a good story.

Barbara Elleman, Editor, Book Links

Introduction

It was a small square book bound in red leather and on its cover were the words *A Line a Day*. Opening it, there were four lines for each day, going through a year with weeks and months, and under them were the same number of lines for the next year, and under them more lines, until five years were accounted for. It had been given to me by a family friend and I accepted it as a trust. So I began on January first, 1917, four lines a day, writing small when there was much to say, writing big when events were minimal. Through the years my handwriting changed but the lines were there to catch the moment and the mood, the great happenings as well as the minutiae that all were a part of growing.

When completed, it *had* to be continued for another five years. A taller, wider book was found and a freer, more journalistic style was used, for events now were not so important as the thoughts they engendered. The daily exercise was proving to be right for someone who wanted to be a writer. At twenty-two I was well on my way to using words as my chosen work in life and my journal was still my confidante.

Looking back over this memorabilia of the years I can laugh at myself, and I can cry, too—the joys were so real, the anguish so intense. Seeing both from the vantage of ongoing years I can see the difficult balanced by continuing challenge and the satisfaction of recognition. Drawn from the diligent daily accounting, a narrative has emerged. Beginning in 1917, it goes up to the time of the Newbery Medal, in 1951. From then on the words speak for themselves.

Elizabeth Yates, Concord, New Hampshire, 1996

Editor's Note

Elizabeth Yates' diaries, on which *Spanning Time* is based, continue to touch the hearts of children—even those living in the 1990s. The author is proud of this. Recently when I was visiting her in Concord, New Hampshire, she shared with me a letter written by Kristi Sadowski of Canton Center, Connecticut. Kristi, who portrayed Elizabeth Yates in a school project, wrote to the author saying that she found her life interesting and that Bobby, Bluemouse, and Brier must have been good friends. The Diaries proved so interesting that Kristi asked Elizabeth Yates to tell her *more* about her life.

As you read the following pages, which combine all of Elizabeth Yates' early diaries—*My Diary, My World; My Widening World;* and *One Writer's Way*—you will definitely see how this interesting life came to unfold and you will get to meet Bobby, Bluemouse, and Brier. Elizabeth Yates is clearly a lover of words and is able to weave them together into wonderful stories. Ever since she was a young girl she dreamed of being a writer, and she held firm to this belief. Kristi Sadowski easily recognized this—she ended her letter with a P.S.: "I very firmly believe that your dream came true."

Elizabeth Yates was extremely helpful in preparing this new edition, and supplied us with many personal and family photographs from her collection.

Carolyn P. Yoder, Editor, Cobblestone Publishing, Inc.

Part I

My Diary, My World

MY DIARY — *My World*

I hear them calling my name, but I have no intention of answering. I'm in one of my secret places and there is so much to think about, because it's my birthday, December 6, 1917, and I'm twelve years old.

Birthdays are always special in our family. Mother put the first present under my pillow, and when I woke up I could hear the crinkle of tissue paper. Last year it was a small wooden horse, just something for me to feel and love. This year it's a hair ribbon, which I wore to school. Even though I don't say anything, I feel that people must know it's my birthday—as if my face were shining.

Last year, Miss Hyde gave me a book without any words in it. It will have only words that I write myself. On the red-leather cover is the title *A Line a Day*. There are really four lines for every day, and they are spaced so the book can be used for five years. I felt shivery with excitement when I made my entry on January first. If lots of things happen I write small, and when nothing particular happens I write big; and there's always the weather. Almost a year has gone by now and I haven't missed a single day.

I have a secret inside me about writing books. When I was little, I liked to draw pictures of letters instead of stick figures and houses and suns. An *R* was beautiful, and an *S* curvy, and an *O* had a way of keeping something inside it. But making letters won't make a writer. It takes words and thoughts. That's what my diary is helping me to do.

Brier has just pushed the door open and snuggled up beside me. He may be the family dog, but he spends more time with me than anyone else. It's cozy here in Father's clothes closet, and there are such nice smells from his suits and from the leather of his shoes.

The opening Brier made brought in some light and I can see on the top shelf the Santa Claus suit folded away carefully. Harry, who is two years older, kept the secret from me until I found out for myself, and I'll keep it from Bobby, who is four years younger than me. When he finds it out, he'll probably feel, as I did, that he had always known. Perhaps that's the way with everything: we make our own discoveries and keep them to ourselves.

Today is my birthday and St. Nicholas Day, and deep inside me I feel both serious and happy. Remembering is like a light that shines out of the things that have been, into the things that will be.

Brier is pushing against me and telling me we should go. Dinner will be extra special tonight. There will be presents, a cake with twelve small candles and one big one "to grow on." If I'm lucky, I'll blow them all out at once, but not until they've burned quite far down. It's something to be twelve years old—a last time and a first time at the same time. I wonder what this year will be in my life? Whatever happens, I'll be writing it down in my diary.

The story begins…

1918

January 7, 1918

Christmas ended last night with the burning of the tree, but I think it was the best Christmas ever.

As soon as Jinny got back from college we started learning our lines and rehearsing the play she had written. It's our present to Mother and Father. We gave it on Christmas Eve in a corner of the living room.

Before we began, Mother lit the big candle that has such a lovely waxy fragrance. "It must always be the first light in the house," she said, and the only reason she gave was that her mother did it and her mother's mother before her. "It's a tradition, an Irish custom that goes far back into the past." When Mother touched a match to the wick she said, "Wish or pray." I wished, but I think she prayed.

Then we did the play. There was a time when all seven of us could be the cast, but now that Teresa is married and Walter is in the Army, there's just Dick and Harry and Bobby and me, so we get our friends in to help. The play was about Mary and Joseph and the Baby, shepherds and kings. After it was over we had supper. Oyster stew—that's another tradition—followed by little mince pies.

Bobby and I left a snack for Santa in the kitchen before we went up to bed; then we hung up our stockings and promised ourselves to stay awake. Suddenly it was morning and there were our stockings all knobbly with things in them. Downstairs, the big tree filled the air with fragrance, and presents were piled under it. Holly wreaths were in the windows and laurel was twined through the banisters.

Santa had eaten his snack and left a note, written in red ink in handwriting so tiny that we had to use a magnifying glass to read it. We knew his writing because we'd been sending letters to him for weeks, placing them in the unused fireplace in the guest room, and he always answered. Even when I was little, I never wondered how a big man could write so small, or get down a chimney, or travel around the world in one night. It was part of the magic of Christmas. Now I know that the magic is made by people who care, and those people are Mother and Father.

We didn't get a chance to open our presents until Father had his tradition, something that goes back into his English past.

After breakfast we all gathered in the living room. Maria came in from the kitchen, Andy came, and Lizzie, and Miss Hyde, of course. To each one, Father made a little speech of appreciation. Then he gave them their presents—a pocketbook for a woman, a wallet for a man, each with a crisp new $5 bill in it. Then it was our turn. The presents I get most excited about are books. There were several, because we try to help each other build up our sets. Bobby wanted to try his new Flexible Flyer right away, and Harry his skates. They could. That's one of the best things about living in Buffalo, New York. It's always cold at Christmas and there's plenty of snow.

I could hardly wait to get into my books, but knew it wouldn't be possible until evening. Vacation nights are like Friday nights during school. No homework, and bedtime an hour later. I could hardly wait until I could curl up in the big leather chair in the den and read. Soon I'm in another world and the people are as real as the members of my family or my friends at school.

Nothing ever tasted so good as the roast beef and Yorkshire pudding we had for dinner, and when Lizzie brought in the big round plum pudding for dessert, it was all on fire. Mother spooned some of the brandy onto each plate, but the dancing blue flames went out before any of us had a chance to blow on them.

The Party and the Play were the next great events. By midafternoon the house was swarming with relatives and friends, all ages and shapes and sizes, and everybody wishing everybody else a Merry Christmas. In the midst of the hubbub came a beautiful silence when Mother lighted the candle again. After that, the house lights were turned on and the tiny colored bulbs on the tree. We gave the play, and then we had things to eat. Best of all were the ice-cream Santa Claus figures, each standing in a nest of spun sugar, with a tiny lighted candle sticking out of Santa's pack.

We did the play again on Twelfth Night, and there was another party. That was the third time, and we were really word perfect with our lines because Jinny insisted on our rehearsing even though it was vacation. Twelfth Night is different, and special in its own way. All day we took down Christmas, the wreaths from the windows, the laurel from the stairs, and packed away the ornaments from the tree. Then Andy took the tree to the snow-covered lawn back of the house, and everything that could burn was piled on it. Not a vestige of Christmas was left in the house.

When Father touched a match to the pile, the fire spread quickly through the dry needles. Holly crackled, laurel sputtered, and the flames looked as if they might reach up to touch the stars. Everybody had a piece of the greenery to toss into the fire, and make a wish. Then we joined hands and walked around it, singing carols for the last time. The house looked plain and empty when we returned to it, but right. There have been twelve lovely days. Now I must tuck them away in the little box of memory, the way we did the ornaments from the tree.

January 10, 1918

Before Jinny went back to college she gave me a reading list—Dickens, Scott, Thackeray, Hardy, Conrad, George Eliot, and ever so many others. Three whole pages with all the titles of the books and the authors in her strong handwriting.

"It will take you years and years," she said in that clear, sure way of hers, "but if you don't read the Classics before you're eighteen, you may never read them."

"Most of the books are on the shelves in the den."

"Yes, most of them. You're too old now to read The Little Colonel books and the Five Little Peppers. You've reached the age when you should read books that stretch your mind."

Something in her tone made me want to do just that, but I knew that I could still read the books on the shelf in my room, the books I'd been growing up with. *The Cuckoo Clock* and *The Little Lame Prince, The Secret Garden* and *Little Women, At the Back of the North Wind* and *Nils, The Wind in the Willows* and others that I would always love.

Jinny is seven years older than me. She's beautiful and brilliant. Her hair is long and fair, and now that she is doing it up in a knot, she looks more than ever like one of the Greek goddesses in my mythology book. She can do everything well, even to tying the tie of her Peter Thomson suit, which I can never do with mine. And she doesn't get into trouble, which I do all the time. She writes not only the plays but other things, like a song for the Jugs and wonderful letters. She will be a very great writer someday, I know. I would do anything for her, and yet I can't seem to tell her, the way I can tell Brier, my secrets or my dream of being a writer.

When she asked me why I was still playing with my dollhouse, I said I wasn't playing.

"What are you doing, then?"

"I don't know." Somehow I couldn't seem to explain. Maybe I thought she would laugh at me. When people do that it makes something inside me go into a knot.

The dollhouse is almost as tall as I am and it's been in the family for a long time. First it was Teresa's, then it was Jinny's, and now it's mine. It's like a world, the way the inside of a book is. When I get home from school in the afternoon I like to go to it, pull up my little green rocker, sit down and look at the people, wondering what they've been doing while I was away from them and what they will do now that I'm back. Imagining—that is the most fun I know. It gives a little thrill of power to know that they'll do what I make up for them.

It doesn't matter, now, whether the day went well in school or not, whether things have been happy or not. Here in this world, with this family, I can make everything go right. I move the father into one room, the mother into another, and the other people one by one. When I hear what they are saying to each other, extraordinary things begin to happen. The dollhouse and its family take on a life of their own, and I'm at the center of it. That's what I was doing when Bobby came and sat down on the floor beside me.

I moved Mr. and Mrs. Stockton close together, as they had things to say to each other. Then Mr. Stockton went to the window to look at the thermometer. He turned and said something to Mrs. Stockton, who suddenly flew upstairs to the children's room.

"What are they doing?" Bobby whispered.

"They had a disagreement and their words were quite unkind, but everything is all right now."

"What was it about?"

"Whether the weather was warm enough for the children to wear socks to school. Mrs. Stockton said it was and Mr. Stockton said it wasn't."

"Father doesn't let us wear socks until the thermometer says sixty."

"That's what Mrs. Stockton said it was and Mr. Stockton said it wasn't. They really had quite an argument. Then Mr. Stockton went to the window and saw that the thermometer said sixty-two—he had read it wrong! Didn't you see Mrs. Stockton fly upstairs to tell the children?"

"Yes, I did. Did Mr. Stockton say he was sorry when he found out that he'd been wrong?"

"No. There wasn't time."

"I think he should."

"Do you? Should he go upstairs now or wait until Mrs. Stockton comes down?"

"Wait, then he can say it privately."

So I brought Mrs. Stockton down to the parlor and stood her before her husband.

"What are you going to do now?" Bobby asked.

"I don't know. I've got to think. It takes a lot of time to make up something real."

"Don't go on thinking so much that it makes you late for supper.

Why don't you come downstairs now?"

"I'll come in a minute. I want to say good night to the Stocktons before I leave them."

When Bobby went away I thought more about him than about the Stocktons. I love him so and wish he could always be the way he is. But he has to grow up, too, the way we all do. Perhaps it's just the dollhouse family who stays the same.

I put them in different places—the father in a chair near the table where a newspaper was open, the mother in a chair by her sewing basket, the children in bed and the cook in the kitchen. They will be like that when I see them tomorrow, but what adventures will they have had to tell me about?

I was almost late for supper, but not quite, and, as usual, Father asked me if I had been at the head of my class today.

It's nice when I can say yes, because Father's smile and the twinkle in his eyes mean more than the gold star on my report card, but I had to say, "Not in arithmetic."

He looked so sad that it made me resolve to try harder than ever tomorrow. Then I told them about the important thing that had happened.

"I learned a new word."

"What is it?" Mother asked.

"Heretic. I was even called one."

"Why are you a heretic?" Father wanted to know.

"Because I said that Brier would go to Heaven when he died, that all animals did."

"Have you looked the word up in the dictionary?"

"Not yet, but I shall this evening when I'm doing my homework. Aren't you glad I'm a heretic?"

I told them that in Mythology class we were discussing the story of Romulus and Remus being suckled by a wolf. I said that that wolf must have a very special place in Heaven, and Miss Kelly said animals didn't go to Heaven because they didn't have souls. I said I knew that Brier had a soul and that he would go to Heaven someday. Miss Kelly called me a heretic, and I felt sure that it must mean something brave and strong.

Mother said that religion and politics were not topics for conversation at a meal. That made me so mad I exploded, because I wasn't talking about either one. Before I had a chance to say any more, Mother excused me from the table. So I went up to my room to write it all down in my diary.

But I found I couldn't write anything! As soon as I sat down at my desk I started to cry. I put my head down and cried and cried. It's bad enough to miss dessert, but it's worse not to be understood. I was still crying when Bobby came up with a plate of caramel custard.

Later, much later, because I'd finished my homework and was in bed, Mother came in to kiss me good night. A few minutes later Father came. "Just be sure you know the meaning of words before you use them," he said. Then he patted me on the shoulder and put out the light.

February 5, 1918

If I write very small and use a pen with a very fine point, I can get fifteen lines in a space for four. That's what I had to do to describe a wonderful dream.

There was an apple tree with many apples on it, looking especially red because the sky above was so blue. The tree was on the other side of a brick wall, but there was a ladder leaning against the wall. It was a high wall, but the ladder was high, too, and its top reached right up into the tree. I started to climb up the ladder. It was so real that I could feel the way my hands grasped the rungs and my toes curled around them. I climbed and climbed toward the red apples and the blue sky. Then I woke up.

The harder I tried to go back to sleep to make the dream go on, the more I woke up. What did it mean? What do dreams mean, anyway? Maria has a dream book, so I went down to the kitchen to talk with her. She was just starting to get breakfast and didn't want to be bothered, but she got the book from its place on her shelf of cookbooks and opened it to "Ladder."

"It means you're going to work hard for what you want."

"But will I get it?"

"It doesn't say. Now, run along and get dressed and let me get on with breakfast."

March 2, 1918

Mother calls housework "privileges" and maybe it's true, because something besides the doing is always there, too. When I help Lizzie clean the silver, she tells me stories about Ireland and leprechauns and odd, lovely things.

Sewing one afternoon a week with Miss Hyde is generally hemming sheets or darning stockings. We don't talk much, but it's very peaceful, and if I have something to tell her, she listens to me as if she had all the time in the world. I do a lot of wondering about Miss Hyde and make up stories in my mind about her.

Saturday morning it's ironing and that's best of all. Mrs. Schmidt comes on Thursdays and Fridays to do the washing, and on Saturdays it's ironing. The flatwork is set aside for me—handkerchiefs, table napkins, towels. Before Jinny went off to college she was doing blouses and petticoats. I'll get up to them sometime, but for now it is just the plain things.

The laundry room in the basement is warm and steamy. The flatirons that sit on top of the coal stove always look ready for work. Mrs. Schmidt tests the one she hands me to be sure that it's not too hot, and then she cautions me not to get to dreaming, because she doesn't want me to scorch anything. I tell her I'm not dreaming, that I'm thinking. Father's monogrammed handkerchiefs, Mother's that are trimmed with lace, all have stories to them.

Even better than ironing is when we take a little rest and Mrs. Schmidt tells me stories. Hers are mostly fairy tales that came with her from her childhood in Germany. They're different from Lizzie's, for they often make my skin creep, while Lizzie's make my toes feel like dancing.

Today Mrs. Schmidt wiped her face, not from the steam in the room but from tears for her Germany, and she told me that I must call her Mrs. Smith.

"But why? My best friend, Carl, is German. His father is a doctor, and he's not going to change his name just because there's a war."

"Maybe he can stand to lose. If I lose a little, I have nothing left."

My heart cried with Mrs. Schmidt, but not my eyes. I think of the Stockton family and know that with them I can make everything come out right, but I can't do that with the world. Year after year, since 1914, the war has been overshadowing everything. When our country went into it, about a year ago, it became a part of all our lives. Walter is in training camp, Jean's brother is fighting in France, and everybody is different. People don't eat sausages anymore, and dachshunds have disappeared, even music by composers like Mozart and Wagner has been torn out of books.

At dancing school I'm the only girl who likes to dance with Carl. The others say his father is a spy. What a lie! He's one of the best doctors in Buffalo, an American citizen too, but few people go to him now. The other day Carl was walking home with me from school and we got pelted with snowballs. I turned quickly enough to see who was doing it and ran fast enough to get one of the boys by the collar. I shook him until he apologized.

"Carl and I have been friends since we were five years old, Mrs. Schmidt, and I'd defend him with my life."

"*Ja, ja,*" she said. "Now we go on with our work."

There was still a pile of handkerchiefs, so when she handed me a hot iron I started in on them.

In addition to the war news, which seems to get worse all the time, there's another influenza epidemic sweeping the country. I had influenza last year, which makes me immune, and I'm glad. I've got a perfect attendance record at school and don't want to break it. So many are absent that we can't get on with lessons as we should, and the death notices in the paper take columns. Mother seems to spend her evenings writing letters of condolence. Her days are spent at the Red Cross, and she's often not home even when we get back from school. But Miss Hyde is there. I don't know what we'd do without her.

Jean and I go down to the Red Cross on Saturday afternoons to roll bandages, pack Comfort Kits, and write letters to go in them. It's hard to write a letter to someone you don't know and will never see. Father is on the Draft Board and often doesn't get home until late. Sometimes it seems as if there's nothing in our lives but the war. Then it came so close that it felt like a cold wind blowing over me. Miss Kelly has died!

March 15, 1918

"She was frail and far from young, but a very good teacher," Mother said. "The funeral is on Friday. It may not be too well attended because so many people are sick and others don't want to risk being in crowds."

March 22, 1918

We went. I wore my Sunday coat and hat, and gloves. Just think, I've lived more than twelve years and this is the first time I've known anyone to die, or seen a dead person. The casket was open and when the service was over we walked solemnly up to it to say good-by. Miss Kelly looked as still as a statue and so white. It tore a hole in my heart just to see her, and I thought of all the times I had made trouble for her in class. I made a promise then and there to try to be better. It was raining when we came out of the church. It seemed right that the sky should weep for Miss Kelly.

I want to be worthy of my country and do all I can to help win the war. One way is with our club, the Just Us Girls. Last year we helped the animals in the war zone. We raised money for the Blue Cross when we had a bazaar of things we had made ourselves, and a Maypole Dance. The letter we received from Our Dumb Friends' League in England, acknowledging our check of $137.71, is one of our proudest possessions.

"What shall we do this year?" was the question we six asked ourselves when we met in our clubhouse.

I wonder what we would ever do if Dick and Harry had not turned their clubhouse over to us to use? It's a shed next to the barn where horses used to be, but where the Pierce Arrow now sits. We have it only one day a week. Bobby and his friends use it as their playhouse on other days. Our meetings begin with a patriotic song like "Pack Up Your Troubles in Your Old Kit Bag," or "It's a Long Way to Tipperary," but we always end with the national anthem. We knit and make things for our sale, sachets and pincushions and pen wipers, and we make plans. Sometimes it seems as if each one of us had a different idea. Brier attends our meetings and it's good he can't talk. Seven ideas might be too many.

"Last year you wrote Mr. Potter to ask if we could use his garden for the Maypole Dance," Jean remembered, "and he said yes and sent us a check for $25 to start us."

"And he did say not to hesitate to call on him again whenever our services were enlisted in a worthy charity," Sue reminded us.

As president of the Jugs, I was the one to write Mr. Potter again. He replied, not only offering his house but his magic lantern machine and pictures to go with it. Working hard, we sold two hundred tickets at 25 cents each. The sale of our nosegays and needlework brought in more money, and the total we raised was $123.82. An "anonymous friend"—I suspect that it was Mr. Potter—brought the sum up to $125, and we were very pleased. We try to do our bit to help win the war, and everything makes us feel that we don't want to do anything else.

The films now are all about the war, and there's a play called *Lilac Time* that Father took the six Jugs to. It made us laugh and cry at the same time and feel even more patriotic than ever. A week later there was a Special Benefit at which a British soldier spoke. His name is Guy Empey and he has written a book called *Over the Top*. I can hardly believe that I have listened to, then shaken hands with, a man who has killed a Hun and written a book.

April 26, 1918

Today Mother said she wanted to have a talk with me. I didn't understand what she was saying and I didn't like it. It seems that something is happening in my body and I'm developing into a woman. She gave me a book: *What Every Young Girl Should Know*. It made me mad. Does this mean I'm not going to grow any more? How awful, and I'm not tall enough yet to be a center in basketball! As soon as I could, I called Jean and said I had to talk with her. She told me to come right over. I did, and told her what Mother had said about my being developed.

Jean explained, in words that I could understand, what was taking place in my body. "I know, because I've had it. It's like a special kind of secret."

"But you have to have a secret with somebody."

"This one you have with yourself and with the future."

"The future?"

"The woman you'll be someday."

"Then I'm not going to stop growing?"

"Of course not. You've really just begun. You'll be as tall as Jinny and you'll be rounded, not so scrawny."

"Mother gave me a book—"

"I know that book. It's silly and it doesn't really say a thing. Mummie got one for me, but we just laughed over it."

Jean's mother came in before we'd finished talking. It made me wince when I saw how natural they were with each other, like two sisters.

Back home again, I put the book in the farthest corner of my clothes closet and called to Brier—he's never very far away. We sat on the floor together. I put my arms around him and started to cry. I don't know why, but Brier did, because after a while he licked my face and it made me feel better.

June, 1918

School is over and we've moved out to the farm, to the big brick house on the hill. From it you can see in every direction—fields and woods and sky. Father's office may be in Buffalo, but Hillhurst Farm, Orchard Park, is the place he really enjoys. So do we. Jinny is home from college, Harry and Dick have jobs but they're on the farm, Bobby and I have our tasks, but there is always time for riding, wading in the creek, picnics, and fun.

When I lean my arms on the windowsill of my room I can see cows grazing in the pastures, the Holsteins that Father is so proud of. When they go to county and state fairs they win ribbons for their records in milk production and butterfat.

In the fields the teams are working the first hay. Some of it is being winnowed, some is being loaded onto wagons to be brought up to the barns. The air is sweet with the smell. The draft horses are all strawberry roans. Father has a special feeling for them.

I can hear chickens cackling in the hen houses across the road. Some of them are the Bantams that will be my care. There are pigeons cooing from the rooftop and flying in circles, round and round. In the barn near the house Al has the horses ready for us, Bobby's Buster and my Joe and three new hunters that Father got this spring. Jinny has had them all out and says they are high-spirited and responsive. Perhaps next year I'll be old enough for a big horse, but I love Joe so much and we understand each other.

July 14, 1918

Today is perfect; that's because it's Sunday. Father doesn't go in to Buffalo to his office, Mother puts her Red Cross work aside, and we're all home.

After breakfast, Andy brought the Pierce Arrow up to the door and we went down to the village to church. Father drove. Maybe next week Al will bring the phaeton up to the door and Mother will take Waverly Belle's reins in her hands. Of course, it takes longer to go the two miles with a horse, but there's always so much to see along the way. When we got home, Al had just finished turning the ice-cream freezer for Sunday dinner. He saved the dasher for Bobby and me to lick. It was delicious, made with raspberries from the garden and cream from the cows that graze the Hillhurst pastures.

After dinner Father took up the Sunday paper, but before he got lost in it he read the *Katzenjammer Kids* to Bobby and me. At least they haven't changed their names! They are German through and through and couldn't possibly be anything else. They say *ach* and *ja*, and Father always reads with emphasis in the right places. As far as we're concerned, the Funnies section is the best part of the paper.

For supper, Mother made tabasco eggs in the chafing dish on the table, and there was a big bowl of salad from the garden. Sunday is so beautiful! It makes me wish that every day could be Sunday, but if it were, we'd never get any work done.

Even here, where the life of the farm goes on as it always has and there's so much to do and so much fun, the war is like a shadow over everything. The news in the papers is more and more serious. Defeat follows defeat, but the Allies carry on, confident of victory. So many men have gone off to the war that the farm would suffer if we didn't all help and so do our bit.

July 19, 1918

One of the big fields has been planted to beans and potatoes so there will be more food to send abroad. This morning we went to it to weed and hoe. Leaving the house, we sang "Pack Up Your Troubles in Your Old Kit Bag," and it made us feel very patriotic. It was hot in the field, and dusty, but the work is important. I counted the bugs I knocked off the potatoes with a wooden paddle, into a tin pail, and there were exactly one thousand! It was tiring, really tiring, but when I think of the soldiers fighting in France I tell myself that our battles with weeds and bugs are helping to win the war, too.

At noon we marched up the hill home singing "It's a Long Way to Tipperary." We asked if we could go back to the field in the afternoon, but Mother said no, that she'd rather have us go riding or play with some of the children who live near. Mother is like that. She doesn't believe in work all the time, or play either.

Near the barn is a long, low building that once was used for pigs, but it's empty now. We've fixed it up as a clubhouse, but I've made the farthest sty into a writing place. An orange box is a good desk, because it has a shelf for my notebooks and pencils. A milking stool is just the right height for a chair. On rainy days, or when other work is finished, I go there to write. I've begun a story called "A War Love." It keeps getting longer and longer. It may grow into a book.

August 7, 1918

It's Wednesday afternoon. So, after luncheon, Bobby hitched Buster to the basket cart and went around collecting the members of the Old Glory Knitting Club. We meet in the clubhouse—six girls and five boys—and we're making washcloths and mufflers and mittens. It's hot work some days, but cooler than weeding in the fields. We're making plans for a circus at the end of the summer to raise enough money to care for a Belgian orphan. Taking turns reading aloud helps the knitting. The boys always ask for one more book of the Rover Boys and the girls want another of the Bobbsey Twins, but the week Jean came to visit I decided to read them "A War Love."

It didn't take so long to read as I thought it would, and when it was finished nobody said anything. They all just went on knitting. I wanted to ask them if they had liked it, but somehow I couldn't get the words out. After a long time, Ferris said he guessed it was time to go, so Bobby went to get Buster and the cart.

"See you next week," was all anybody said. When Jean and I were alone, I looked at her, hoping she would say something, and she did.

"It sounds like all the books you've been reading. It doesn't sound like you."

I felt as if my best friend had turned against me. "You mean it isn't any good?"

"That wasn't what I said."

I took up the papers and looked at them, written carefully in purple ink, words spelled with the help of a dictionary, and more punctuation than I'd ever used before. Way down inside me, even though I felt as if I'd been turned to stone, I began to know what Jean meant.

"Someday I'll write something that—"

"Of course, you will," Jean said.

To keep from crying, I tore the pages up and, on our way back to the house, dropped them in the ash can.

August 31, 1918

The circus was a great success. We made $297, and that is a lot of money. The one hundred knitted articles we have made for French children is a lot of knitting. At our last meeting, I read to our eleven members the letter of thanks which assured support of a Belgian orphan, and the letter from the New York office of the Comité pour la Protection des Enfants de la Frontière. I'm glad it was in English or I could never have read it. It said, "The sweaters and caps and mufflers and mittens have all been greatly admired by us here, and you will never know what comfort and warmth they bring to the poor little children for whom you have made them. The Comité thanks you and your little group for their continued interest and help."

We congratulated each other on what we had accomplished and told ourselves that if the war was still on, we would have to double our work next summer.

September 26, 1918

Suddenly it seemed, summer is over. I always feel as if it's going to last forever, but it doesn't. We've moved back to the city and started school. I'm in the Sixth Grade. Lessons will be hard, Grammar especially, but if I'm going to be a writer, I'll need it. Arithmetic will always be impossible, but History and English I can look forward to. There are Swimming Lessons one afternoon a week, and Dancing School every other Friday.

Mother insists that I take "Lessons in Gracefulness" on Tuesday afternoons. I don't like them and would far rather be playing baseball with Bobby and his friends than jumping around and striking poses, but Mother says it won't hurt me to do something I don't like. That leaves Wednesday afternoons for club meetings.

We've been getting the shed all fixed up. Harry whitewashed the walls, Bobby cleaned the windows, I did the floor, and it looks very nice. I hope the Jugs will do as well with knitting as the Old Glory Club did. We'll be making caps and mufflers for the Fatherless Children of France this year as well as things we can sell to raise money for the Blue Cross. It hurts us to think of the terrible suffering those noble horses and brave dogs must endure, and we want to do what we can to lessen it.

October 10, 1918

On Tuesday afternoon when I got home, Bobby met me with the most dreadful news. Our clubhouse had been *vandalized*! When he took me to see it I felt sick. The walls were splashed with red and green paint, as if someone had hurled cans around until they were empty. The floor was littered with torn paper. The six chairs that had been bought for the Jugs meetings had been broken as if they were kindling wood. Then I didn't feel sick, I felt mad.

"I could kill the persons who did this."

"But who would do such a thing?"

"I know who, but why? Those boys who live down the street. They've always been mean, throwing snowballs at us when we walk to school, and remember the time they tied a can on to Brier's tail?"

As soon as Father got home we took him to the clubhouse. Mother came too. I told them who did it and that I'd find a way to get even.

"You do not know for sure."

"But—but—" I was so angry I could hardly speak.

"Andy will paint the walls and put a lock on the door. Your mother will buy some new chairs. When is your next meeting?"

"Tomorrow afternoon."

"It should be ready by then if you and Bobby start picking things up now."

"But aren't you going to *do* anything? I'd like to kill those boys."

"We are doing something, in our own way."

I'll never forget the way Father looked when he said that—sad but strong. When he and Mother went back to the house, I began to see that there are other ways than wanting to get even. What is the use of trying to win a war in France if we can't win in our own backyards?

October 11, 1918

Jean wasn't in school today, and when I got home Lizzie told me she had phoned and wanted me to call back. Her voice sounded far away when she said that Alan had been killed in France three weeks ago and the news had just reached them. I told her I'd be right over, but for a minute I just stared ahead of me. The war has meant rolling bandages and knitting mufflers, weeding fields and raising money for the Blue Cross and orphaned children. Now it meant Death. I would never see again someone I knew, and that someone is my best friend's brother.

When I got to Jean's house, there wasn't anything I could do but hug her. Then we went for a walk, round and round the block, scuffing through leaves, not saying anything but knowing we had each other. That night, instead of doing my homework, I wrote a long poem about Alan. It made me feel better to get my thoughts down on paper. When I give it to Jean, I hope it will make her feel better.

November 11, 1918

And now the war is over! On the seventh of November there was a false Armistice and we started to get excited. Then on the eleventh the true one came and we got really excited. When it was announced in school we banged our desk lids, stamped our feet, and shouted. All we wanted to do was make a lot of noise. Then the twelve grades were called to the gym and Miss Keyes read the announcement again. We sang "Over There," and it meant something because it really is over, over there. Then we sang "America." Miss Keyes said there would be no more school, so we went home singing.

The whole city was wild with noise—church bells were ringing, whistles blowing, and many of the houses had flags hanging from them.

When Jean and I got to her house we sat for a long time on the porch steps and didn't say anything. We were both thinking of Alan. He made his life count. I hope I can make mine count. People have been saying that this was "a war to end war," "a war to make the world safe for democracy." Because it is finally over, this must be the most important day in the history of the world.

December 6, 1918

I'm thirteen today, and I feel older in my mind when I think of all that has happened. I don't play with my dollhouse anymore, and I can't remember when I stopped. Thinking about real people, or people I make real in stories I write, is what I like to do now. The dollhouse has come down through our family, and it's time for it to go on to one of my cousins. The little green rocker will go, too, for when I tried to sit in it the other day I didn't fit! I'm five feet six inches now and weigh a hundred and fifteen pounds. Another inch and I can play center in basketball.

During Christmas vacation Father took the Jugs to see *The Blue Bird*, by Maurice Maeterlinck. Then he took us to Huyler's and we had fudge sundaes. It isn't the first time I've seen *The Blue Bird*, and it won't be the last, because Father says no one is ever too old for it. The part I like best is the Kingdom of the Future, where Father Time says that each child born in the world must bring something to the world.

I think I came with a pencil in my hand.

1919

January 1, 1919

This year I've decided to give up candy, just to see if I can. It will be good for my figure. It's a pact I'm making with myself, so I'll not say anything about it to anybody.

January 28, 1919

There seems to be more and more to think about, and I've found a lovely quiet place for thinking. It's a church I pass on my way home from school. Sunlight through the stained-glass windows looks like rainbow fragments on the stone floor. A candle flickers in a red glass bowl near the altar. It's warm there, and quiet. My thoughts feel as if they were taking root in the silence, the way seeds must feel when they take root in the earth. I like to talk to God, but I generally end up talking to myself.

Yesterday something happened that made me feel all mixed up. Brier had followed me to school; he often does, and waits for me until I start for home. When I stopped at the church, he found a corner on the porch and curled up to have a sleep. When I came out it was snowing and Brier wasn't there. I was surprised and worried, because once he sees me go into a place he never leaves until I come out. I hurried home. Brier was there all right, and Mother was very cross.

"Where have you been and what have you been doing?"

I tried to explain.

"Miss Anna Rochester of the Humane Society has been here and she brought Brier with her. She said she saw a dog cowering for shelter in the portico of the cathedral. She went up to him and saw the name on his tag. She tried to get him to follow her, but he would not budge. She was afraid he would come to harm in the storm, so she sent for the Humane Society's van. They got Brier in a net and brought him home. You can be very thankful, but where were you and what were you doing?"

I stroked Brier with my left hand, trying to make up to him for the indignity he had suffered, and I clenched the fingers of my right hand to hold back my feelings. I tried to explain that I had gone to the church to think.

"Think! And for so long and on such a day, knowing Brier was

Elizabeth MacKinstry's

portrait of

the young writer

outside in the cold?"

"Maybe I was praying, too."

"Both could have been done at home."

"This was special."

"Consideration for others, animals among them, is special."

"Don't you want me to be good, Mother?"

"Not too good, just natural."

"You mean if I'm too good, I may die like Beth in *Little Women?*"

"That's not quite what I mean."

"I think I'd like to die."

I stamped out of the room and Brier padded behind me. When I got to my own room and closed the door for privacy, I didn't cry as I often do. I wrote it all down in my diary. When Mother lectures me her words hurt more than a hundred bullets, and why can't I ever say anything in my defense? Why can't I ever do anything right?

Maybe I am selfish and inconsiderate. If so, I'd better do some kind of penance the way monks did in the old days. When I went to bed I decided to sleep on the floor, rolled up in a blanket. Brier could have my bed all to himself. Jinny says that to have a dog sleep on your bed is to ensure good health, because a dog can absorb disease and nullify it. That's a new word for me, I had to look it up in the dictionary. Perhaps that's why I never have colds, or almost never. The first night was hard and I woke up stiff, but I felt virtuous, and I'm sure this will give me better posture, help me to stand straight and walk like a queen. But the next night! There was a rainstorm. Mother came in to close my window and stumbled over me, but she didn't fall or hurt herself.

"What does this mean?"

I tried to explain, but as so often happens, words seemed locked inside me. Mother asked me to get back into bed. Then she sat on the bed and put her arms around me and we talked. Later, after she had tucked me in and gone, the promise I gave her not to do such foolish things again kept me as warm as the blankets.

February 15, 1919

Miss Elizabeth MacKinstry has been commissioned to do my portrait, and sitting for her in her studio is an experience. I have to keep very still, with my eyes toward a spot on the wall before me. Miss MacKinstry tells me about her early days as an artist. I asked her how she knew what she wanted to be, and she said that when you are sure that what you want to do is what you must do, then you will go through anything to attain it. This may be true for me, as I want to be a writer. When I think of it, a shiver of expectancy goes through me. It's like being at the foot of a mountain I know I'm going to climb.

Miss MacKinstry talks to herself a lot, and now and then she puts down her crayons and comes forward to straighten my bow or pull a strand of hair over my shoulder. She didn't let me see the portrait until it was finished. Then we both stood before it, and for once she didn't keep staring at me.

"Twelve years old and looking out on life with eyes of wonder."

"I'm thirteen, Miss MacKinstry."

"Of course you are, and there's a great deal of difference, but I think the older you grow, the more the eyes will see to wonder at and about."

February 28, 1919

The skating on the lake in the Park is great this winter. Sally and I go almost every day after school. Today we had an adventure. We were at the far end, having fun doing figures, when we heard a crash and saw that a boy was in the water. He was yelling like anything. We were the only ones near enough to hear, so we skated fast to get to him. We pulled him out; then the ice gave way and all three of us were in the water. We kept breaking the ice until we got to shore. Then we made our way back to the warming hut. The little boy was shivering terribly, and so were we.

Everybody made a fuss over us and said we were so brave. Later, after we'd warmed up and taken our skates off so we could walk home, Sally and I couldn't see what was brave about it. If a person goes through the ice and you're near, you pull him out, don't you?

"We never asked him his name," Sally said.

"And his mother never asked us ours."

All the way home I kept shaking my head to try to get the water out of my ears. Sally said that if I'd worn my cap pulled down instead of on top of my head, my ears wouldn't be so waterlogged. My cap has disappeared. It's probably somewhere under the ice.

The next afternoon when we skated down toward the far end of the lake there was a big sign—DANGER—and the whole area was roped off.

March 25, 1919

Winter is almost over and I've had a perfect attendance record at school, not absent or tardy once since September. I want to keep it, but it may be hard because my ear has been hurting so, the one that got so much water in it when we went through the ice. Today I got behind in everything. Miss Keyes called me into her office just before the final bell rang and gave me a note for Mother.

"Will she be home?"

"She's always home."

"Please give it to her immediately."

I nodded. It hurt too much to talk.

Bobby was waiting for me at the school door, but I couldn't keep up with him, even when he urged me to walk faster, saying we'd never get home. I pulled my tam down over my ears to keep out the wind and told him I couldn't walk any faster. He looked at me and I shut my eyes tight to keep from crying, but it was no use. Tears came spilling down my face. Bobby snatched the letter from my hand and ran the rest of the way home. Mother was standing at the door, and even though I kept saying it was nothing, I let her take off my coat and arctics, but not my tam.

"Don't, please. My ear hurts so."

April 15, 1919

It's remembering I'm doing now, for this all happened three weeks ago!

Mother undressed me and put me in her bed and sent for Dr. Buswell. He felt my pulse, took my temperature, and when he prodded my ear I couldn't help letting out a cry. Maybe it was my pride that hurt more than my ear, but it was hard to admit that in the battle I'd been having with pain it was pain that won and I had to give in. It seemed to be all there was in the world. I felt surrounded by it, like an ant in the bottom of a teacup. After Dr. Buswell left I asked Mother if I would have to miss school the next day.

"We're not going to think of anything, dear, but getting well."

Mother's room was like a hospital. She slept in Father's bed and he went to the guest room. I must have been drowsy most of the time. I remember Lizzie bringing me soft and slippery things to eat, Miss Hyde reading aloud to me, Father standing by my bed and patting my shoulder, Bobby coming and just looking at me. Mother was always there, pouring warm oil into my ear, changing the bandage my head was wrapped in, or just holding my hands in hers that felt so cool. I couldn't talk and I tried not to cry, but one night I overheard Dr. Buswell talking to Father and Mother. He said it was acute mastoiditis and that only an operation could drain the fluid that was pressing on the bone.

"Is there any risk?"

"There is always a risk with an operation, Mr. Yates, but the risk of not operating is greater. The child is strong. Her system should be able to withstand the shock."

"Will it leave a scar?"

"Yes, Mrs. Yates, a scar behind her right ear. Fortunately she is a girl. Her hair will cover it. It is a scar or her hearing."

"When—"

"Tomorrow morning. Unless drainage commences during the night, we must open the passage to relieve the pressure. I shall make the necessary arrangements at the hospital."

"She is in God's care, Dr. Buswell."

"Yes, Mrs. Yates. I feel that as profoundly as you do."

I woke up often during the night, and every time I saw Mother she was not in her bed but kneeling beside mine. I tried to say something just so Mother would know how comforting it was to have her there. I pulled my hand out from under the sheet and put it on hers that were clasped together. She closed her hands over mine, and the cool, strong hold was all I knew before slipping back into sleep.

Suddenly I woke up, not because it was morning but because of a shattering sound as if all the china in the world was being broken and it was all inside my head. The pain was worse than it had ever been and I screamed. Then there was no more pain, but a thin warm stream running out of my ear and soaking the bandage. Mother was standing beside me and her hands were feeling the wetness. She started to remove the bandage.

"My ear doesn't hurt anymore."

"It's draining."

Mother started to cry. It was the first time in my life I had ever seen her cry, and I couldn't understand it, because everything was all right, or going to be.

Dr. Buswell came in a little while. It was morning then and Bobby had gone to school, but Father had not yet gone to his office.

"Thank you, Doctor," Mother said.

His hands were feeling around my head, putting another bandage on. They felt soothing and I didn't want to pull away from them as I had before.

"Don't thank me, dear lady, thank God," Dr. Buswell said.

Everybody smiled, me most of all.

I wasn't allowed up for a week and I felt like a queen.

Miss Keyes sent me a bunch of freesias, and their fragrance filled the room. The Jugs all wrote me letters. Jinny sent me a book. It's a Life of Joan of Arc, and reading about her fills me with a fighting spirit to get well. Bobby gives me news from school every afternoon. Maria makes all my favorite foods and Lizzie brings them to me on a tray. As soon as I could sit up, I began to write in my diary to bring the events of these past days up to date.

April 25, 1919

Easter is almost as late as it can be, April 20, so we really are in spring. My new hat, which I wore on Easter Sunday, has almost as many flowers on it as are coming up in the garden, but different. So much else says it's spring. Miss Schaenut came for a week to do the household sewing. She made two new dresses for Jinny and shortened two of Jinny's for me. I hope the day will never come when I can't wear Jinny's clothes, cut down or made over. It's like Elijah and Elisha. If Jinny's mantle falls on me, someday I may write as well as she does. When I said that to Miss Schaenut, she looked at me as if she had never heard the story. I told her it was in the Bible and she just nodded. Perhaps she's so used to not talking when she has pins in her mouth for hems that she has almost forgotten how to talk. I can't get anything out of her.

Jean and I aren't roller-skating to school, because we have bicycles. I call mine Comrade, and I expect he'll be a trusty friend for many years. On Friday, after basketball practice, we stopped at Thurston's Drug Store for sundaes.

"Fudge sauce," Jean said.

"Me too," said Ethel as she put her 15 cents on the marble top of the table.

"Strawberry on mine."

Jean stared. "But I thought you liked fudge best of all."

"Not this year," and that was as much as I would say.

We spent a lot of time talking about the Jugs and decided that we should have another name, something that would suit us better now. I said that I would ask Jinny. She's home on vacation now and she always has lots of ideas. She did, after I explained to her that we were all keen on tennis and hiking as well as finding some needy cause to help.

Jinny came up with O.A.O., or, when deciphered, Out And Out good sports. The others agreed that would be the exactly right name for us, that we would keep it a secret and it would be our Code of Behavior. Anyone giving our secret away would be dropped from the club. That was my idea. Jean said no, that we'd have them pay some sort of penalty. Jean is always easier on people than I am.

We've been thinking of ourselves as the Tipped-Tam Ten because we all wear tams and at rakish angles, but it's good to have a name without a number so we can add new members if we want. We set up our quarters in the old playhouse, wrote a Constitution and By-laws. When it came to officers, I was elected President, Jean was Secretary, Ethel was Treasurer.

We had our first real meeting yesterday, and when I had to make a speech I was terrified! My knees shook, my hands got cold, but it went all right. Everyone likes our new name and the Cause we've decided on for this year. Last week we had all heard Mr. Hoover speak, and we are going to pledge our savings to his starving children. One dollar will feed a child for six weeks!

June 17, 1919

I have a place of my own! A new garage has been built, and the top of it is to be a pigeon loft someday, but Father said I could use it for the time being. I climbed up the ladder this afternoon and got myself established. It is clean and bare, the new wood has a lovely smell. The top of the nesting box is slanted just right for a desk and the inside holds all my papers and even has room for some books. There's a window that looks across the fields to the pinewoods.

I sit in the middle of the floor, looking out, and I think; then, when I'm ready to write, I turn around to the slant-top desk. Often it seems that writing is mostly thinking. Sometimes I go down the ladder hours later and not a single word has been put down on paper, but they're all in my head, getting themselves ready.

Today I've been working on a play—*Called Coward*. I couldn't seem to get it to come right, so I went for a ride on Old Joe. It helps to talk to a horse and I trust Old Joe. He won't say something is good if it isn't, and he won't belittle me either. He listens to me and when he flicks his ears in a certain way I know that he understands.

June 28, 1919

Jinny writes all the time. When I went by her room this morning she was sitting at her desk, writing. I went in and asked her if she would read me something of hers and she smiled in a secret sort of way.

"I'm writing a description of my well-beloved."

"Just for yourself or is it a story?"

"Just for myself. Would you like to hear it?"

"Oh yes, please, Jinny, please."

"The well-beloved: He will be tall and straight of limb, tender and true. When we meet, our eyes will say more than our lips, and we will know that we were meant for each other. So sure will we be that we will be willing to wait for each other, if we must. When we are married, our home will be a beautiful place, and the children who come to it will be the manifest of our love."

"Oh, Jinny, he's somewhere in the world waiting for you as you are for him. You'll find each other, I know you will."

Jinny had used a word that was new to me, so I looked it up in the dictionary after I left her room. Manifest. It was the exactly right word. How did she know? How does anyone know when a word is the only word that can be used?

July 12, 1919

Old Joe has cast a shoe, and Bobby and I decided to ride over to the blacksmith's after breakfast on Saturday morning. There were cantaloupes on the table, and I know I don't like them, so I pushed mine aside and had another bowl of cereal.

Father likes to linger over breakfast when he doesn't have to go into his office in Buffalo and Mother sits with him over a final cup of coffee. We are excused as soon as we are finished. Jinny was the first to leave the table, then Harry and Dick, and soon Bobby. When I pushed my chair back, Father said to me that I had not eaten my melon.

"But I don't like it."

"Have you tasted it?"

"No."

"How do you know then that you don't like it?"

"I just know, that's all."

"You will remain at the table until you have tasted your melon, and I will remain here, too."

I had no intention of touching the melon, even though Mother finished her coffee and went out to the kitchen to talk with Maria and Father picked up the morning paper and got behind it.

The clock in the hall struck nine. Bobby came back and stood in the doorway of the dining room, motioning with his lips and gesturing toward the barn. I pointed to the melon and made a face at it. Bobby left.

In another few minutes I heard hooves on the drive and saw Al and Bobby riding off to the blacksmith's, leading Old Joe between them. Father turned a page.

Lizzie cleared the table, all but the plate with the slice of melon. I was not going to eat something I knew I didn't like, even if I sat there all day. Father turned another page and another, and the clock struck ten.

A whole Saturday morning was going to waste, all because of a stupid cantaloupe. I disliked melons more than ever but decided I'd have to do something or we'd be sitting at the table all day. So I dipped my spoon in and brought a small piece up to my mouth. A taste would satisfy Father and then I could go. It did have a very nice smell. I put it in my mouth, chewed it, swallowed it, then—however can I write this? It was delicious, like peach ice cream or charlotte russe. It was ambrosia. Perhaps it was what the lotus-eaters gave Ulysses when they lured him from his course. Over and over again I dipped the spoon into the melon until there was nothing left but an empty shell.

"You may be excused now." Father's voice came from behind the newspaper.

I didn't say anything, just left the room, and, as nobody was around to do anything with, I climbed up the ladder to my pigeon loft. Maybe a new taste is like learning a new word. I resolved then to try anything once. Maybe I'll write a story about this someday, because it was like a battle and *we both won*—Father won his point, and I made a discovery I might never have made in my whole life.

September 9, 1919

Before we left the farm and moved back to Buffalo for the big brown house on Delaware Avenue and the Franklin School, I had my last ride on Old Joe. Father says I'm too big for him now and that he should go to Bobby. It's time for the little Shetland, Buster, to be turned out to pasture. Buster is twenty-three and that's quite an age for a pony; it is for anyone, I think. Father is going to get me a horse next spring, a hunter like the three that Jinny and her friends ride. He says we may start entering them all in horse shows.

I told Old Joe I'd never forget him. When we got back to the barn I rubbed him down, gave him some oats, and whispered into his furry ear that someday I'd be writing stories about him. That was a promise I knew could be kept.

September 17, 1919

Seventh Grade is going to put me to the test. Latin and Algebra and History and English and French. Miss Keyes certainly wants to have her girls well grounded. Algebra doesn't make any sense to me, but Latin is going to be exciting, particularly because we have it with a new teacher. Her name is Miss Watkins. She is tall and beautiful, and looks as if she had stepped down from an Elgin marble to breathe the life of the past into the present. She has one brown eye and one blue and a lovely smile. I could kiss the very ground she walks on and I'll do anything to merit her approval.

When I got my report card for the first week, I showed it to Mother and Father after dinner when we were alone. Bobby had gone to bed. Harry and Dick were at a friend's house. It was not a card to be proud of, and I think it was harder on Mother and Father than on me, because I was high in some subjects, bottom low in others. I tried to explain that with subjects I liked and teachers I admired I could do well, but with some things I just couldn't.

Father reminded me that Jinny had been good in everything whether she liked it or not. Then he opened the *Wall Street Journal* and started to read. It's like his going into another room and closing the door when he does that. Mother and I were alone together. She shook her head sadly.

"There's no standing still in life. We either go forward or we go back, and I think you're going back."

Her words stung; they always do and I suppose it's because I deserve them. I really want to go forward. I said I'd try to do better. I didn't want to cry, but I did when she put her arms around me. It made me think of the time last winter when she spent a whole night praying for me. I want to be worthy of her, and of Father, so I said again that I'd try and I meant it.

December 6, 1919

Something wonderful happens in our family when you get to be fourteen. You have a room of your own! For so long I'd been sharing one with Bobby. I knew that things had been going on in Teresa's old room on the third floor, but I'd been told not to go up there. The house often had the smell of new paint when I got home from school, and there were sounds that made me have a suspicion, but this morning I really was surprised.

We went upstairs after breakfast. Father opened the door and Mother said, "This is your very own room." It was different from the room I remembered and prettier than anything I could have imagined.

Because the room's at the top of the house, the ceiling is low and there are angles, made by the roof, at the corners. Three small windows face west, another one faces south, and at each one there are frilly white curtains. The wallpaper has sprigs of tiny roses against a pale-blue background. There is a narrow mahogany bed with a white counterpane. Beside it is a table with a reading lamp. Nearby is a small bureau. Bookshelves run along one wall near a desk with many pigeonholes. There's a fireplace with a little gas log. Beside it is a low rocking chair and a spirit lamp with a shiny brass kettle. There's another chair and a dressing table. The carpet is blue, a deeper shade than the wallpaper. I just looked and looked and tried to take it all in.

"Aren't you going to *say* anything?" Bobby asked.

My eyes got all full of tears, happy tears, and all I could do was put my arms around Mother and Father and say I hoped I'd be worthy of it. It's a turning point in my life to have a room of my own.

After school, Bobby helped me carry up books and get them on the shelves. Miss Hyde and Lizzie helped me move my clothes and get them in drawers and closet. I was busy putting things in their right places when Bobby appeared in the doorway with a book in his hands.

"Look what I found in the back of your clothes closet, *my* closet now." It was *What Every Young Girl Should Know.* "I don't want it," he said scornfully.

"No more do I."

I took it from him and he went back to get his room settled. I despised the book and the prissy way it was written, and the fact that it didn't really say anything. When I write, I'm going to face up to facts, and if I don't know things, I'll find them out from honest books or from people who have knowledge.

I had to get rid of it, so I went down the back stairs to the cellar, opened the door of the furnace and threw it in. The coals were bright red, quivering with heat, and the blast of air was fierce. The book was soon consumed, and only a dance of little darting flames showed where it had once been.

1920

January 1, 1920

The first entry in my diary for this year is that I haven't touched candy for 365 days. I wanted to see if I could do it when I made that pact with myself, and I did it! As I look ahead into the empty pages that will fill as the days and months go on with my own handwriting, I ask myself, "What will this year hold?"

January 10, 1920

Now that I'm fourteen I have an important household privilege and that is helping Lizzie serve when Mother and Father have a dinner party. It's like being in a play. I wear a black challis dress—the same one Jinny wore when she used to do this—a white apron with a frill around its edges, and a white cap that sits on the top of my head in place of the bow from my hair ribbon. My hair is held back by a barrette and it makes me feel very dignified. Lizzie has taught me how to pass and remove, when to refill glasses or add another pat of butter, and when I'm not busy I'm to stand quietly.

"You're to see without being seen, as it were, and you're not to do any dreaming or you'll be no help to me."

"I won't—I mean I'll try not to."

It's all so beautiful. The table is covered with a white damask cloth and laid with the cut glass, silver, and best French china that come out only for parties. Flowers make the centerpiece and two candelabra, each one holding four tall white candles. Father looks handsome in his tuxedo, and Mother looks lovely in an evening gown, with her hair piled high on her head and her diamond lavaliere, which hangs from a gold chain around her neck, flashing in the light. The guests are handsome, too. Never more than eight, for Mother likes small parties.

The food is as different from everyday as is the table service. Everything is special, and there's always wine, white or red, served in the Venetian glasses that Lizzie handles as if they were crown jewels. I like to watch her pour the wine, filling Father's glass first, just a quarter full, then waiting for him to taste it and give her his nod of approval.

"If anyone notices you and speaks your name, you're to drop a wee bit of a curtsy and incline your head, so. You're not to answer back."

Hillhurst Farm,

Orchard Park, New York

"What if I get asked a question?"

"Leave it to your parents to answer. A good servant is to be seen only—her work will do the speaking."

Almost never does anyone notice me, because the guests all know that one of the Yates girls helps at parties, and now it's the youngest's turn. I listen and I pick up interesting things about the world from the conversation. I try not to get too interested, but last night Lizzie had to nudge me with her foot to pay attention and refill Miss Martin's water glass. The reason it was empty is a story in itself.

Miss May Martin is one of the great ladies of Buffalo society. She has traveled all over the world and I think she has met everyone. She's tall, with white hair, and she positively glitters with jewels. She's the only one who ever notices me and she does it in a fascinating way. As she comes into the room she unfurls her fan, puts it up to her face and looks over it right at me. Then she arches her brows, folds her fan and gives her attention to her dinner partner. She's like Marie Antoinette, or Madame de Pompadour, but she's like anyone, too, because she can get hiccups! That's what happened last night.

"There's only one way I know how to handle them and it's never failed me," she announced as she pushed her chair back, took her glass of water and moved away from the table. She bent low over the glass and drank all the water from the far side; then she returned to the table, sat down, and went on with the conversation. That was when Lizzie pushed her foot against mine and cocked her head toward the empty glass.

So it's not just interesting information I get during dinner parties but actual knowledge. I can't wait to have hiccups to put Miss Martin's method to the test.

I filled Miss Martin's empty water glass and Lizzie did the wine glasses again and that seemed to make people go into the current topic of prohibition.

"It's an unjust law and I don't intend to keep it," one of the men said. "I have my own bootlegger and he keeps me very well supplied."

"I would never patronize a bootlegger," Father said. "I have a cellar inherited from my father and, with care, it should last us until this unjust law is repealed."

I was proud of Father. To him a law is a law and he intends to keep it. Then the conversation moved on to other things. It never stays very long on one subject or with one or two people. If it should, Mother has a way of steering it to something else or someone else.

March 25, 1920

We were in gym class today when the bell rang summoning all grades to their rooms and their desks. Miss Keyes appeared in our room with a sheaf of papers in her hands. She explained that the Franklin School was this year and thereafter to take the General Information test given to the boys at the Nichols School.

"There are a hundred questions divided into six categories—Current Events, Literature, Art, Music, Personalities, Quotations. You have an hour to answer according to your ability. I ask you to remember what Marshal Foch said to his soldiers: 'Think, and yet again think, I tell you this day to learn to think.'"

She handed out the questions and special sheets of paper with lines numbered from one to a hundred. Then she said that when the bell rang we were to turn the papers in to Miss Conary.

Some of the girls read all through the questions before they started to write anything. There were a few groans and sighs, which were silenced by the tapping of Miss Conary's ruler. I decided to answer the questions in order and not worry about what was ahead. I'm always happy with a pencil in my hand and a sheet of paper under it. The first question was easy and the more I went on, the more I realized that the conversations heard at dinner parties had given me lots of information. So had the books I'd been reading, and the games I played with my brothers. Sometimes I just had to guess, but it seemed better to take a risk than leave a blank. When I signed my name at the end, I was pretty sure that I had answered sixty correctly.

Walking home from school, Jean and Martha and Ethel and I stopped at Thurston's to have a sundae and compare our answers. Ethel got all the ones on art. She should; her father is an artist. Martha was sure of the current events ones. And Jean was probably right on the music questions.

"Sometimes I wasn't sure, so I didn't put anything down."

"You could have guessed."

"Would that have been fair?"

"Of course, and you just might have been right."

"I think I got all the quotations except that last one. Whoever said it, and where?"

"Oh, you mean 'Amyas, do thy duty like a man, to thy country, thy Queen, and thy God, and count thy life a worthless thing.' That's Sir Richard Grenville in *Westward Ho!* It's one of my most favorite phrases. I say it to myself often."

April 1, 1920

A whole week has gone by and the scores have just been announced. I got 87 out of the 100 correct. My prize is a book, *The Autobiography of Benjamin Franklin.* When I told everybody about it that night at supper, Father smiled and patted me on the shoulder, Mother looked as if I had done what she expected of me. Bobby turned the pages of my book, but soon gave it back to me saying he liked adventure stories. Maybe I can get him to see that reading about another person's life is an adventure story, an adventure in your mind.

June 11–15, 1920

Mother and Father have taken Bobby and me to Jinny's graduation from Smith College. It was a perfect day. We sat in a great crowd of people, all proud of their daughters, but no one so bursting with pride and joy as I was when Jinny walked across the platform and received her degree from President Nielson—*summa cum laude*! Her Phi Beta Kappa key was her only ornament. In her long white dress and with her fair hair done in a low knot, she looked regal. There's nothing she can't do, I thought, when I heard her receiving special commendation for her work in dramatics and her prowess in athletics. And to think what she will do!

In the afternoon Jinny and I went for a walk around the campus. At the library, Jinny looked at me and said she had something wonderful to tell me. A secret. Her face was alive with smiling and it made her more beautiful than ever. We sat down on the bottom step and she told me what had happened.

"This morning, before the ceremonies began, the Dean called me into her office. The college is offering me an assistant professorship in the English Department, beginning next fall. It's never happened to anyone before—here, that is. I'm going to ask Father tonight, when they take me out to dinner, if I may accept."

I was so thrilled for her that I could hardly speak, and then I couldn't say much but how wonderful it was. What I wanted to say, because the words kept hammering in me, was, "Don't ask him, tell him."

Looking beautiful and radiant, she went out to dinner with Mother and Father while Bobby and I had dinner by ourselves in the Wiggins Tavern. I was so bursting with excitement over Jinny's secret that I suggested we order everything on the menu to celebrate.

"What?"

"Jinny and her triumphs."

"She's doing that with Mother and Father. Let's celebrate being ourselves."

Jinny didn't get back until late. I had gone to bed in the room we shared, and, though I wanted to stay awake, I had fallen asleep over *Jane Eyre*. The strangest sound wakened me, and when I sat up I could see by the light from a streetlamp that Jinny's clothes were on a chair and she was in the other bed, all humped up and crying. That was the sound. But from Jinny? It was one of her prides that she never cried, not even when she broke her arm.

"Jinny?"

"You should be asleep."

"I am—I mean I was."

"Well, go back to sleep."

"What did Father say?"

"About what?"

"The secret you told me when we were sitting on the steps of the library."

"I don't know what you're talking about."

"The professorship, the teaching."

"Oh, that."

"Yes, it is so wonderful."

"People only work to have leisure. I have it, so why should I work?"

"But Jinny—"

"Mother and Father want me to be a debutante. They're going to give me a big coming-out party next Christmas; then I'll probably get married. Now go to sleep. You're just a little girl. You can't possibly understand."

"But I can! I can!"

Suddenly I felt as if I'd been hit in the stomach. It wasn't that I didn't have any words, it was that I didn't have any breath. It was like the time during a basketball game when I tripped and fell flat on my stomach and the wind was knocked out of me. It was awful —the nothingness, the feeling that there was just my body and nothing in it.

It took a long time then for the air to come back; this time I wondered if it ever would. But it did, and what came with it was a cold fear. Something had happened to change Jinny. Could this happen to me? Could someone take the pencil out of my hand, tear up my notebooks, say I was to write no more? No! Then and there I vowed an awesome vow that what I had to do I would do, and that no one would stop me.

We're home now, but there's a wall of silence between Jinny and me. The joy she shared for a little while with me is still my secret, but it feels like a stone in my heart. I wonder and I wonder. What makes people do the things they do? What? What? Round and round go my questioning thoughts without finding any answers. I had dreamed of showing my poems to Jinny this summer. Now I know that I can't.

June 19, 1920

The minute we got out to the farm I went to the barn to see the horse Father got for me. Her name is Bluemouse. She is six years old and sixteen hands high, gray with speckles, a short mane and a flowing tail. For three years she was one of Man o' War's running mates, so she is fast. I put my arms around her and she nuzzled me with her velvety lips. We are going to be great friends. Al wants her to rest for a day and he says my first ride should be with Jinny. Perhaps the strangeness between Jinny and me will disappear when we ride together.

June 27, 1920

This year I'm to be a real working part of the farm. It won't be just the vegetables I raise in my garden plot, or the eggs from my Bantams. I am to do the buttermaking! Father told me about it at breakfast, and he said it would be a business venture.

"Ed Wado has a room in the cellar all ready. It's cool and light. The walls have been whitewashed and a sink installed. He thinks a barrel churn is the most efficient, so he has put one there along with a worktable, bowls, paddles, pail, and scales. He's coming in this morning with fourteen quarts of cream and will show you how to turn it into butter."

"And then?"

"You'll be billed for the cream at cost; after you have made the butter, weighed and packaged it, you will bill your Mother at the current market price. The difference between the two will be what you make for yourself. The profit, to compensate for your time and labor."

"I'll do my best to show a profit."

"Arithmetic hasn't been easy for you, I know, but earning your own money may help you with figures."

Then Lizzie came in to say that Mr. Wado was in the kitchen with fourteen quarts of cream!

We went down to the cellar. Mr. Wado poured the cream into the stone barrel of the churn, took hold of the handle and pushed it back and forth with one hand, evenly, easily. Then he said I should take over. He leaned against the table and told me a lot about but-termaking, especially the way the weather affects the process. On a bright, dry day butter can "come" in thirty minutes; on a sultry day it can take hours. I used my right hand for a while, then shifted to my left, and tried to keep the tempo steady. All of a sudden there was a thump. The butter had "come"!

Mr. Wado showed me how to open the little hole in the bottom of the churn and drain off the buttermilk into a shiny new pail; he showed me how to uncap the churn and take out the huge lump of almost-white butter and wash it thoroughly, work it up, salt it slightly, weigh it, shape it, and wrap it in five-pound packages.

"That's all there is to it, and you've got some twelve pounds of butter and about six quarts of buttermilk."

Before he left, we poured out two cups of buttermilk to drink. It was good, quite thin, with a flavor all its own, and had tiny flecks of butter floating around in it. There was washing up to do, but it was soon done, and everything could be left to dry in the air and in the shaft of sunshine that came in through the open window. When I took the packages upstairs to Maria to put in the big icebox, I felt very happy.

One day a week is Butter Day. It's Reading Day, too. I can hold a book in one hand, the churn handle in the other, and not mind if it takes a long time. I'm reading *Lorna Doone* now.

Last week it was hot and sultry—even a thunderstorm didn't clear the air. It seemed as if the butter would never come, but Mr. Wado told me it always would, just to keep on churning. It came when I was at an exciting part of *Scottish Chiefs* and couldn't wait to turn the page. But I had to put the book down. It could wait; the butter shouldn't. So I ran the milk off into the pail, drank a glass of it, then washed the big mound of butter, paddled it into shape, weighed it, wrapped it, and took it upstairs.

All the time I was doing that, I could think about the people in *Scottish Chiefs*, but when it came to my account book I had to put all my mind on it. So much for the cost of the cream, so much for the butter, and then I made out the bill for Mother. Fourteen quarts of cream at 11 cents a quart, butter at 27 cents a pound, left a tidy sum for me. It made me feel rich, with a book half read, too. I never charged for the buttermilk.

July 10, 1920

Today I was on my way up to the pigeon loft, for the characters in *Called Coward* are still on my pages and I don't like to leave them too long, when Jinny called to me from the barn. She had Canadian Belle saddled and bridled, and Al was just bringing Bluemouse out of her stall.

"Thought you might like to go for a ride."

"Oh, yes!"

By the time Al had Bluemouse ready, I had changed into my jodhpurs and boots, and we were off.

"You've sat a horse almost before you could walk," Jinny said when we let the horses amble after our first canter across the field, "but that's it, you've sat. Now, with a real horse and a chance to ride in shows soon, you've got to do more than sit. You must think of your form."

"You've always told me to hold the reins as if they were silken threads."

"Yes, and to keep talking to your horse. The bit in the mouth isn't your only contact. It's your voice that makes your horse feel a part of you. And keep those toes turned in! See how Belle and Blue are flicking their ears? They're as interested in our conversation as we are in them."

"What if Blue should take it into her head to run, really run, the way she used to with Man o' War?"

"She isn't likely to unless she senses that you've lost contact with her."

"But if she did?"

"Sit tight, grip with your knees, and don't pull on the reins hard. Tense them and loosen, tense them and loosen, but gently, never jerkily. Move her head a little to one side to divert her attention, and as soon as she responds, run your hand down her neck, stroke her and let her know you're pleased with her. Let's give them their heads and see how well they take the brook."

"Oh, Jinny, I don't know whether I can sit Blue when she takes a flying leap."

"Of course you can!" Jinny leaned toward Belle's mane and made a clicking sound to which Belle responded, changing from a walk to an easy trot, then a canter. She called back over her shoulder, "Don't ever doubt your own ability."

I held Blue in for a minute, long enough to lean low on her neck and whisper to her, then I gave her her head. The long strides she took were glorious. She broke from a canter into a gallop and soon passed Belle. Almost before I knew it, she took the brook in a high, wide leap. I reined her in to wait for Jinny and Belle.

"You did it!"

"Bluemouse and I did it!"

August 2, 1920

Something wonderful has just happened to me! On the space for today in my diary I have pasted four silver stars. Whenever I see them they will tell me of the event that shook my life.

The house is overflowing with people, family mostly. Teresa and Ed are here, Walter and Ibby, and little children seem to appear everywhere. Jinny has her roommate from Smith visiting her, as well as two men from Yale; then there's Harry and Dick and Bobby and me.

After supper Jinny said they were going for a ride in the moonlight and asked me to join them. It was beautiful. The fields were so wet with dew that it splashed from the horses' hooves. The moon made the world mysterious, and the air was damp and fragrant. The horses kept whickering to each other, and whenever we broke into a real run they snorted and tossed their heads.

When we got back to the barn, Jinny asked me to rub Belle down so she could go to the house and start making cocoa. One of the Yale men went with her; the other one, Brad, stayed with me. We unsaddled and rubbed the horses down, giving each one a measure of oats. Just as we started toward the open door into the barnyard, Brad pointed toward a little door.

"What's this?"

"Manure chute for the ponies' stalls upstairs."

He pulled me into it, closed the door, held me in his arms and kissed me! After a minute, or two, or three, he opened the door, took my hand in his, and we followed the path of moonlight out of the barn and toward the house. Brad hummed the tune of a song everyone is singing this year, then he said the words—

> *"Just a voice to call me dear,*
> *Just a hand in mine,*
> *Just a whisper in my ear,*
> *'Darling you're divine.'"*

I wanted to tell him that he was divine, but the words wouldn't come. When we reached the house, he dropped my hand and went up the steps and into the kitchen to join the others with their cocoa, and I raced upstairs. In the hall I met Bobby.

"What's happened to you?"

"Nothing."

"Something must have. You're all out of breath and your eyes are shining. You look beautiful."

"Do I?"

"Was it fun riding in the moonlight?"

"It wasn't the ride. It—oh, Bobby, Brad kissed me!"

"In the moonlight?"

"No, in the manure chute."

"Oh."

"But I love him! Can't you see that the main thing has come into my life?"

"Aren't you going down to have cocoa with them? Everybody's in the kitchen and they're all talking and laughing."

"No, I can't."

"Then I'll go down and bring you up a cup. Don't take your first kiss so seriously."

I wanted to say something cross to Bobby for having broken my beautiful bubble, but somehow I couldn't. He's just so dear. As I watched him go down the stairs, my heart ached with love for him, something very different from the feeling I had for Brad.

August 24, 1920

This afternoon I rode down to see the Triers. When I go I'm never sure what will be happening, but there's always something. Their small place is mostly kitchen inside and garden outside. They treat me as if I were the child they never had, and I think of them as fixed points on my compass because I can always be sure of them. They never go anywhere except to the village once a week to shop, and to church on Sunday. Their old black horse is as old as their old black buggy, but they wouldn't trade either one for a motor car. They listen to me and I listen to them because they have stories to tell. Today I helped Mr. Trier thin the carrots in the garden, then went into the kitchen to watch Mrs. Trier make bread.

"How long have you known me, Mrs. Trier?"

"Since you were a little small girl riding down on your fat pony. You'd tie him to a tree, then crawl around under the currant bushes and pick the ones we never could get."

"I've always known you. You're in the flowers and the sunshine and the good smell of that bread coming from the oven."

"That sounds very poetic."

"I'm going to be a poet someday."

"So?"

"I am one now, but I don't show my poems to anyone. They might laugh."

"We wouldn't laugh."

The Triers always have to tell me when I should be going, because time doesn't seem to be when I'm with them. Something in each of us seems to fit into the other and it has nothing to do with hours or days, or even years.

September 10, 1920

Today I made butter for the last time. After I washed and dried my equipment and put it away, I settled down to my accounts. I have made a profit of $42.86 and I've checked and rechecked the figures, so I'm sure they're correct. After supper Father went over them carefully. It didn't take him nearly so long as it did me, but everything tallied!

"That's a nice sum to have in your savings account and it will go on working for you. You have the making of a businesswoman. I'm proud of you."

His words pleased me, so did his smile, but something sent a little runnel of fear through me. I'm becoming more sure of what I want to do and be when I grow up, and it doesn't have anything to do with business.

September 22, 1920

Rules! Rules! Rules! Now we're having them in Rhetoric, or English Grammar as Miss Clements prefers to say. I dislike her class as much as I dislike her. Why can't I just write the way I feel, instead of having to learn all about parts of speech and parsing sentences and things like that? Today she said, "Learn the rules. When you gain mastery you can find freedom within the structure you have made yours."

That impressed us, but Miss Clements doesn't. We take it out on her by whispering and passing notes and giggling when her back is turned when she writes something on the board. She's so sloppy. Her hair straggles, and one day a clothes hanger fell out of her dress when she got up to do something. We howled with laughter. Then it was awful—she burst into tears and dismissed the class!

Walking home from school, we began to feel sorry for Miss Clements and thought of reasons why she is the way she is. Ethel thinks she may be suffering from a fatal disease. Jean says she has probably been disappointed in love. Caroline, always practical, says that now we are in Eighth Grade we ought to be able to show some kind of intelligence in dealing with her. We decided to prepare a solemn document of behavior and we made it up as we walked along. Ethel took it home to letter it, and when she brings it to school tomorrow morning we'll sign it and get others in the class to sign it, too.

This afternoon Charlotte put the document on Miss Clements'

desk when she was out of the room, and there was no danger of our seeing her as it's Friday and there won't be any class again until Monday morning. We'll have two whole days to get used to what we've done. This is what we said—

To Miss Clements
in Defense of English Grammar

We, the members of the Eighth Grade, who wish to form a more perfect union, establish justice, insure tranquillity, and promote the general welfare, do ordain and establish this LEAGUE OF HONOR, accepting as our motto the words Confidentes esse vim audeamus officium facere. The following conditions must be implicitly obeyed, or the member breaking this trust given her forthwith will be banished from the LEAGUE.

1. No rudeness.
2. No undertone remarks.
3. No complaining of lessons.
4. Give full attention.

Separately we pledge our sacred word that we will not disobey any of the above rules.

It was signed by the members of the class, all ten of us.

It's unbelievable! Monday morning, after we had taken our seats in Miss Clements' room, she smiled at us and said "Thank you." She looked tidier than we'd ever seen her, and almost pretty. Then she said something to each one of us about the homework she had given us.

"I read your paragraphs illustrative of the various figures of speech over the weekend and I shall now make my comments so we can all learn from each other. Ethel, I did not know whether you were writing fact or fiction in the experience you chose to relate."

"Does it matter?"

"Not for the writer of fiction, but when you deal with facts you must be careful not to tangle your skeins. Beatrice, you said the day was so exquisite you could not describe it."

"That's true."

"No, Beatrice, if you see a thing, you can describe it. If words fail you, you have not seen it."

When she got to me, she said my penmanship was improving. "It is finding its own style. It looks better on the page and is easier on my eyes, but watch the way you use punctuation. It must aid the sense. It is not like pepper and salt to be sprinkled indiscriminately."

Penmanship! Then it had been worthwhile all those days in Miss Clay's room in the third and fourth and fifth grades. Mr. Bennet used to come once a week. Standing by the blackboard, he would make loops of *l*'s and curving lines of *s*'s and rows of *m*'s which we copied on the paper on our desks. Sometimes I wondered why we had to do so many, so often, and the same kind of exercises.

When the hour was over and we walked out of her class, we stood in the hall and stared at each other. "She said we would all learn," Ethel whispered. "That means she included herself with us." And I, who had been rebelling against Rules of Rhetoric, found that I was suddenly excited by them. Penmanship had been the beginning; now figures of speech were the next step.

December 6, 1920

Something special always happens on my birthday! Under my pillow this morning was a little slim leather-bound book of prayers from many sources, many nations. And there are several blank pages so I can write my own prayers and make them a part of the book.

Tonight we heard Fritz Kreisler at the Music Hall. It's his first appearance since the war years and such a proof that all the hatred and meanness has been forgotten. It was wonderful to close my eyes and let myself be wafted up in tune with the infinite by the strains of that magic violin. It is said that "art makes the whole world brothers," and listening to him makes such things as nations and nationalities seem trivial. My prayer is that someday I may be a master of the pen, as he is a master of the violin.

1921

January 5, 1921

My resolve, as I face a new year, is to know myself, and that means doing something about myself. Benjamin Franklin had a system for self-improvement. So shall I, but where do I start? I'm all mixed up. My marks in school are degrading; never in subjects I like, but in ones that don't make sense to me, like Algebra.

And it isn't just lessons, it's socially. I feel awkward and tongue-tied with people older than me. Even studying the *Encyclopedia of Etiquette* doesn't seem to improve me. At dancing school I like it when Carl asks me to dance with him, because we've known each other so long, but with other boys I can't think what to talk about, even though I once played marbles with them.

I braid my hair at night in a dozen pigtails to make it curly, the way I used to braid Old Joe's mane, but all it does is come out frizzy.

I'm a wallflower and it isn't any fun, but the worst of all is that the older I grow, the further away I seem to get from my parents. They just don't see why I want to do some things and can't do others. I wouldn't dare show them my poems. When words flow from the point of a pencil, why can't they flow from the tip of my tongue? If I don't speak their language anymore, and they don't speak mine, what is language?

In the privacy of my diary, which is for my mind what the privacy of my room is for my body, I face the fact of myself and know that I want to be a poet. The writings I am doing now are practicings for greater works I shall do someday. I dream, but to have this dream fulfilled I must work to obtain knowledge. Henceforth, I will try with my lessons, in school or out, not to waste any time and to concentrate on one thing for a specified time. I will care and I will make a desperate effort. In each study I will set a standard mark for myself, such as in French 9, English 8, 9, or 10, Latin 7½, 8, or 9, and so forth. Each night I will inquire for my marks, and if any one of them has fallen below the standard, I shall consider myself disgraced until a week of excellent marks redeems the bad one.

At home I promise myself that I will be more cheerful and obedient, and each day to do some unselfish act, though it is hard for me. I will try to stop criticizing people and their clothes and be charitable.

Franklin School years

February 18, 1921

Tonight I really tried to study, but I ended up writing a poem in Latin when I should have been doing three pages of translation of Virgil! And instead of doing English History, I rewrote some of *Called Coward*, which is laid in the time of the Wars of the Roses. On the title page I put that it was by Barry Compeyson, because a man's name looks more important.

I like to write by candlelight because it makes a glowing circle just for me, and it doesn't show under the crack of my door when Mother or Father make their late rounds to see if we're sleeping. Some nights I get only four hours' sleep, but that's all Napoleon ever had, and tonight I'm not going to bed at all.

There is so much I want to read: Keats, Shelley, Byron. Homer and his wine-dark sea make me leap ages and miles to be with him in ancient Greece. The more I read, the more I want to write. How can I ever hold to my high resolve to study when there is so much else I would rather do?

March 10, 1921

The family are all out tonight. Miss Hyde and I had dinner together, and I had such a longing to talk with someone that I asked her to come up to my room. I lit the gas log and we sat beside it. On my desk was the red "A Line a Day" she had given me and it now has four whole years of my life inside its covers.

"Remember, you told me to write in it every day and I have. No eyes but mine have read these pages."

"None should, for a diary is a private place. Someday you may go back and find that this record of your growing has much to ponder."

"Someday? That's like Peter Pan's Never Never Land, or More's Utopia, or the lost Atlantis. Is it real? Is someday ever today?"

"For you it will when you write for other eyes to read."

"Oh, Miss Hyde, do you think I really shall?"

"Of course I do, if you keep on writing."

"Someday, then, I may put a book of mine in your hands for you to read. It will be like the child of the red 'A Line a Day,' for there it had its beginning."

"I may not be here then, but I think I'll know and be glad. I've been in your mother's service a long time, since before Virginia was born. I'm not young anymore."

"I thought you'd be here forever."

"Forever is a word we use when we are young without knowing its meaning. As life goes on, we learn that there is no such word."

"I've never shown my poems to anyone, but I'd like to show some to you. I feel safe with you."

"Please, do let me see the ones you're willing to share."

I put the copybook in her hands—"Poems, Book I." It has seventeen poems and *L'Envoi*. As she sat in the little rocker by the fire, I pretended to read from an anthology, but I really watched her. She has a half-smile that never deepens, nor does it fade. Her hands held the book the way a mother holds a baby, and I knew that whatever she said would be good for me to hear. When she closed it she handed it back to me as if it were something precious.

"You don't have to say you like them if you don't."

"I like them."

"Which one do you like best?"

"The one called 'Study.'"

"Why? I didn't think it was nearly so good as 'Twilight.'"

"'Twilight' sounds more like Alfred, Lord Tennyson than you."

"I wrote it after I learned his 'Ulysses' for recitation."

"You've been learning some of Wordsworth, haven't you?"

"Yes. Last month I had to memorize 'Ode on Intimations of Immortality.'"

"And Browning?"

"Oh, yes. I love Browning. He's so valiant."

I wondered how she knew, but when I asked her she smiled as if she had a secret with herself. Then she asked me to read to her some of my favorite poems. They were all in the book I had on my lap, so I read her Wordsworth's "The World Is Too Much with Us," some of Browning, Blake's "The Little Black Boy," and Emily Dickinson's "I Never Saw a Moor." She let a minute or two go by before she said anything.

"Each one is distinct. You can't mistake Wordsworth for Browning. Blake is quite himself, and Emily Dickinson—"

"Emily! Nobody could ever be like her."

"No one can ever be like you, nor can you be like anyone else."

"How can I say things my own way when my mind is filled with others' words?"

"Perhaps it will be when you're ready to trust yourself."

We talked some more. When Miss Hyde left, she seemed to go from the room as softly as a shadow and I went back to my desk. I reread *Called Coward* and it was as if my eyes were new. There were places where I had used lines of Christina Rossetti's because I had loved them so much; then I read some words of William Morris', used because I had not thought I could say it as well as he did. Staring at the pages, I realized it had never occurred to me how out of place were the words of nineteenth-century writers with the setting of the fifteenth century. And it was all because I had not trusted myself! Maybe that is what I need to do more than anything else: believe in myself. I closed the notebook with *Called Coward* on its cover and put it in the bottom drawer of my desk.

March 14, 1921

Today I did the household marketing and it was an adventure. Last week I went with Maria to see how she did it. This week I'm on my own and will be, two mornings every week, from now on. (It's another one of those household privileges which seem to get more interesting and responsible the older I grow.) Mother gave me the housekeeping money in a special purse and a notebook in which to list purchases and their costs. Maria gave me a shopping list and told me to keep my eyes open for what was in season. She gave me other instructions, too, and I hoped I'd remember them all.

Andy brought the Pierce Arrow to the door promptly at seven. I'd had my breakfast in the kitchen. We drove down to the big Open Market near Chippewa Street. I felt as if I were in a play, walking up and down the aisles. Some of the stalls were under cover, some like fruit and vegetables were in the open. Everything looked tempting, but I had my shopping list in one hand, the purse in the other, and Andy walked beside me with a huge basket.

Maria told me not to be taken in by appearances, to use my nose as well as my eyes, and always to smell butter before I bought any. With something like strawberries, she told me to ask the man to tip the box to be sure they were good all the way down, not just on top. She said garden lettuce was preferable to hothouse, that the reddest meat was not always the best, and that strong-smelling fish was the freshest. Steak to be tender should be nicely marbled, and a chicken to roast well should have joints that move easily.

When I saw cantaloupes, I departed from the shopping list and bought three that were fragrant and whose stem ends gave to the pressure of a finger. Artichokes were on the list, but they didn't look fresh, so I didn't buy any. At one of the stalls I was offered a cherry to taste. It was so good that I bought a pound. Andy got me to school just before nine o'clock and went on home with the car laden with our purchases.

This afternoon, as soon as I got home from school, I went over my accounts with Miss Hyde. She found a mistake in subtraction and we corrected it. This kind of arithmetic makes sense!

March 27, 1921

Mother and Father took Bobby and me to New York for Easter vacation. I couldn't possibly write in my diary except to make a tiny note. Now I'm spreading it over all five days as if it was one experience, which it was. Plans had been made weeks ago and in them were concerts and plays, visits to art galleries and museums, as well as the shops. There was some point of interest every day—like the top of the Flatiron Building, where I marveled at the city spread below and felt a funny feeling in my insides. Another day we had a leisurely drive through Central Park in a horse-drawn carriage.

Every night, before going to the theater, we dressed in our best, and dinner was always at a different restaurant, Rumpelmayer's, the Brevoort, the Astor to see people of the theater, the Waldorf Astoria to see people of fashion.

And the plays! *Dear Brutus, Medea, Abraham Lincoln, Othello,* and at the opera *The Magic Flute.* Hearing Zimbalist play and Jeritza sing, watching Raymond Massey act, seeing Sarah Bernhardt in her farewell performance (reclining because she had recently lost a leg to an illness), I felt numbed by beauty and raised to new heights.

Mother said that this was all part of our education, and when I got back to school Miss Conary had written on the blackboard a line from Aristotle: "All teaching is through art." I could agree. I feel as if my mind is a seedbed of ideas, and when my fingers close around a pencil the page will seem too small for me.

May 26, 1921

Miss Conary gave us an assignment, not compulsory, but to do if we wanted to. However, doing it would enrich our minds and deepen our understanding. It is: to read the Bible straight through from beginning to end, four chapters on weekdays, six on Sundays. That would get us through it in a year.

"Read it as literature and history," she said, "but don't be surprised if you find inspiration in it, too."

I began, as several others did, and tried to keep to the schedule, but I was bored by the pages of "begats." Some of the laws seemed unreasonable, and much of the behavior was revolting, but there were passages of pure poetry that exalted me. The more I read, the more I found to hold on to, like Blake's "I give you the end of a golden string."

Oh, if only I could write like Job or Isaiah! I don't lack ideas, but a way to express them. My metaphors get all mixed up and sometimes I never can find the right word no matter how I search the dictionary. Maybe when I'm in Ninth Grade, in Miss Keyes' room and we do more serious writing, I'll feel more able to say things the way I—and nobody but me—can say them.

August 4, 1921

I rode in my first Horse Show at the County Fair. Bluemouse behaved admirably. She tossed her head happily when a yellow ribbon was attached to her bridle. It fluttered in the breeze we made as we cantered around the ring on our way to the paddock. People in the grandstand and along the rail clapped, and I was so proud of my lovely gray mare.

Jinny got a blue with Red Rambler, the thoroughbred hunter that Father got for her a little while ago. She got the Silver Trophy, too, at the end of the show.

There is a party tonight at the Country Club for all the horsey people. Fortunately I'm considered too young to attend. I don't like big parties, where everyone talks and there's a lot of noise. I like small groups, where conversation is like a tennis match, first the ball in one court, then the other, volley after volley, with every stroke counting, then one shot well aimed to make a finish.

September 28, 1921

Ninth Grade! Greek and Geometry are new subjects, and there are to be themes every week. We are in Miss Keyes' room now. She has ideas that don't seem to have anything to do with education but are interesting. One is sharpening a pencil to a fine point. I'm good at this, because long ago Andy taught me how to handle a knife and keep the blade sharp. Another thing she has us do is wrap packages, folding the paper neatly and tying the string securely. She gives a spelling test on Friday afternoons before we have basketball and reminds us that at the end of the year there will be awards for the girls who have not missed a word in the tests.

And then there's the Reading Aloud—ten minutes or more a day to an older person, starting the first day of school and going right through to the last in June. Miss Keyes talks all the time and quotes from every book that's ever been written. She tells us that we can often learn more through the pores of our skin, and that everything we learn will be useful, if not now, then later on.

There are three new girls in school this year, and some of my friends have left for Hutchinson High. I asked if I could change because they have cooking and chemistry and lots of exciting things, but Mother was firm. She said I would get the sciences in college and what I needed now was the solid basic grounding that the Franklin School gave. Maybe it is the best kind of education if I'm going to be a poet. When I said this to Mother she smiled in a tantalizing way and said, "We'll see about that when the time comes." A shiver went through me. When she says, "We'll see," it generally means that her ideas and Father's are not the same as mine.

Joy upon joy, I am to correct themes this year with my adored Miss Watkins! Two themes a week is the rule, a page in length, never more than a page and a half. Sometimes a subject will be given, sometimes we can choose our own. The title is important, as are paragraph subtitles. There is no classroom available for individual work, so we will sit on the stairs for privacy. Oh, to sit beside *her*!

October 7, 1921

Today was the first time. My theme was on buttermaking. It had been submitted early in the week, so Miss Watkins had had time to read it. I wondered what she would think of me. She underlined one word and circled a punctuation mark.

"'Climactical' is not the adjective from 'climate,' but from 'climax.' Don't let yourself be so captivated by the sound of words that you forget it is their meaning that matters. Keep your themes in a folder. After some time has gone by, you can measure yourself against yourself and see how you have improved. I hope you will show this one to your Father."

She took her pencil, made a red 9 up in the left-hand corner, gave it back to me, and *smiled*!

I did show it to Father that night. He read it as slowly as he reads the *Wall Street Journal;* then he gave it back to me. "Anyone would know you had made butter," he said and squeezed my hand for a minute. I knew what he meant and happiness tumbled around inside me. Mother didn't take quite so long to read it. "That's very nice, dear, very well done. I'm glad your teacher liked it."

So I put the theme away in a special folder. Now I live for those lessons on the stairs and Friday couldn't come soon enough.

October 14, 1921

"I didn't know you went to Wyoming last summer."
"I didn't."
"You did your research well, and your familiarity with horses supplied the feeling."
"Thank you, Miss Watkins."
"Did you go to the International Horse Race at Belmont Park?"

"Oh, we went. Father took Jinny and me. It was thrilling."

"You have made it so. Your use of words is good. You must have listened well to all that was going on around you. You were not there alone, you had your reader with you. I like the way you link meaning to observation. This, in your third paragraph—'There was something significant of the nations, Britain and America, in the horses as they pranced to the starting point—Papyrus, confident, calm, proud, phlegmatic; Zev, nervous, excited, keen, eager. High-strung both of them, but both keyed to a different pitch.' Were you sorry Papyrus did not win?"

"Oh, no, I'm an American."

The theme got a 10 in Miss Watkins' red pencil in the upper left corner and something sang in me. I had pleased her and myself too.

Description is one thing, philosophizing quite another. I've found that out. When I read Thoreau's words "The mass of men lead lives of quiet desperation" I felt such a part of the mass that I wrote a theme about them.

"I think you do not yet know enough about desperation to write convincingly. Stay with what you know."

"But I have known depths of despair."

"You can learn much from Thoreau without trying to interpret him. Your use of words is often overdone—words like 'grandilo-quent,' 'asseveration,' 'pusillanimous.'"

"But I like to find new words."

"They must be right in the context or they are meaningless. Study for simplicity. It is a hard lesson to learn. And don't tell me that an experience was unforgettable. You must make me feel that it was unforgettable, and your right use of words will do that."

She talked to me about my mixing of metaphors and asked me to bring her a single sentence that would be explicit. I worked hard and this is what I brought to her: "The forge of the years is before me: I know that only on the anvil of persistence with the hammer of hard work can I shape my dream into reality."

Keeping her red pencil in her lap and smiling, she said, "You're really serious about your work, aren't you?"

Of course I said yes.

December 6, 1921

Life gets more and more wonderful! This morning at breakfast Father told me that, now I am sixteen, I am to have a monthly allowance of $25. "For all reasonable expenses. It will be your own money and consequently your responsibility. You will make no accounting, such as you do with the marketing money, but you must learn to live within it."

"That's a fortune!"

"You've handled money well. You've shown a profit in the butter-making and your weekly marketing has been prudently done. Now, see what you can do for yourself."

The check looked to me as if it would buy the world, but I think it was because I had been given not so much a gift as a trust.

After dinner, with all the wonder of cake and candles, Mother took me to see Pavlova. Oh, she was glorious, never did she seem to touch the ground, always she was in the air or in the arms of her partner. I was so inspired that when I got home I worked for a long time on the poem I want to send to *St. Nicholas.*

December 31, 1921

What a Christmas this year! We all seemed to get what we were longing for, and my gift was an opal ring from Mother and Father. Ever since I saw one years ago, it has been my deepest wish, and now it seems that all my material desires are satisfied. Mother reminded me that it was not my birthstone, and Miss Hyde told me never to let it fall on a stone floor or it would shatter into a thousand fragments. Jinny said not to wear it if I ever felt sick, for its color would change and it would give me away. I don't care a fig for superstition. To me my opal is imprisoned beauty flashing in the light.

Christmas vacation seemed to go in getting ready for Jinny's coming-out party. The debutante ball on New Year's Eve would be the social event of the season. I addressed envelopes for the invitations and helped in many ways, but I was not at all sure, when the great moment came, that I really wanted to go.

My best white organdy dress with the blue silk sash makes me feel like a little girl, but when Mother said I could put my hair up I felt older. Jinny looked like a queen. Her first dance was with Father, of course; then she was whirled off in the arms of different partners.

My first dance was with Bobby. Then one of Jinny's friends asked me for the waltz. I must really look quite grown-up because he whispered in my ear that he loved me and would wait for my coming-out party, then he would ask me to marry him. I could have slapped him! I'm an inch taller than he is and I'm probably still growing. He's nice enough, but there are so many things I want to do before I get married. Besides, I want to choose for myself, not have a man thrust himself on me.

1922

January 5, 1922

All my good resolves to study Latin when I go up to my room after dinner evaporate when I get an idea for a poem. I've just finished working over the one I started while watching Pavlova. I've printed it out carefully and am sending it to the St. Nicholas League. I wonder how long it will be before I hear from them.

The Ovid translation never got done, because I fell asleep over it, so I had nothing for Latin and it was the first period! Miss Keyes asked me to stay after school. She lectured me until nearly 6 o'clock, when I could have been skating with the O.A.O.'s. Walking home, I decided that I'd have to take myself in hand, so I wrote a declaration—

I swear with a solemn oath that I shall never, during the remainder of this year, enter Latin Class without having spent forty-five minutes of concentrated study on my preparation.

I asked Ethel to witness it and had already written out her part of the declaration—

I promise that if my best friend does not observe her self-made rule that I will neither speak to her nor have anything to do with her for one week.

Now I'll see if this works.

February 12, 1922

Madame Curie is visiting Buffalo and Mother took me to hear her speak. Jinny came too. Sitting in the crowded hall and listening to the small, frail woman who had done so much for her country and the world, I felt renewed excitement about my own life—not to be great as an ambition, but great for something worthwhile. "Not tomorrow, not next week, but today," Madame Curie had said at a time when the words had been a rule of life to her. I took them to heart as my rule.

When the lecture was over and Madame Curie left the platform, I sat still in the marvel of all I had just heard. Jinny nudged me and told me to wake up, that Mother wanted to take me shopping. I shook my head, still in a daze, but I wanted Jinny to know that I

On Bluemouse,

ready for the show-ring

had not been sleeping. I came out of my daze when I remembered that another great event was ahead.

February 13, 1922

DePinna from New York is in Buffalo today. For three years, every time DePinna has come, I've begged Mother for a suit and she said that I would have one when I had the figure for it. Now I have and, after looking at several, we chose one that is a sky-blue tweed with four pockets in the jacket and a skirt with two pleats. My measurements were taken, Mother gave the order, and delivery was assured within the month.

"How can I ever wait that long!"

"You'll have to remember to carry yourself well when you wear a suit, to hold your shoulders back and your head high."

"I shall!" Madame Curie's words came back to me, the words she had used when told that formalities regarding the precious gram of radium would be taken care of the following week. "Not tomorrow, not next week, but today. Now." I straightened my shoulders and thought of my sky-blue suit.

February 14, 1922

If school were just writing themes, all would be well. I never lack for subjects, while some girls spend half their study period chewing the tops of their pencils, wondering what to write about. To me, everything, everyone, has a story. Sometimes, when I'm at my desk at home and Brier snuggles close to me, I imagine myself inside his wiry coat and try to think what life is like to him.

Miss Watkins gets more strict in her marking all the time; appearance, handwriting, punctuation seem to count as much as the idea. A word misused or misspelled, a carelessly placed comma, unnecessary repetition, faulty paragraphing can bring a mark down from a high of 10 to 9, 8, 7. A theme turned in late, no matter how good it is, gets zero. Today she gave me the highest praise I've ever had, when she said, "You do have ability, and that can take you far."

February 18, 1922

The pact I made and Ethel witnessed is working. This week my work merited a White Card, signed by Bertha A. Keyes. I put it at Father's place at dinner. It isn't so much what it says, that I am "entitled to this token of approbation for faithful performance of all school duties during the past week"; it's what it means!

The Reading Aloud to an older person ten minutes every day has nothing to do with school, but it's important to me. Reading is my life, the way writing is, and there are plenty of older people around our house. Mother is generally the nearest, and we never stop at ten minutes. Last night I read to Father. He fell asleep and I didn't know what to do, so I just kept on reading—twenty pages of Lord Chesterfield's *Letters to His Son*. When Father stirred, I closed the book rather loudly and slipped out of the room. Miss Hyde is always around to listen, if Mother is out, and she corrects my pronunciation in her gentle way. Last night I read the newspaper to Lizzie; dull for me, but she liked it.

April 18, 1922

Mother and I have just begun a *Life of St. Francis of Assisi*. When we finished the first chapter, we talked about all that he had done for his own time, and for people ever since.

"Mother, why doesn't Jinny do something?"

"She's doing a great deal. Her coming out was a success and many pleasant things have been moving her way because of it. She's active in the Junior League. She's on the committee for the Spring Horse Show. What more would you want her to do?"

"Not more, just more important, like writing plays the way she used to. Teach. Work. Do something."

"Jinny has been born to a certain way of life and she is doing what is expected of her. For her to work when there is no need would be to deprive someone for whom there is need. Her education and training have equipped her to fill a position of influence in society. I hope she will write more plays for the pleasure of her friends and the benefit of some worthwhile charity. There is an interesting word which you might well add to your vocabulary. Dilettante. It applies to people in our position."

"In the book we're reading, St. Francis was a nobleman's son and look what he did with his life."

"Oh, but that's so different."

"Why?"

"Because he was a saint."

Grown-ups have a way of giving answers that are no answers, and there's nothing to be done about them. We had read more than ten minutes and the book was closed, so I kissed Mother good night and went up to my room. Brier was already there, waiting for me, so I talked to him. "I feel like Hector on the ringing plains of windy Troy, for I am about to do battle, but the battle is with myself."

Brier always listens to me. He looks wiser than he used to because of all his gray hair and I sometimes think he is the only one in the house who understands my position. I told him that in another few years I would write poems, stories, books. "The kind people want to read. I will do it and I will be happy." He wagged his tail and in his eyes was agreement. I remembered the word Mother told me to look up, but I closed the dictionary as soon as I read the definition, knowing it was not for me.

May 5, 1922

Today *St. Nicholas* came. I raced up to my room with it to see how my poem looked in print, but all I could find was my name on the Honor Roll. It's a bitter blow. My poem was not good enough to print and I had considered it my best, so far. But, *allons!* I can't let a first discouragement drag me down, for there may be many worse ones later.

Sir Philip Gibbs, a charming Englishman, is lecturing in Buffalo and Father took me to hear him. He spoke about his book, *The Middle of the Road*, which I had just read. I liked what he said. His philosophy matches with the ancient Greeks' *sophrosune*—that was their great virtue and Miss Keyes keeps the word written in big letters, Greek letters, on the blackboard in her room. Moderation. I need it. One day I'm up, one day I'm down; one day everything goes well, the next day I'm in disgrace. I'm lectured at school and lectured at home.

Midterm examinations were a real test, but I came through them, even with an 88 in Greek. It was a double-red-lined report that I could take home and I was so thrilled by that achievement that I wrote a paraphrase of Kipling's "If" for my theme. The first two verses were all about playing the game of learning and obedience so you could earn white cards and red-lined reports, but in the last verse I let my deepest feelings out:

> *If you can have a time for work and still a time for play,*
> *Using your opportunities with conscientious thought,*
> *If you observe three bywords carefully each day*
> *That with mental, moral, physical your life must be*
> *   inwrought;*
> *If you can shun temptations, forcing your will to aid,*
> *And ever strive to higher far ascend;*
> *If you can be undaunted, as well as unafraid,*
> *You'll gain the gole of college, then, my friend.*

May 10, 1922

Sitting on the stairs with Miss Watkins today I watched her as she read my theme, my paraphrase. I couldn't really tell what she was thinking, but soon I knew.

"Well done," she said, "except for a word misspelled." Her pencil drew a red A– at the top of the page. "I didn't know you wrote poetry, and I'm glad that you can print so nicely. It's a useful skill."

Miss Watkins glanced at me as if she saw me instead of my paper. She said I looked feverish and to go to the school nurse and have my temperature taken, then report to Miss Keyes.

I was horror-struck! I did feel achy and hot, but I had no intention of being sent home when a basketball game was to be played. On my way to Mrs. Ellington I stopped in the cloakroom and took a long drink of cold water and swished it around in my mouth.

When I presented myself to Mrs. Ellington I told her there was absolutely nothing the matter with me, but as I was wearing my opal ring I turned the stone into my palm so it could not give me away. She took my temperature twice and shook her head both times, then told me I was subnormal.

Knowing Miss Watkins had already warned Miss Keyes that I would be reporting to her, I went to her office and said that I was normal. It seemed better to leave the sub off. I never intend to be sick, I said. Miss Keyes looked at me and said she approved of my attitude. The basketball game was a hard-fought one, but our team came through victorious.

When I got home, Mother took one look at me and told me to take a hot bath and get into bed, that I had every evidence of a cold, and rest and warmth were the rule. An hour later she came up to me with her infallible remedy for every ill—a tiny little glass of hot toddy. It was sweet, and as it went down I could feel its warmth tingling all through me.

Mother sat beside me and held my hand, but what she was really doing was taking my pulse. She said colds are soonest over when we keep them to ourselves and she wanted me to stay in bed all day tomorrow. I don't mind. Tomorrow is Saturday and I've just started to read *The Three Musketeers*.

May 16, 1922

Roller-skating and bicycle days have come. Hatless, coatless figures are seen flying through the streets. Jacks and marbles are played on house steps. Wizened old Italians playing hurdy-gurdys stop before our house in the evening. Popcorn men stroll slowly by. (I wanted to put an exclamation mark after every sentence, but Miss Watkins says not to be too free with them or they lose their meaning.)

I never seem to outgrow the ecstasy of the spring, not that I should or anyone should. My bicycle has been painted a gorgeous green and it seems to go even faster than ever. I race everywhere on Comrade and scorn other forms of conveyance. We play tennis after school and go home munching popcorn and walking to the rhythm of a squeaky street organ somewhere in the distance. Oh, these spring days and their long, light evenings that make us all like children in our thoughts and actions!!!

June 10, 1922

Prize Day brings the school year to a close and I have some records to put down. In gym, 3'8" in the high jump, 13'11" in the broad, so I've won my F.S. '22 letter. In pencil-sharpening I did the finest point in the least time. Wrapping up a package with cardboard, brown paper, and string was won on all three counts—time, security, neatness. Perfect attendance, neither absent nor tardy all year, brought commendation. But I missed one word in a spelling test, so the award, a cake of pink soap, does not come to me. I spelled "judgment" with an *e* after the *g*. That's the way it is in the Bible and Shakespeare, but Miss Keyes says we must be consistent and spell the American way—"judgment" without an *e*, "honor" without a *u*, and such. So, for the addition of an *e* I lost and must bite the bullet of disappointment, resolving to be more aware of national differences. All those who had kept faithfully to the ten-minute Reading Aloud received a book as a present from Miss Keyes. My set of the Brontës is almost complete.

June 25, 1922

Father must be as glad to get out to Hillhurst for the summer as we are. This morning after breakfast he said to me, "Let's take a look at things with the horses." Al soon had Red Rambler, the big gelding, and my beautiful Bluemouse saddled and brought around; then Father and I trotted off. He likes to see how the trees he has had planted along the farm roads and even the main road are growing, how the cattle look in the pastures, and the way the crops are coming. Stopping at the farm office, he had a long talk with Ed Wado. Before we left, Mr. Wado said he had cream set aside for my butter-making and that he would bring it around.

We rode down one of the lanes that dips into a little valley where the heifers were grazing, then climbs to a ridge. At the crest we reined the horses in for a rest and Father pointed to some woodland. He told me he had just made arrangements to buy it, all fifty acres, for he had learned that the timber was to be sold. He said it was important to have strong stands of trees throughout the country to keep water in the land. It sounded almost Biblical the way he said it—"to keep water in the land."

July 31, 1922

I think the times I like best of all are when I go off on Bluemouse, as I did today, all by myself and for the whole day. I put a sandwich and an apple in my saddlebag, with my notebook and pencil. The whole day is mine and so is the country. I talk to Bluemouse and she replies with a flicking of her ears, a whinny sometimes, and a snort when I nudge her into a gallop up a hill. At noon we stop by a creek for water. I flatten myself on the stones and have as good a drink, but not such a long one, as Bluemouse does; then I loosen the saddle girth. While she grazes, I lean back against a tree and write in my notebook. I've been thinking about aloneness and realize that it is the price a writer must be willing to pay. I have to be by myself to think out my thoughts.

On the way home it started to rain, then it turned into a steady drizzle, but it felt as good to me as it did to my horse. Back at the stable when I told Al where we had been, the back roads traveled and the different villages gone through, he said I must have been thirty miles and that Bluemouse deserved an extra measure of oats. Thirty miles of thinking: what a day!

Riding I think; up in the pigeon loft I write. This summer I'm writing a novel, *The Songs of the Angel*. It goes on and on. It may be years before I finish it. I'd like to read some of it to the Triers, but maybe it's better not to read it to anyone until it is finished.

When Jinny isn't working with the horses to get them ready for the shows, she has friends in for parties: tennis in the afternoons, bridge in the evenings. Last night, short a fourth, she asked me to join them and taught me how to play bridge. I expect that will be as useful an accomplishment as the other bits and pieces of learning that come my way. Maybe. I say that because of something I've just learned not to do, again.

At breakfast, Father read in the paper about a girl who had swum the length of the Panama Canal with her wrists tied together and her ankles also tied to each other. It sounded interesting and I decided to try it. I rode Old Joe down to Green Lake. I didn't take Bluemouse, because I didn't want to have to tie her to a tree while I was in the water. Green Lake was made years ago by damming up a small creek that flowed through a valley. It's deep enough, but murky, and there are woods all around it. It had been a rainy day, so no one else was there and I had it to myself for my experiment. Old Joe didn't mind being tied loosely to a tree, so I got into my bathing suit, took two pieces of clothesline and swam out to the float. I tied my ankles first, and then my wrists, and jumped in, thinking it would take me only a few minutes to swim back to the shore, but I sank like a leaden weight and couldn't swim to get any kind of motion from either my arms or my legs. I could see dimly through the murky water the skeletons of trees all around me and knew how deep down I had gone. By a superhuman effort, I broke the bonds at my wrists and struggled up to the surface, gasping and choking. I lay on the float for a long time. Then I got the line around my ankles undone and swam back to shore. It felt so good to have Old Joe under me instead of all that water around me. My wrists are raw from the rope and I wore long sleeves at dinner so no one would notice.

August 24, 1922

Jinny has been working with the three hunters—Rob Roy, Larkspur, and Red Rambler—schooling them, putting them over the jumps Al made in the field, and all sorts of general handling, while I've just been riding Bluemouse. At the County Show the horses were entered in all the classes they could qualify for. One of them was "Seat and Hands," and I felt smart in my trim habit, shiny black boots, bowler hat, gloves, and holding a crop, which I never used. Just before I went into the ring on Bluemouse, Jinny, standing by the gate, whispered, "Light hands and a firm seat. Don't think of the people watching you, but of Blue's perform-ance." When the class was over—all the gaits shown as well as backing, standing, dismounting and mounting before the judge—Bluemouse had a red ribbon pinned to her bridle! I thought my heart would burst with love and pride when I trotted around the ring for the last time. Jinny came out of that show with six blue ribbons, a silver cup for Rob Roy as champion saddle horse, and in the lightweight hunter class she got a blue and a silver plate with Larkspur. After the show there was a big party at the Coun-try Club, but I didn't go to it. Jinny is in her element. Father says we can go on to the State Fair in Syracuse in September, but we'll be up against much stiffer competition. Jinny's dream is Madison Square Garden next winter.

September 22, 1922

There are some new faces in school and some of my old friends just look different. They've either bobbed their hair or put it up, and I still wear mine shoulder length with a band to hold it back. I don't feel as opposed to study as I have some years. Maybe I'll even do better with Algebra, though I doubt it. At home our family has shrunk. Father and Mother have taken Jinny to Europe for two months, the boys are in college, so it's Bobby and me and Miss Hyde, and Brier, of course. The house on Delaware Avenue seems awfully big.

Miss Keyes talks more than ever. I guess that is one thing that will never change. At the last period, which is always hers, either History or English, she didn't hear the bell and just went on talking, but she made one startling statement. She said, "A lady might commit murder, but she would never throw a scrap of paper on the street." Walking home, Ethel and Barbara and I had to think that one out, so we stopped at Thurston's for sundaes and tried to reason how that could be. Creating a situation and trying to resolve it is better than a problem in Algebra, as far as I'm concerned. Finally we left, each one of us putting our 15 cents on the marble top of the table.

We're not supposed to, but we often slip notes to each other in classes and today Ethel slipped to me the paper she had been writing during Study Period. It was folded sixteen times and she gave me instructions not to open it until I got home. When I did, I saw that it was a poem about me! It's so beautiful that I'm copying it into my diary on one of those blank pages at the end that are for special thoughts.

> IN SCHOOL
> *She sits here, close beside me, silent—*
> *Silent save for the quick, sharp scraping of her pen.*
> *I too am still. The busy room*
> *Throbs with the heavy, even pulse of school.*
> *Her head bends low, intently, over her work.*
> *Her brown hair, dark and smooth and lustrous,*
> *Lies gently against the soft curve of her cheek,*
> *Delicately modeled, yet ruddy*
> *With the clear, fresh bloom of radiant health.*
> *Her eyes, deep fringed, are warm,*

Like dark, clear amber, burning
With suppressed thought—burning
As she writes, in Greek, so carefully,
Lips parted, just a little—firm resolution in her chin.
I am glad that your Greek is so interesting—
For if it were French you were doing,
I could not sit here, idly, watching.
Yet were I studying ever so hard from a book
My profit would be of far less worth
Than are the deep thoughts I am thinking now,
Watching your face.

School nights or not, I'm always allowed to attend a play or concert when either comes to Buffalo. Miss Keyes and Mother have the same idea about education—that much of it comes from exposure to our cultural inheritance. When Walter Hampden came in *Hamlet,* the O.A.O.'s went, inviting Miss Comey (the new teacher, whom we adore) to be our chaperone and guest. Miss Hyde took me to see *Mr. Pim Passes By,* and I was so charmed that I'm considering being a playwright instead of a poet, in spite of my faults with *Called Coward.* Last night it was the New York Symphony with Walter Damrosch conducting. I felt so carried away on a surge of sound that I wondered if my feet would touch the earth again. It was like when I heard Rachmaninoff, I thought that he was speaking to my soul. Even with all these marvelous events, my lessons are going just a bit auspiciously.

December 6, 1922

It was so small that my hand had to search for it under the pillow, and it was not even in a box, but wrapped in soft paper. When I went down to breakfast I knew who had put it there and I showed it to Father, fitting perfectly on the little finger of my right hand.

"You're seventeen," he said, as if that explained everything.

The ring is the Yates crest. The gold is so new and shining that the design and wording are clear. Father's, inherited from his father, has been worn so long that the lettering is faint and the design has almost disappeared; but he lives by it and the motto is engraven on his heart, so it does not matter what the wear of the years has done to it. On a shield there are three gates, for long ago an ancestor of ours was keeper of the King's gates. Above them is a crown from which emerges the bearded head of a goat. At the base of the escutcheon is a scroll with two words, *Sois Feal,* "Be thou faithful," and they are in Norman English. That is my motto and my direction, as it has been Father's. I wear the ring with pride, and I honor its challenge.

December 14, 1922

Today, when I came home from school, Mother was having a tea party, so I crept quietly and, I think, invisibly up the stairs, but their voices followed me and I knew with a sinking heart that they were talking about me.

"I hear she writes poetry." That was Miss Martin.

"Perhaps it's just a phase," Mrs. Slee said.

"She's very young to write poetry."

"That's why she does, my dear, because she is young; but they get over it."

"Virginia is settling down nicely and we feel that Betty will do the same, in time."

I turned the crest on my finger and thought of its words, "Be thou faithful." To what—my family? myself? Is this where the test comes? I felt angry. I wanted to go downstairs and stamp into that stupid tea party and tell them I was going to do what I had to do whether anyone liked it or not; then I felt sad and tears rushed into my eyes as they do so easily. But the words of King Arthur that Miss Keyes had us memorize came to my mind:

> *If thou hast sorrow,*
> *tell it not to thy foe;*
> *tell it to thy saddle-bow*
> *and ride singing forth.*
> *Hide it deep in thy heart*
> *that it leave no smart;*
> *nor let it be guessed*
> *what is hid in thy breast.*

If only I could have ridden Bluemouse across the fields, but she is in the barn at Hillhurst, and I in my room in Buffalo, so I told myself I would have to ride singing forth in my mind. And so I did.

1923

January 1, 1923

The chimes have been ringing the old year out and I have written the last words in my red-leather "A Line a Day." Five years of my life are within its pages, five years during which I've grown from a little girl to being someone who can measure herself against what she wants to do with her life. I'm 5'7" and I weigh 125 pounds. That's probably what I'm going to be, as I haven't changed for a year.

January 15, 1923

I've started a new diary. This one has a green cover with space for four years and it is called "A Diary by Days." These will be important years for me as I finish at the Franklin School and then go on to college. Looking at so many blank pages, I wonder to myself what they will hold.

Today we had our first class in English Folk Dancing and Songs. A Mr. Rabold comes from New York and it is exciting. We did Morris dances and swung our way through the Helston Furry. Next time he comes, which will be in two weeks, he's going to start us on a Sword Dance. The songs—"Greensleeves," "The Foggy Foggy Dew," and others—make my heart melt and my feet tingle. Now, more than ever, do I long to go to England. Father says it will be my graduation present, but that is a year and six months away.

January 29, 1923

Jinny's social life makes me feel farther apart from her than the seven years between us. I don't see much of her, even though we're living in the same house. Occasionally, just occasionally, we do have a talk about books. She keeps me reading, just as did the list she made for me when I was little. I don't always enjoy a book, but she says I shouldn't read just for enjoyment but to stretch my mind and develop new tastes. Jinny used to be so studious. Now laughter and lightness fill her days and she's more beautiful than ever. Today it dawned on me that she is in love! As soon as she gets back from New York I'm going to ask her. She's there, staying with a college friend, for the Horse Show at Madison Square Garden. Father didn't send our horses this year, but Jinny took her riding things just in case.

Maid of Honor

at Jinny's wedding

February 27, 1923

Jinny's back, positively shining, but with an air of mystery as well as triumph. She told us all about it at dinner tonight. I think she spent most of her time at the Garden and with the horses. There were parties every night, and the last night there was a ball. She did get a chance to ride and even brought a horse from the Bard Stables through to a championship. I wanted to know more, so I asked her to come up to my room and sit by my little gas fire. My homework was all done by the time she came, because she had a long telephone call. Her eyes were sparkling, her cheeks glowing, and there was an electric quality about her. I asked her if he was tall and straight of limb, tender and true.

"Oh, so you guessed! He's that and more. We met last summer at the State Fair. He rides for Bard and I've never seen such handling, such rapport with a horse. We've been writing every day, and telephoning. Then last week in New York—"

"He asked you to marry him?"

"Yes! He's coming this weekend to see Father."

"It's like a story in a book—'and they lived happily ever after.'"

"I hope so, but—well, I don't know what Father will think. You see, he really doesn't do anything but ride and he doesn't have any money."

"But what does that matter if you love each other? If, as you said to me long ago, when you looked into each other's eyes you both knew?"

March 4, 1923

I didn't get a chance to meet the "well-beloved" because that weekend the O.A.O.'s had a house party at Charlotte's on the lake shore. We had been making plans for weeks and invited both Miss Watkins and Miss Barker to be our guests. (We had to have at least one older person around to listen to our ten-minute Reading Aloud.) When I got home Sunday evening the house had an empty feeling to it. Miss Hyde said Father had taken everyone to the Buffalo Club for dinner, then to a concert.

"And Jinny's young man? Oh, do tell me what he is like."

"Young man? Oh yes, someone did come yesterday to see your father."

"Didn't he stay overnight, like a guest?"

"No."

It was puzzling. I had looked forward to meeting him, to welcoming him as one of the family, to seeing that shining radiance that Jinny was keeping to herself spill over on us all when it was no longer a secret. When I got up to my room, a piece of paper on the bare surface of my desk caught my eye. It was Jinny's handwriting, that strong, angular hand that is so distinctive. It said, "Forget what I told you the other night. Destroy this." She did not sign it. There was no need.

I unpacked, took a bath and went to bed to settle into a book, but it was no use. My mind kept whirling. I put out the light, knowing I wouldn't sleep, but wanting everyone to think I was asleep when they got back. I heard their voices, then soon the silence of the house.

After a long enough time for everyone to have gone to bed and when I felt the darkness was safe, I crept down to Jinny's room and made a scratching sound at her door. She didn't say anything, so I went in. She was sitting at her desk, but she turned to look at me. Her face had its stony look.

"What do you want?"

"I found your note."

"Yes."

"Tell me what's happened. I can't stand not knowing."

"I'm not announcing my engagement. Ever."

"But, why, when you love him?"

"If you must know, it's because I would have to give up too much. We wouldn't be able to live in the way I'm accustomed to live."

"But, you'd have each other."

"You're too young to know about these things. People must have something more than love to live on."

"But—"

"Please go back to bed and forget what I said to you the other night."

I left the room and felt my way up the dark stairs. Once in bed I pulled the blanket up to my chin to stop my shivering. It wasn't that the night was cold, but I felt I'd never be warm again. Something I could not name had an icy clutch on me. There was nothing I could do about it, but I was afraid of what life could do to people.

April 22, 1923

Recitation in English is my joy. The poems I've learned and those I'm learning I say to myself walking back and forth to school and at night before I fall asleep. Tennyson, Wordsworth, Shelley, Keats,

Byron, and so many others are my friends. It's as if I had a book-shelf in my mind and instead of reading I can remember and say their words. Next week we will start memorizing our parts for the play we are doing this year. It's *As You Like It*, and I'm to be Jaques. I hope I won't be self-conscious. That's my bane, the way shyness was when I was little.

May 10, 1923

I'm almost too tired to write anything in my diary but I must make a note, for it was all such fun. Last weekend, Martha's mother took the O.A.O.'s on a camping trip. We walked miles, slept out-doors, cooked our meals over a fire, swam where the creek ran deep holes, and we managed to keep up our Reading Aloud. Ten minutes from each one of us for two days and we read all of Christopher Morley's *Inward Ho!*

May 12, 1923

Buffalo society is agog! Jinny's engagement to a rising young lawyer has been announced. The wedding is set for early June and Jinny wants me to be her Maid of Honor. What could I say but yes, even though with a heavy heart. Shall I go through life the only one knowing her two secrets? Presents keep arriving at the house; every-one talks about what a good match it is, and Mother looks very happy. Jinny is having so many parties given for her that we scarcely see her at home. My dress is going to be beautiful, but it is a nui-sance to take time from tennis to go for fittings. Jinny's dress is ele-gant, but I wish she could be married in her riding habit and I could attend wearing jodhpurs. It would be much more suitable. However, my dress is the most exquisite one I've ever had, very long, gold color with a brown velvet sash and lace collar. I'll use it for years and years as my best dress. But all of this—the dinner party before the wedding, with duck and champagne, then the wedding with crowds of people—makes me feel as if I were going to be in a play. It doesn't seem real, somehow, and what does it have to do with love? When I get married, if I ever do, I want to have the wed-ding be just between me and my well-beloved, and God.

June 6, 1923

The last day of school and a really great event in my life—not a word missed in the spelling tests all through the year, and Miss Keyes presented me with the Cake of Pink Soap. It's big and fragrant, a very special kind of French soap. This means everything to me and I can look back on all that has made it possible. When we first began Latin in the Seventh Grade, Miss Conary said it would help us to know the meaning of English words by knowing their roots and if you know roots you can spell. Also, reading observantly fixes words in your mind, and knowing the rules, like *i* before *e* and such, helps too. When I showed the soap to Bobby he smelled it suspiciously. I assured him that I was never going to use it for washing.

"But that's what soap is for."

"Not this soap."

"Then tell me what you're going to do with it."

"I shall give it to Father."

"But it's a ladies' soap!"

"If it were not for Father and his wanting me to do my best, I would never have won this."

"He won't use it. It smells too much."

"He'll use it if I give it to him."

June 28, 1923

Everything has been the same for so long, and now it seems everything is different. Jinny is married and she and Henry are living in a house Father gave them for a wedding present, the boys are away in summer jobs, and I'm to go to camp, Tegawitha in the Pocono Mountains of Pennsylvania. Bobby will be the only one home. It all got decided as if it was to happen anyway. No butter-making, no garden, no horse shows, none of the things that have been summer for so long.

Mother says in her reasonable way that it's good for everyone to have a change, and Father assured me that the horses would be kept exercised and two of the mares might be bred. I had my last ride on Bluemouse and told her all the things I can't ever tell people. On my way back I stopped at the Triers to say good-by to them, and for the last time Brier slept on my bed. There's a terrible aching inside me, even though I'm excited about the adventure ahead. Why, oh why, do we want things to stay the same when we know they can't?

July 10, 1923

It's the first time I've ever been away from home. I thought I'd be lonely, but the life has caught me up so quickly that I haven't time to be bothered with myself. The counselors are really great and the six other girls in my cabin are the kind I like to know. My diary can't possibly hold all we're doing, so I'm keeping an extra notebook. During our last theme session on the stairs, Miss Watkins said to me,

"Seek to be one of those people on whom nothing can be lost."
(That's Henry James.) I want to save everything of this experience
for themes next winter. From the time the bugle sounds reveille to
taps at night, the day is full—baseball, track, tennis, swimming,
canoeing, riding, crafts, and *people*. Each one is new to me, and interesting. There are ten horses and each one of them is as different as
the people. Rainy days are for crafts and I've already made a ceramic
bowl that will be a drinking dish for Brier. On Saturday nights we
sing around the campfire and next week we're going to do a play.

Best of all is the woodland world—the lake held by hills that rise
to mountains. And the weather, whatever it does, I relish it—sunny
days, or gray, or rainy. Last night there was a glorious display of
northern lights. We all went out to the athletic field, lay on our
backs, and watched the colors changing and shifting, streamers of
light being gathered into the center of the sky, then being scattered
to the disappearing distance. We're generally a chattering bunch,
but it was so awesome, so celestial, that we were silenced. No one
said anything as we went back to our various cabins and snuggled
into our cots.

The only time I have to be alone with my thoughts is rest hour.
We can't talk or read, but must lie on our cots quietly; there is no
rule against thinking. I try to think fast and make notes. When I'm
home and can take Bluemouse off for one of our days together, I'll
be able to think longer and more slowly.

July 28, 1923

Mrs. Lynch called me to her office today. I couldn't think what
I'd done wrong, and I hadn't done anything. What she said left me
as speechless as the northern lights, but in a different way. She said
that one of the counselors had been called home and that during
August she would like me to teach riding to the little children. She
was serious, and even mentioned that I would be paid.

"From the first day we have seen that you have a natural ability
with horses, and that you also have a respect for children. We would
like to assign you to two hours' teaching every afternoon, and to act
in general as a Junior Counselor. We feel that we can trust you."

"Me, teach?"

"The little ones. They are the most teachable, for they have confidence in the horses and in their instructor. It is the older ones who
sometimes treat a horse as if it were a mechanical thing that gives
trouble."

On my way back to the cabin I went down to the lake. I wanted to sit still for a few minutes and remember things Jinny had said to me—that riding is rhythm with the horse, that balance is instinctive, with a firm seat and knees that grip, that a horse senses through the telegraphy of the reins whether a rider is trusting or timid and will act accordingly. Remembering that made me realize that, more than anything, I must help the children to understand that they and their horses are friends, working together, being happy together. If they feel comfortable, and sure, technique will take care of itself. Just thinking about Jinny made me ache for all we once had shared. But nothing could take from me my joy in reading, my delight in riding, and those were paths she had started me on years and years ago. I can hardly wait for tomorrow and my first time with the children.

August 14, 1923

Mail time is just after luncheon and I'm often lucky. Mother writes twice a week, and between Miss Hyde and Bobby and some of the O.A.O.'s I have a letter almost every day. Familiar handwriting is like a picture of the person. It makes me feel happy just to see it. Today there was a small square envelope. The writing was cramped and trembly, and on the back it said G. A. Trier, Orchard Park, New York. I didn't want to open it right away, because I thought he must be telling me that Mrs. Trier was sick and I was too far away to go and see her and be of some help. I asked Mrs. Lynch if I could be excused from rest hour to go and sit by the lake. She saw the letter in my hand and said yes.

After I read it I looked out across the lake to the distant hills and the faraway sky. His words kept repeating themselves inside me, "You'll never know how much you meant to her." I couldn't cry. Somehow I thought she wouldn't want me to. I can only try to lead a better life, to be more like her. She was always so calm, so sure. She believed in people. She believed in me.

September 4, 1923

This is my first day home after the wonderful summer at camp. I saddled Bluemouse and rode down to see Mr. Trier. He was sitting in the rocking chair near the window where she used to sit. Everything was the same. The plants were still blooming. The big iron stove was warm, but there was no fragrance of new-baked or baking bread. I pulled up the chair I always sat in and put it beside Mr. Trier, then I took his hands in mine. We didn't say much, but when I knew it was time for me to go he kept hold of my hands as if he didn't want me to go.

"It almost seems like home again to have you here," he said. I told him I'd come down every day until school started and we went back to the city to live. Riding home I cried, not for her but for him and me.

September 16, 1923

So many doors have been closing, but there's one that is opening and that is the Twelfth Grade at the Franklin School. As usual, Morning Exercises begin the day. The lower classes march into Miss Keyes' room singing a hymn. Then she reads from the Bible, we say the Lord's Prayer, announcements are made, a new teacher is introduced, then another hymn and the classes march out to their own rooms and we sit down at our desks, facing Miss Keyes' desk and the blackboard with that one Greek word written on it and the line from Marshal Foch. I love Morning Exercises. They give the day dedication and direction. What will it be like when the days don't start this way? Well, June and graduation are a long time off and I've got work to do between now and then.

September 27, 1923

The first marking period has come and in spite of all my hard work with Algebra and Geometry, I'm still no better. But themes! If that were all I had to do, I'd be at the top. This year it's one a week and they can be up to three pages in length and corrected with Miss Keyes at her desk. Penmanship still counts, and she told me not to keep trying different styles but to let my hand go its natural way, except when I'm printing for a special reason. And I have a special reason, but it is very, very private. I've been working hard over my poems and am beginning to hear my own voice in them. I'm much more critical than I used to be, and when I read them back to myself, I know that something has been said in a way that only I could say it. I've decided to put my poems to the test. I've printed thirty of the best, put them in an envelope with some postage, and sent them to a publisher. I said in my letter that I hoped they would want to put them in a book.

October 25, 1923

Twenty-eight days have gone by, each one a year in length. When I got home from school this afternoon there was a fat envelope for me, but not the one I had been hoping for. Up in my room with the door closed, I opened the package and read the letter that was enclosed:

My dear Miss Yates:

    We are returning your work herewith. You ask for our criticism. Here
it is, although as a rule it is impossible to do much along this line; we
have so many MSS. submitted. For one thing, you have too much verse
that is like blank verse. There is not enough rhyme to what you have
done, neither does it scan. You should be careful of the words you use, as
sometimes you use words that only sound like words. The number of feet
in the lines should also be carefully regulated. In other words, you have
some excellent ideas and the whole thing is very sweet, but the mechanics
are not good. You can improve them greatly. When you have done so and
when you have a little longer collection suitable for a book, we shall be
glad to give it our friendly consideration.

The Editors

Reading the letter over and over gave me the same feeling as
when I first rode Bluemouse in the show-ring and we came out with
a yellow ribbon. I'm not worthy of a blue yet, but this letter is like a
rung on the ladder or a milestone on a long, long journey.

October 26, 1923

At recess today I told Ethel about the letter and said that perhaps
I should show some of the poems to other people, submit one as a
theme, read them aloud to Mother for the ten-minute stint.

"Perhaps you should, and perhaps you should still wait a little
longer. Some things are best kept secret. Lots of growing goes on in
the dark, but there comes a time when it bursts into light. You've
got it in you to get somewhere."

"You too, Ethel."

"I doubt it. When I fall in love it will be husband, home, and
family for me."

"I'd like that, too."

"I'm sure you would, and you'll have it, but you've a responsibility first to the gift that is in you."

"Sometimes I think I'd like not to have a responsibility, but to be
like other people."

"You couldn't be even if you tried."

After we said good-by and went our separate ways, I wondered if
being different was worth the price one had to pay.

Jinny was sitting at my desk when I got up to my room. I knew
she was coming to supper, because Henry is away, but I hadn't
expected to find her in my room. She was reading my poems. I had
left the big envelope on my desk, but I never dreamed that I would

be sharing them first with her—she who started me on the road to reading that led inevitably to writing. If she likes them, I won't care how long it takes for me to be worthy of publication; if she doesn't, I think my world will tumble.

"Do you like them? Oh, Jinny, please say you do. It will mean everything to me to have your approval."

"They're sentimental drivel. Juvenile. What's more, you've plagiarized. Love! What do you know about it? All your friends are girls."

"Someday you'll be sorry for saying that about my poems."

"Someday! Don't you know it never comes?"

Before my eyes she closed her hands around the pages and crushed them, then dropped them into the wastebasket.

That night at dinner she told the family about my poems. That I wrote poems was not exactly news to them, but that I had been rejected by a publisher was. Father said that he'd like to see me do something at which I could succeed and we would talk about it when my education was finished. From what Mother said, I realized that to have a poet in the family might be a little difficult to explain. Bobby was the only one who didn't say anything. He just looked at me with those warm brown eyes of his. There wasn't much I could say, either in explanation or self-defense. I'll just have to play a part, the way I did in *As You Like It*, and get on with this way of life until I can lead my own life.

After dinner, Mother and Father and Jinny went to hear the Ukrainian National Chorus and I went upstairs to study. Before leaving, Father reminded me to study, not to spend the time writing poetry. Life is hard. I just hope it won't make me hard.

My room is like a sanctuary. Once there, with the door closed and my little gas fire for company, I lit a candle and put it on my desk. Candlelight takes away harsh edges and laps everything in a warm glow. I brought the crumpled pages out of the wastebasket and laid them flat, with my dictionary on them. Looking into the candle flame was like looking into my future and I realize that if I really want to be myself, I'll have to fight to claim my right. The candle gleamed on the crest on my little finger. *Sois Feal.* But what does one do when fidelities conflict? No matter what the cost, I know I must keep faith to the urge within me, but I hope I can do it without hurting other people.

I heard a small knock at my door and saw the handle turn. It was Bobby in his blue pajamas, his hair tousled, his feet bare. His eyes blinked as he came from the darkness of the hallway into my candlelight. He put his arms around me and asked me to read him some of my poems. When I said I would, he curled up tailor fashion on the floor and I reached under the dictionary for my pages.

The first one I read was "The Baying of the Hounds," and I read whisper-soft so the sound would help the eeriness of the words. More than once he shivered, and it made me feel that my words were going home. Oh, what it is to have an audience! I read three others, and I could have read many more, but I decided that moderation was good in this case, so I told him he should go back to bed. When he stood up, he rested his head on my shoulder. He's almost fourteen, but he still has a little boy smell to him and I breathed it as if it were a rare perfume. "I love you," he said, and when I asked him if he believed in me, he said, "You know I do."

After he left and the door closed behind him, I stared into the candle flame. The more difficult life becomes, the more grateful I am for the things of which I can be sure. Bobby is one of them.

December 6, 1923

Under my pillow this morning was a letter from Mother. If only I'd been awake and heard her, I would have hugged her tight, because I love my parents and hope not to disappoint them. She said, "We want only what is best for you, and may each year bring you more of the good things—health, success, friendship. This is more than a wish, dear daughter. It is a prayer." She didn't say happiness and I'm glad, for I wonder if anyone is ever happy. Life has such strange evolutions, death must be a blessing. I do feel so queerly about everything, and I'm so discouraged. I feel that I've made a failure of my entire life. Not one thing of worth have I put behind me in all my seventeen years, and now I'm eighteen. Sometimes I feel a stranger in the house where I was born. In my notebook I have copied some words of Thomas Stribling's. They say just what I feel: "The woes of eighteen are absolute. Untempered by philosophy, unsoftened by comparison, they are the worst a human being must face." Would that I were twenty-eight today instead of eighteen!

When Father got home from the office he brought me a typewriter. "For your correspondence," he said, and his eyes had their twinkle. I shall teach myself to type. It was good to be able to tell the family at dinner that at school I had proved a proposition in Geometry. Somehow it made the birthday cake aglow with eighteen small candles and one big one "to grow on" all the brighter.

It's late but I go to bed with this resolve and call Brier to witness: I am going to make this year mean something. Eighteen, that's really old, "old enough to have some sense," as Miss Stoner said to me in Greek class today.

1924

January 1, 1924

Never has there been such a New Year's Eve and never have I looked into the new year with such determination and with so little questioning. I'm alone, with sounds of merrymaking drifting up to me and around me. Mr. Potter invited the O.A.O.'s to Lake Placid for a week of vacation. He wanted to share with us his joy in the mountains and give us a taste of the winter world. Only four of us could come, because the rest had mumps! The first day we got here I felt a little queer, but I wasn't going to let it interfere with a cross-country ski trip and skating after supper on the floodlit lake. But the next morning it was hard to swallow and something that felt like a marble was under each jaw. I had to tell Mr. Potter, but I begged him not to send me home.

He talked with the doctor at the Inn, who said that as long as we were outdoors the swelling would be frozen where it was and would not be contagious, but that indoors I would have to keep to myself. So that's why I'm alone.

January 4, 1924

Today was one of dazzling sunshine and glistening snow. Every Adirondack peak that could be seen looked near enough to touch. We snowshoed five miles in 20° below temperature to a small lake high in the mountains. Mr. Potter made a fire right on the ice, and we helped gather wood for it. Soon we were having mugs of hot soup and toasting thick pieces of bread on sticks held over the fire. The only thing I can't do is talk, but listening makes me more aware of others and the towering mountains. Now, everyone is downstairs in the big room dancing the New Year in while I'm sitting with my coat on in a cold room writing it in. I just put my hand up to my jaw. It's not marbles that I feel, but peas. Perhaps by tomorrow even they will be gone.

May 24, 1924

These last few months at school are like going down a ski slope. Everything is whizzing faster and faster—the play, the Folk Dance Exhibition, the tennis tournament, house parties every other week-

In her graduation dress,

with Brier

end with the O.A.O.'s and special teachers, and soon College Board Examinations. I don't know how I feel. Mixed up. Everything we've known for so long is coming to an end and a whole new way of life will be beginning. Most of my friends are going on to college. Maybe I won't, because I know what I want to do and college might hold me up for four years. I feel like two people—one is lighthearted and lively, the other sober and tormented. Writing is my shining light and today I turned in my last theme. As far as I'm concerned, it's my best. It is six pages, a comparison of the works of Browning and Tennyson against the background of their day. It is the culmination of weeks of study. Writing it made me feel so good that, once it was done, I did nothing but write poetry. I am full of songs!

May 26, 1924

Miss Keyes called me to her desk to correct my theme. I felt scared at what she might do to it, because she's so particular, but her red pencil had made only one mark—a 10 in the upper-left-hand corner. Beside it but near my name and the date—Grade XII, May 24, 1924—she had written in her flowing hand, "A very delightful paper to read." I stared. It's one thing to be correct; it's quite something else to give pleasure. Then she proceeded to read aloud parts of it to me.

"I like the way you have expressed yourself—'which impelled the man to discover, the poet to reveal'. . .'words of philosophic truth issue forth and take root in our understanding'. . .'words revealed in a vivid, flashing form but standing immortally as one man's supreme belief in a great Divinity'. . .'a new exponent of beauty, freedom, self-assertion' . . . 'Life cannot always give us what we ask, but poets can give us dreams.' This is good thinking, expressed in your own way. Your style is emerging. You still like Tennyson's 'Ulysses,' don't you?"

"It's my favorite poem. I say it often to myself."

"In your words, 'Ulysses has become to me almost a prayer—a hungry yearning for other things yet past human boundaries, but a suggestion, half a promise, that we too may leave our well-ordered homes behind and strike out upon the waves *to strive, to seek, to find, and not to yield.*' And I surmise that you are speaking for yourself as well as for the ever-roaming Ulysses."

"Yes, Miss Keyes, I am."

"But now for another matter. I have seen the results of your College Board Examinations. You have failed Algebra and Geometry. If you are willing to be tutored this summer, you could take them again and pass."

"Maybe I won't go to college."

"What would you do?"

"Go to New York and get a job. Write."

"Your parents may have other plans for you."

"I want to lead my own life."

"You're very young, but at least you know what you want to do. Many people go a long time without discovering that."

June 6, 1924

The great day of Graduation has come and gone. It was inspiring and impressive. We twelve seniors, all in white and with our hair done up, stood in a bower prepared by the juniors. Miss Keyes was on a raised platform. Her green, long-sleeved, high-necked dress hung straight from waist to ankles, just showing her sensible shoes; her straight hair was drawn back into a tight knot, with a black ribbon holding it. She looked to us as she had during all the years we have known her, spurring us to achieve good grades, wakening in us intellectual curiosity. Seeing her like that for the last time, I had a sudden ache in my heart and wondered if I had ever really appreciated her. She, who usually says too much, said very little and I'll always remember her closing words: "Beware what you set your heart on, for you are sure to get it." Then she gave us our diplomas. Mine didn't have a *summa* or a *magna cum laude* on it, but I did receive three prizes— another Cake of Pink Soap, a Life of Charlotte Brontë for the Reading Aloud stint, and a dictionary for the General Information test.

We congratulated each other, laughed and cried, wished each other the very best and said we'd see each other soon. Family by family went with Miss Keyes to her office for what she called her "personal farewell," and *Υ* being where it is, we were the last to go in.

Father said something about college and Miss Keyes said that it might not be for me. I could have hugged her for taking my side.

"What your daughter will lack in higher education may well be made up in wide reading and travel. The field of journalism appeals to her."

"Has she ability?"

"Yes, and something of equal account—persistence."

"But she's so young!"

"A year at a good boarding school might bridge the gap."

On the way home, sitting between Father and Mother in the car, I thanked them for all they had done for me and said that I was sure they would be proud of me someday. Mother said they wanted me to be happy, but I could feel behind her words that she wanted me to be happy in their way, not in the way I saw for myself.

They went out after dinner and Bobby and I were alone in the living room. We lit a fire, because, even though it is June, the evening was cold and it's always so cozy to sit by a fire and talk. Bobby seemed surprised that I wasn't going to make up my marks so I could get into college.

"I know what I want to do with my life, so why shouldn't I go ahead and do it?"

"You're awfully young to go out in the world on your own."

"I'm four years older than you. Oh, you all sound like a Greek chorus—too young, too young. When am I ever going to be allowed to grow up?"

"Don't take things so seriously. Have a wider mind and try to see things from Father's and Mother's side, not just your own."

"What do you want to do with your life, Bobby?"

"You're always thinking about what's ahead. I'm going to wait till I get there."

"Don't you want to do something special?"

"Why bother about it now? I'll do what Father and Mother want me to do, I guess."

"But—"

"I'd really like to make moving pictures, but you have to have some capital to start with and I don't believe Father would give me any, because he doesn't like the movies. Maybe if I made a picture of a farmer with some cows, it might be all right."

"If that's what you want to do, go ahead and make your plans. Don't depend on anyone's help. I'll write stories for you to produce. We'll be a team."

"Maybe we'll have to wait a little while. Getting famous isn't going to be so easy as you think."

"You're wise, Bobby, much wiser than I am. How did you get this way?"

"Maybe it comes from listening to you."

Brier came in and pushed himself between us while we were sitting on the floor by the fire. I felt a rush of happiness. I was with two who loved me and whom I greatly loved.

June 15, 1924

The far future may be unsettled, but the near future is sure, for we are going abroad! Father and Mother, Bobby and me, and we'll spend two weeks in France and almost that long in England. I'm so excited. I'll see things I've been reading about for years.

Tonight, after dinner, everyone left the living room except Father and me; then he came out from behind his newspaper and said he wanted to talk with me. My next year is apparently all decided. Miss Keyes suggested a boarding school, Oaksmere in Mamaroneck, New York, and I have already been entered!

"You must credit your mother and me with some knowledge of you and, whether you wish to admit or not, some interest in your future."

"And then what?"

"After a year away and a summer at home, we hope you will see things a little differently."

"You don't want me to be a writer."

"Frankly, no. I had thought, if you felt you had to do something after your education was finished, that you might have a small business of your own. A flower shop, perhaps, to combine your love for growing things and your business sense. For, however poor the showing you've made in mathematics, you've proved to have a head for personal finance."

"I don't want to be a businesswoman."

"You have done well in writing at school, but that is a long way from being a writer. Writers, like artists and musicians, are born. Such talent is not in our way of life. For you to try to be one might only be to break your heart. Your mother and I want you to be happy."

Words rushed through my mind, but I found it hard to say them. How could I ever make him see that I've got to be me, that I've got to do what is mine to do or something in me will die? Success or failure is not the question; doing is. I think it was turning the crest on my finger, *Sois Feal,* that gave me the courage to say what was in my heart and mind. He listened. I told him I'd do my best during the year at boarding school. After that I would like to find a summer job to earn some money and get used to being on my own, then go to New York in September. He understands investments and what I was saying was about an investment in my own life.

"I give you my word of honor, Father, that I'll do what you and Mother want me to do for a year."

"I give you mine to respect your intention."

I put my hand in his and we looked straight into each other's eyes. How brown his are, I thought. The agreement was sealed with a handshake; not the pat on the shoulder he used to give when I was little, nor the good-night kiss that I would as a matter of habit have given him. The clasping of hands made me feel grown up. Perhaps Father saw me for the first time as an individual, even though I am his daughter.

When I left him and went upstairs to my room, I saw a piece of paper pinned to the pillow on my bed. It was a note from Bobby:

> Good night, dear Betty. I just thought I would have to drop you a line before I went to bed.

Had he heard the drone of voices from the living room and thought things might be hard for me? He could not be sure, but he wanted me to be sure of him.

July 28, 1924

It's our last night on the S.S. *Paris.* Tomorrow we land at Cherbourg. Somehow I haven't felt like writing poetry. I want to put down in plain, solid words what this experience is meaning—perhaps so I can relive it again, perhaps to use later on in writing. There've been smooth seas and rough, spray from big waves with the taste of salt on it, sunsets always different, people, and the coziness of just us four together. My problems have disappeared, my questionings are swallowed up in enjoyment.

August 7, 1924

I'll never forget my first sight of Paris as we drove to the hotel through dimly lit streets—little cafés and people sitting outdoors, taxis with squawking horns, graceful trees, carts coming to market with vegetables all scrubbed. . . . We're going everywhere, from the highest towers to the lowest crypts, even riding in a flatboat through the sewers, really just a clean, swift, underground river. I felt as if Jean Valjean was with us. . . . Museums, galleries, shops, restaurants, and every evening a play or the Opera. . . . Last night we had dinner at Foyot's and Father danced with me. . . . Bobby and I walked down the Champs Elysées, then prowled along the bookstalls by the Seine. We climbed to the top of Notre Dame, 397 narrow, winding steps. Paris is beautiful from that height; the gargoyles almost near enough to touch are grotesque. In the Louvre I felt trembly when I saw the Winged Victory at last, after all that Miss Keyes had told us about it. To see the real after a lifetime of reproductions is tremendous.

Miss Martin has arrived in Paris and with her is a Mrs. Ogilvy from New York. They joined us in a trip to Versailles and Fontainbleau. Oh, to see where people I've read and studied about lived, to touch things they used, makes me quiver. On the drive back, Miss

Martin suddenly put her hand on mine and said, "Don't ever lose your enthusiasm, dear child. Promise me." I promised her!

August 12, 1924

One more night and then we leave for England. At dinner Mrs. Ogilvy gave me a fan. I wish it had been a fountain pen, because I've lost mine. She fascinates me! Beautiful, regal, and commanding, she is exquisitely coiffed and handsomely gowned. At the same time, she charms and awes me. Perhaps I'll put her in a book some-day. I love Paris and am sorry to be leaving. We've been so happy here, and in this strange world where happiness is constantly sought and rarely found, that is an achievement. Surely of all the world, Paris must be the most wonderful. The French live as if the happiness in this life were all that mattered. Maybe it is.

August 13, 1924

In England I feel as if I have come home. The Channel crossing was smooth and then on the train tea was served in the most im-peccable way. The countryside looked like a park where cattle and sheep graze at will and horses belong. The towns through which we passed were neat and the signs readable, the voices understandable. After dinner in our hotel, Father and I went for a walk down Pic-cadilly, and it was as if I'd been there before—Dickens, Burke, Goldsmith, Thackeray all came alive for me. Miss Keyes said that when you see what you've read about, you find your place in it.

The days are filled to overflowing—museums, galleries, churches, libraries, Kew Gardens and Hampton Court, the Houses of Parlia-ment and the Zoo, Madame Tussaud's, Kensington Gardens and Peter Pan and rowing on the Serpentine, visiting the Tower and eat-ing at the Cheshire Cheese. And at the theater to see an actress like Sybil Thorndike and an actor like George Arliss makes me glow with admiration. I am awed beyond expression. A cloud of history seems to dance before my eyes. To think that I am really seeing all this, more than seeing—being a part of it!

August 17, 1924

Today was different from every other because Mother telephoned to a family cousin—rather, a distant relative, but family all the same —and asked if I might come and call on her.

"Why me, not all of us?"

"Because Cousin Bella is interested in writing and I thought that you and she might have much in common."

I was terribly scared and terribly excited when I took the rightly numbered red bus out to Kensington, yet somehow I felt important. I wasn't just anybody, I was somebody interested in writing. Every now and then something happens to bridge the gulf between Mother and me, and this was one of those times. When I reached the block of flats and was sure of the one that was Cousin Bella's, I rang the doorbell. A maid in a black dress with a white cap and apron—just like the kind I used to wear—answered the door, addressed me by name, and took me in to a room where a spare, angular woman with gray-white hair was sitting by a small coal fire. With our first clasp of hands, I felt we knew each other.

The maid brought in tea, with it a plate of thin bread and butter and one of plum cake. Cousin Bella and I talked of many things while we were having our tea, then we got to writing. She reached toward a desk that was close beside her chair and picked up a red-leather portfolio. It had beautiful gold tooling and her name was lettered on it. She opened it so it lay flat on her knees and I could see there were many pages of elegant handwriting, the lines and paragraphs and margins all as exact as if they had been measured. "I dreamed of being a writer," she said, "and indeed I have written many stories, but no eyes other than mine have seen them. Here are the seven I consider my best."

"But—but—"

"They are my life, more than my life. I could not have endured it if they had been rejected."

We talked more. She did not show me the stories, nor did I ask her to read from them. On the bus going back to the hotel, I tried to figure out how anyone could go to so much work—thinking, writing, copying—and not take the next step of sending to a publisher. What good is a story unless it is read? At dinner, when I told the family about my visit, I said that Cousin Bella might be a Jane Austen or a George Eliot. Mother shook her head.

"I think it highly unlikely. People who gain greatness are born to it, they don't just happen."

"George Eliot began as plain Mary Ann Evans."

"Cousin Bella was born to a certain station in life. She is filling it adequately. Writing is a pleasant avocation."

August 25, 1924

And now it's our last night in London after a glorious week driving through the English countryside, visiting castles, staying in little inns. Often Bobby and I went exploring on our own, and that was best of all. Tomorrow we'll be on the S.S. *Majestic,* westward bound. I'll have five days to think, to write down all I've seen and done. I wonder if someday I'll ever return. If I do, things will be different, and I'll be different, too.

August 31, 1924

Only a few more hours, only one more sun shall I see rise before I am home again among all the trivial things that make up my life. No world can ever be the same after one has been to Europe; just as the horizon widens before my gaze as the ship heaves steadily onward, so does the outlook on life become broadened and enlarged. Travel is to me the biggest kind of experience. Now I really have become a Ulysses "always roaming with a hungry heart."

I woke up at four this morning. It was exciting. There were lights along the shore and lights far off in the distance that were New York. A little boat crept up alongside and let the pilot on; then we swung ever so slowly into the channel. It was nearly daylight, so I hurried out on deck to watch the sun rise out of the mist. Shore was on both sides and what an emotion there is in seeing land after only water for five days! Far off, ahead of us, the skyline of New York loomed up from the pink and gray haze—like fingers pointing up. The channel was full of little boats.

Will marvels never cease! I am to stay in New York for a night and a day with Mrs. Ogilvy. Mother was delighted at her invitation and I am thrilled.

At Grand Central Station when Father was getting their pullman tickets to Buffalo for tonight, he got mine for tomorrow night. He told me what to tip the porter, and Bobby reminded me to put my shoes outside my berth, for they would be shined free; then they went to their train and I went in a taxi to Mrs. Ogilvy's apartment on East 86th Street.

Luxury! Mrs. Ogilvy's maid unpacked my bag and pressed my dress, the one I had worn as Jinny's Maid of Honor, which is still my very best. She drew my bath and made me feel like a princess. The only jewelry I wore was my opal ring and I did remember to slip the cord of my Parisian fan over my left wrist. In the drawing room Mrs. Ogilvy looked more imperious than ever, but when she said I was like her daughter Lydia, who, had she lived, would have been just my age, a tenderness came over her and I loved her. When a Mr. Mortimer was announced, he kissed Mrs. Ogilvy's hand; then she introduced me to him and he said, "Charmed." Soon after that, dinner was announced.

And what a dinner! Filet mignon with watercress, tiny rolls, wine, and for dessert *marrons glacées* and coffee. Conversation flowed between Mrs. Ogilvy and Mr. Mortimer and occasionally it included me, but I'm always happy when listening and observing. I soon decided that when I fall in love it will definitely be with an older man. After dinner we went to a friend of Mrs. Ogilvy's who was having a musicale at which Fritz Kreisler played after his concert at Carnegie Hall. There was a light "collation" served, which was mostly champagne, caviar sandwiches, and little cakes. I had to pinch myself to be sure it was all real. We didn't get back to East 86th Street until after midnight.

September 2, 1924

I'm writing on the train to Buffalo and it's jiggly, but I've got to put this down while it's sharp and clear because it has been a day of heights and depths.

Mrs. Ogilvy's maid woke me at 10 with my breakfast on a tray and said I was to be ready at 11 for a drive in the park to be fol-lowed by luncheon at Maillard's, then Mrs. Ogilvy would take me to my train. It was hard not to be tempted by more than the deli-cious food at luncheon.

"I understand, dear child, that you will soon be at boarding school just outside New York. It would mean a great deal to me if you could spend your weekends with me. I am a lonely old lady and life is empty for me."

"If the school allows it, perhaps now and then."

"We could go to the theater, attend the opera, and I would intro-duce you to many interesting people."

"I'm going to be working, Mrs. Ogilvy, as soon as I finish school."

"Oh, but, my dear, why? Your father could give you anything."

"Not the one thing I want."

"What is that?"

"Someday I want to write, and I'm the only one who can do that for myself."

"You have chosen something very difficult. It is a field in which many fail."

"I know, but even if I fail, I've got to try. Ever since I was a little tiny girl I knew that was what I wanted to do."

"But when you could have everything, why do you feel you must work?"

"To keep faith with myself."

"You make things hard for yourself."

"That's what my little brother tells me."

We laughed and ordered dessert. I had a chocolate éclair, but Mrs. Ogilvy just had coffee. That was the high part, when I held my own and made my point. The low point happened out on the street while we were waiting for Felix to come up with the car. When the car came to the door, two shabbily dressed women were walking by slowly, the hand of one held by a limping child. With a wave of her hand and the brusque words "Let me pass," Mrs. Ogilvy pushed them aside. The women drew back, startled but compelled to obey the imperious voice. It all happened quickly. Following behind Mrs. Ogilvy, I saw the look on their faces, the look of bitterness and hatred; I heard the child's cry as he was dragged forcibly out of the way. Felix held the car door open; Mrs. Ogilvy got in and called to me. The nameless others disappeared into the crowd moving along the sidewalk.

"You won't mind if we leave you at the station a little early, will you? I have an appointment with my dressmaker and your train will be made up a good hour before its departure."

"No."

"You'll come soon again, my dear, and we'll have more lovely times together."

When we reached the station I recovered myself enough to say a civil good-by, but I knew that I never wanted to see her again. I knew, too, that I had to atone in some way for what I had seen, even been a party to. It was not discourtesy. It was cruelty of the rankest sort.

I checked my bag, then went to the ticket counter and exchanged my pullman for a coach. The difference was $19.57. I couldn't get it to the unknown women or the little lame boy, but perhaps it would help in some way. There was time for me to walk to the nearest church, St. Patrick's, and put the money in the poor box, time for me to kneel by the flickering candles and pray that I would always see people as God's children and treat them so. Then I went back to the station, picked up my bag and found a seat in the coach. Before writing all this, I wrote my thank-you letter to Mrs. Ogilvy, even though the only paper I had said "S.S. *Majestic*." I wanted to put her and her way of life out of my mind and get on to other things.

It's a wakeful sort of night, but the sound of the wheels is soothing, even the breathing of other passengers and the occasional whimper of a child. My thoughts are finding a rhythm; words fit themselves into it, begin to take form and ask to be written. I shall soon be making a poem. As for my body, I couldn't be more uncomfortable, but in my mind there's a glow of happiness.

Bobby and Andy beside him, ready to take my bag, were standing on the station platform when the train reached Buffalo. I could have cried, they looked so good to me.

"You forgot to put your shoes out for the porter to shine."

"Robert Yates, you have very sharp eyes."

September 18, 1924

I have said good-by to the special people in my life. One of them is Mr. Trier. We sat in the kitchen, not saying much, just being together. He looked frail, and for the first time I had to admit to myself that he really is old. I feel that way about Brier. It's a strange feeling. My longest good-by was with Bluemouse. She is in great condition. Jinny and Henry have been living at Hillhurst while we were away, and they've been going to all the shows. Bluemouse got a blue in one of the hunter classes. I rode all afternoon and talked with her all the time. When she flicks her ears I know she understands. When we got back to the barn I rubbed her down well, then just buried my face in her mane. Before I left I gave her a measure of oats. Her whickering followed me out of the barn.

Now a whole new life is before me. In a way it will be like riding a horse I've never been on before, so I'll just have to grip a little tighter with my knees, turn my toes in, hold the reins firmly, and watch for the flicking of ears that means rapport has been established.

October 5, 1924

I've been at Oaksmere a week and things are beginning to go smoothly. The girls are different from the O.A.O.'s—much more sophisticated. I like my roommate, Winnie, and I think we'll have some good talks together. The school is right on Long Island Sound and when everything is still, the lapping of the waves fills the silence. I didn't think I'd be homesick, but I cried myself to sleep the first two nights and I kept thinking about the way Bobby asks me why I always have to do things the hard way. The classes are History and French, Philosophy and Psychiatry. No Greek or Latin, but maybe by this time they've been built into me. The Greek ideal "to know yourself" has come to me to mean "to be yourself." Mrs. Merrill, the head, called me in to her office after dinner to talk about my year and how it could mean the most to me. She says I am to have one course away from school with a Miss Albertina Russell.

"She is not a writer, but she has been instrumental in helping many talented people to become writers. She is an old lady now, so you will have the benefit of years of experience. You will take the commuter train in to New York every Friday morning and be back in time for luncheon and afternoon sports."

I asked some questions and Mrs. Merrill told me a lot more. She said that, when my parents had entered me, my father had spoken of my interest in writing, and that she understood I had done consistently well in themes at my former school. This is the best news! I might have cried myself to sleep with joy that night, but I didn't. Winnie and I spent half the night talking. I read her some of my poems and she liked them. Perhaps I won't recount many day-to-day events in my diary anymore, but concentrate on what I do with Miss Russell. Work with her is going to be the most important part of Oaksmere.

October 24, 1924

This has been my first Friday with Miss Russell. I found her apartment easily, only a few blocks from Grand Central Station. It's in a rather shabby brownstone, but when I went in and up the stairs I felt as if my feet were on the slopes of Olympus.

I knocked on the door that had her name on it, and a voice said "Come in." I saw a very large, very old woman sitting at a desk, her hair as untidy as the papers on her desk, and I wondered if I could be in the right place. She pointed to a chair and asked me to sit down. When I did and we looked at each other, suddenly nothing mattered but the quietness in her large gray eyes. I felt at home in their gaze.

"Mrs. Merrill has told me that you seek instruction in the written word."

"Yes. I want to write."

"Why?"

"Because it's the only thing I can do, want to do."

"What have you written?"

"Poems mostly. Themes in school. A play. Two novels, but those were long ago. I've kept a diary since I was eleven."

"And you are now?"

"I'll be nineteen in December."

"Show me something you have written."

"I do have a poem in my purse. It's not very long."

"A few words will be enough for me at this time. You will understand that I read very slowly. Be patient with me. How long do we have together?"

"Mrs. Merrill expects me to take the 11:30 train back to Mamaroneck."

"While I read, write what life means to you."

"Now? Here?"

"Where else? A writer should be able to write on any subject, at any moment, in any place."

"But—"

"Take as long as you like."

In the small room there was another table, quite bare but for a large white pad and a jar filled with pencils. Miss Russell indicated that was where I should sit. I did, facing a wall and a pad as blank as my mind. Then I began to think. When I took one of the pencils and made contact with the paper, words flowed. Of course, I knew life meant fulfilling my dream to become a writer, to work hard and not to count the cost. At the end I added my hope that my words might do some good in the world. It took only half a page to say that, but it was what I deeply felt. I put it on her desk and sat down in the chair beside her, waiting.

"Your work shows promise."

"Oh, Miss Russell, for so long I've been almost the only one who has believed in me. Now there's you!"

"Then that makes two. This will do for today. On your way to the station, stop at a dime store and buy three notebooks. One for your own thoughts, one for the pieces you will do for me, the third for the words of others that you wish to remember; words you may read in books, words you may hear in lectures. Do not spend more than ten cents for each notebook. What goes in them will give them value."

October 31, 1924

And now I've had my second lesson! She's just the same, as slow in speaking as she is deliberate in reading, but her manner gives me a feeling of composure. Only one thing seems to matter when I am with her in that small room and it is putting ideas into words. If it takes my life to learn to do that, my life will be well spent.

I laid on her desk three pages of notes I had made from a lecture Christopher Morley gave when he came to school.

"This will take me a long time to read, so, while I am engaged, write a description for me of your walk from the station this morning."

"How much time shall I take?"

"As much as you need."

Words failed me, for the morning had been such a shining one that everything was touched with splendor, from the tip of the tallest building to a piece of metal in a gutter. I could not, just could not, get it into words. I laid a blank piece of paper on her desk and waited for her to finish reading.

"This is well done for notes. He must have spoken about many other things, but you fastened on what was significant to you. Learn to broaden your range of hearing. When you listen to a person speaking, either in a lecture or personally, strive to catch the full tone and the undertone."

"But how?"

"The way anything is accomplished. By practice. But this is good for what it is. Your handwriting is kind to my eyes. Now, what does this blank sheet of paper mean?"

"Miss Russell, I am not able to put into words the way the world looked this morning. It was so beautiful."

"If you see a thing, you can describe it; if you feel an emotion, you can convey it; or you are not a writer. I do not want to hear you say again there are no words, for there are. There is one in the dictionary to which you have no right—'indescribable.' Take it out of your vocabulary now. And for next week bring me several brief character sketches of people you observe on the train as you travel between Mamaroneck and New York."

"Yes, Miss Russell."

"Be careful not to indulge in generalities; you must discipline yourself to particulars."

On the way back to school I reproached myself. How could I have forgotten what Miss Clements said to her class on English Grammar when I was in the Eighth Grade!

November 14, 1924

When I gave Miss Russell my character sketches, she read them with pencil in hand, drawing a line under a word and sometimes under a whole sentence. Watching the pencil, I began to rearrange words mentally, seeing how a thought could be better expressed. She paused over the last sketch and asked if what I was saying had been clear to me. I said yes, and then reading it with eyes other than my own, I began to wonder what it was that I had meant.

"You use some words whose meaning you do not know."

"I can look them up in the dictionary."

"Only living can give meaning in some instances."

"But—"

"Use what you know now and grow into precise use. Many words are cheap, the right word is priceless. Now for next week, equip yourself with a blue crayon and a red one. Circle in blue every *so* in your character sketches, in red every *very*. See if the sense is communicated with some of the adverbs eliminated. Consider whether you would rather have your style be lush or lusty. Continue with your sketches. This will sharpen your observation and increase your sympathy, but in your notebooks and for yourself. You will not need to show them to me. Bring me some nature sketches when you have them ready. Before you leave, write in fifty words what it is to be an artist."

"But I'm a writer."

"Artist is the inclusive term."

"Miss Russell, it will take a thousand words to do justice to that assignment."

"Say it in fifty, your words or another's."

I moved over to the writing table, wondering when I had ever felt so devoid of ideas. Remembering that I had copied in one of my notebooks a statement of Robert Henri's that had appealed to me, I read it and found that it said in forty-two words what I felt, so I copied it and gave it to Miss Russell. She read it aloud, word by slow word. "To be an artist is to construct, and to whatever degree one shows the genius for construction in work of any sort he is that much an artist. The artist life is therefore the desirable life and it is possible to all."

The words sunk into the silence between us.

"There is not one word in those two sentences that does not contribute to the whole thought."

"But it's so plain!"

"Why did you copy it in your notebook?"

"I guess because it said what I think."

"In time, you will gain the mastery of the artist. Your words, read by others, will seem to be theirs. That is the link the artist forges."

Mrs. Merrill met me at the station in the school car. She wanted to know how things were going. It was hard to explain how well. I said that Miss Russell did not praise my work or dispraise it, but that something was happening within me. "She teaches me to write by having me write."

December 6, 1924

When I woke up on this cold and misty morning, I reached my hand under the pillow. There was nothing there. For the first time in all the years I can remember, there was nothing to mark my very own day. But, of course, I said to myself, I'm not home, I'm away; and I realized that I was growing up. It's exciting and a little frightening. There was just enough light in the room to see by, so I reached for the pad and pencil on my bedside table and wrote a poem to myself.

What is it to be nineteen?
It is to stand on one of the rises
That make up the near mountain of life
And be able to get a view:
To look back at the way I've been traveling
And see what has helped me—
My family, my home, my friends;
To look ahead at the world waiting for me,
And glimpse something of what I will do,
And in seeing realize my part
In a great progression.
People have helped me,
In years to come may I help others.
So I start toward the next rise,
Seeing a little more clearly
The tide that carries me forward
And up the near mountain of life.

And so I turn another page in the book of my life, mixing up my metaphors.

December 12, 1924

Today I submitted to Miss Russell the nature sketch she asked me to do. I've worked hard over it, simplifying, clarifying, strengthening. It had to be a poem, "Fall Night." When she finished reading it, she gave me the highest kind of approval. "You write best about what you know. The words ring true."

"I've never been a leaf."

"You have enough imagination to overcome that situation. Something it is—the countryside long familiar to you, the world of nature—has been allowed to speak through you. Now, go on."

I would not see her again until after the New Year, for Christmas vacation is coming soon and at Oaksmere we are busy with a play whose lyrics I am writing. I wanted to hug Miss Russell, but our relationship has had no show of affection, so we shook hands and wished each other a happy Christmas season. "Keep writing every day," were her words as I went out the door.

1925

January 1, 1925

Distant bells sounding through the cold night are signifying a new year, and without doubt it will be the most important year of my life.

January 7, 1925

Vacation has been fun and there are a few more days left, but I can hardly wait to get back to Oaksmere and my work with Miss Russell. There've been lots of parties and some dances, skating and skijoring with the O.A.O.'s, then going back to someone's house for hot chocolate, sitting by a fire and talking. We've done this for years and we'll probably do it whenever we get together. Most of our ten are in college, two are in finishing school. I hope people don't think that is what Oaksmere is for—I don't want to be finished! Martha is the only one who is on her own. She has always been as certain about being an artist as I've been about being a writer. She's living in New York and studying art. We've made a plan to share an apartment when I come down in September and she's going to be on the look-out for just the right one with two rooms.

Mother and I have had some happy times during vacation, but she still hopes I'll find the way of life in Buffalo so attractive that I'll agree to a coming-out ball next Christmas and "the delightful life of a debutante" until I get married. She can't understand why I haven't been to see Mrs. Ogilvy. My wanting to work "when you don't have to" is as hard for her as a problem in algebra was for me. At the end of one of our talks she said, "Success will justify you; failure will more than prove your folly."

She said it so tenderly that I put my arms around her and kissed her. All I could say was, "Just give me time." Later that evening Bobby and I were out in the kitchen making fudge.

"Mother still wants me to give up my dream of being a writer, but I can't."

"No, of course you can't, because you're you."

"I've been thinking how awful it would be if Mother and Father should die before I prove myself."

"They're not going to die for a long time, but it won't be be-

Harry Yates around 1925

cause of you. They've got all kinds of important things to do for years and years. Come on, want to lick the pan? I'll take the spoon; it's got more fudge on it."

January 27, 1925

Father is different. We talk about the farm, the land, the animals, and I try to be intelligent about Wall Street. Those stock reports mean as much to him as words in a book do to me. He never says anything to dissuade me from my resolve. We made a pact last summer and sealed it with silence. I like the way men do things.

I had nothing to show Miss Russell for my three weeks of vacation, but I felt the writer in me was growing.

"Everyone needs a fallow time and is better for it."

"I'm beginning to know the difference between lush and lusty."

"Good."

"I'll learn the meaning of all my words if I have time."

"Oh, time! Now, for next week, bring me your thoughts about God. You think for yourself, you question, you doubt. This is essential for all who must find their own way. The work you have chosen is your way to God, but what is God?"

"God!"

"Not more than two pages, but one will do."

As I was going out the door, she said quietly that she had sent my poem "The Little Road" to the *Newark Evening News.* "You may have to wait a long time before you hear whether they will use it or not, but a writer is schooled to patience."

On my walk to the station I thought how quickening it was that Miss Russell makes a link from one lesson to another. She gives me something to do, something to look forward to. She puts a semicolon to a morning's work, never a full stop. And to think that she has sent one of my poems to an editor! My mind was busy, one part of it thinking of the poem gone into the world on its own, the other thinking of my assignment. It would be like trying to put Niagara in a teacup. How could I ever do it? And yet I was eager to try. After all, it is just my answer she wants, not a theological one.

Perhaps because of all Miss Russell is doing for me, I am more aware of her as a person. In spite of her bulk, she seems frail, and she looks old, the way Mr. Trier did the last time I saw him. When she said the word "time" it was as if she had done with it. Or almost.

March 16, 1925

These March days are like no other—soft winds blow in off the

Sound, snowbanks are disappearing so rapidly that I wonder if they ever had been there. Winter sports are over and the courts have not dried enough for tennis, so we go on long walks in the afternoons. And we talk. Oh, how we talk!

April 2, 1925

This morning Miss Russell was positively beaming when I came in the door. There on her desk was a copy of the *Newark Evening News* for Wednesday, April 1, 1925. She had opened it to the page where my poem was printed. I stood beside her reading "The Little Road" as if I had never seen it before, looking at my name as if it were someone else! But it was true. Something of mine was in print! I put my arms around Miss Russell and thanked her, not knowing whether to laugh or cry I was so happy, but she knew what to do and that was get on with our morning's lesson. Much of what she said was reminding me of things she had already said, but it was as if she wanted to be sure that I would be sure.

"You will always be your own audience first. Read your work aloud to yourself for the sound, the tone, the meaning. What you write must ring true in your inner ear, and if it does not pass this test, be willing to discard it. And never let anyone compel or tempt you to write what you honestly feel is not for you to write."

"Miss Russell, this work that I have done for you, will I use it in any way?"

"Work done opens the way for work to do. Trust your creative power, and go on."

"To fresh fields and pastures new?"

"Yes."

She turned to face me fully and her large overmoist eyes seemed to absorb me. She smiled, and her smile illuminated her generally impassive face. Then she took my hand in hers. I had a strange feeling that her tired old hands were placing some kind of trust in my young and strong ones. Halfway to the station, I remembered that she had not given me an assignment, and there was not time to go back for it. At the newsstand I bought two copies of the *Newark Evening News*—one to send home; the other to take back to school.

April 6, 1925

Suddenly it seems, in the eyes of friends and family, I am what I have been all along—a poet, and that's because something of mine is in print. Mrs. Merrill practically declared a holiday she was so pleased, and Mother was so delighted that she telephoned me and said that the Buffalo paper was making a news item of my achievement and that she would send it to me by Special Delivery. When it came, I didn't want to show it to anybody. It was on the Society Page and this is what it said:

> Miss Betty Yates, third daughter of Mr. and Mrs. Harry Yates of Delaware Avenue, is the latest recruit to the coterie of local poets. Her little poem, just published in a Metropolitan paper, is delicate and piquant with a certain felicity of expression. When she completes her studies and returns to Buffalo, we predict that she will be one of the most popular of next season's debutantes. Her sister Virginia has done highly creditable work in writing delightfully for her friends and it would appear that Betty is running true to form.

Winnie heard me groaning when I read it and asked what the matter was.

"Why can't they speak more of the poem and less of my social standing?"

"If you're going to be a public person, you'll have to get used to all kinds of things people will say about you."

And that, I can imagine, is what Miss Russell will say when I see her.

April 10, 1925

This is hard to write, but I must put it down, even though I wish this day had never come. When I went to the old brownstone for my lesson and climbed the familiar stairs, I was filled with anticipation. I was a little more than a student. I was someone whose work had been recognized and Miss Russell was responsible. There was a pile of mail outside her door and inserted in the door was a small card:

> Any enquiries relative to Miss A. R. Russell are to be made to her executors.

Then there was the name of a law firm on 46th Street.

No, not yet! I protested inwardly. I put my arms against the locked door and leaned my head on them. I could not believe, would not believe, that what had happened was true. It was as if by sheer force of will I could have made this Friday morning be as other Fridays had been for months past. But I could not. Our lessons were over. The questions I wanted to ask would go unanswered. Time had run out.

As I walked away, I began thinking of all we had talked about. Her words flowed over me like the sunshine of the April day. It comforted me to realize that the memory of things said overcame grief for all the things that now would never be said.

"What do you mean? This must be clear to you; only then will it be clear to others. Words without meaning are like clouds without rain. . . . You absorb so easily, be careful about this. . . . All that matters is that you sound your own note, find your own perfect pitch. . . . Yes, you may admire Thoreau, Cather, the moderns, the classicists, but you will write as yourself. . . . Yes, these are good, but they are exercises. You will not use them. Discard, or keep to look back on only to see how you have grown. They are ladders that have got you to new levels, and at each level you will find the material to make yet another ladder. Let the used ones go, for they have served their purpose."

It was her voice I heard, not the traffic on the street or the wheels of the train. Inwardly I answered her and said I'd do my best. Only that would be worthy of her.

I went to Mrs. Merrill's office as soon as I got back to school and told her. She was distressed, but more for me than for Miss Russell. I assured her that it was not the first time I had faced the finality of death. She excused me from afternoon activities. I spent the hours down by the shore, listening to the gentle lapping of the waves and thinking.

May 16, 1925

The school year is rushing to a close and with it my childhood, or what is left of it. Last night Mrs. Merrill gave us all a party at the Country Club. She told us what some of us had been suspecting, that we are the last class to graduate from Oaksmere, that after May 30 there would be no more school. For good reasons she was closing it. Oddly enough, she used the same words Miss Russell had: "I am very old." Perhaps there does come a time in every life when these words must be said, and willingly, if the years have seen fulfillment.

After dinner she took us to a vaudeville show—not a Shakespearean play, or the Symphony, or the Opera, but a vaudeville! Most of the time we practically laughed ourselves under the seats, but there was one number that was different. A blind man sang a medley of songs that always ended with the refrain:

> *My darling, my wife,*
> *The light of my life,*
> *Has eyes that can see for me.*

We kept singing it on the way back to school. Once there, we went up to Helen's room, made cocoa over her little stove, and talked.

Most of the girls are thinking about getting married soon, and some are even secretly engaged. I said that men were all right up to a point, but I didn't like them when they got slushy and that I was going to wait until I found one I could talk with about the deep things.

"I'm not going to let myself fall in love until I have begun to make my way as a writer."

"You may not be able to help yourself."

"You may have to forget about being a writer."

"Not me. The man whom I shall someday love will love me for what I am."

"I'm glad you said someday."

"Maybe each human being is half a unit and the whole reason for living is to find the other half and make a whole."

"That's a romantic idea."

"When two people find each other, a man and a woman, their separate ideas meld. Neither wants to change the other, but each one wants to share with the other."

"You think too much."

"What if I do? I can't take as mine what other people say. I have to figure things out for myself."

"I hope I'll still be around when you find your missing half."

"You mean it's going to take a long time?"

"It won't be soon."

May 18, 1925

Days are still full with classes, tennis in the afternoon, even swimming off the rocks when the sun is warm, and the world becomes ever more beautiful as spring beginnings merge into summer's promise. In the evening, in one or another of the girls' rooms, we talk endlessly about what we'll be doing when we leave Oaksmere, and we wonder when we'll ever see each other again. Winnie is going to Europe with her parents. I have applied for a summer job at a camp. It was an ad in the *New York Times* and it might have been written for me:

> Counselor wanted for equitation. 9 horses. 90 campers. Girls from 6 to
> 16. Writing ability an asset. All expenses paid, plus $200.

When I showed it to Winnie and said that I had already applied and asked for an interview, she was aghast.

"Are you really experienced enough?"

"Yes. If there's anything I know about, it's horses."

"What about writing? Do you suppose they have a camp paper and you'll be asked to write for it?"

"Whatever, I can take it on. Miss Russell always said that a writer should be able to write on anything at any time. Think of being paid for what I like best to do—riding and writing!

May 21, 1925

I had an interview with Mrs. Brill in her office in New York before I took the train to Buffalo. We had all said good-by to Oaksmere, to Mrs. Merrill, and to each other earlier in the day. Some got weepy, but I was so excited at what was before me that I couldn't have squeezed out a tear. When I presented myself at Mrs. Brill's office at precisely the time she had told me to come, I felt confident of myself. She told me all about the camp, went into some detail about its rules and regulations, then she asked me questions about horsemanship. Apparently my answers satisfied her. She asked if I was a writer, and of course I said yes.

"We would like you to write the editorial for our weekly newspaper. This will also serve as the sermon for our Sabbath Eve gathering on Fridays. Please send your first one to me within the week. You are not Jewish?"

"I am not Jewish."

"You can do this for us?"

"Yes, I feel sure that I can."

"Each week you will have one day off, Friday. If you desire a change of scene, the camp truck goes to Rutland that morning for supplies and you can ride with it. You will most likely find another counselor or two wanting to do likewise. That gives the horses two days of rest, as there is no riding on the Sabbath."

"I understand, and I thank you."

"I think you will do very well for us, Miss Yates."

June 28, 1925

My few days at Hillhurst were busy—a last ride on Bluemouse, a visit to Mr. Trier, packing the trunk small enough to go under a cot in a cabin with all that I would need for the summer. A new notebook and some yet-to-be-sharpened pencils were included. Miss Russell's voice could still be heard: "Write something every day. Keep yourself in training."

July 2, 1925

Here I am at Camp Kinni Kinnic, but more exactly I'm in a canoe on Lake St. Catherine with my notebook on my knee. While this first day is fresh in feeling, I want to write it down. The calm water is mirroring the sky, thrushes are singing in the woods, sunset colors are deepening.

Mrs. Brill gave me a briefing this morning, along with the other counselors. She showed me my cabin, gave me the names of the seven ten-year-olds who will be in it with me, then took me to the stable and turned me over to Tim. He introduced me to the horses and I took each one out for a short ride. I wanted to find out how they behaved. Most of them were reliable, two were flighty, one had a tendency to stumble and one had a hard mouth. I lost my heart to a bay, sensitive and tractable and so like Bluemouse in temperament, but it's the black gelding who shies easily that I'll use. He'll be all right if he knows who's in the saddle. I discovered some near trails and saw several dirt roads that led into the hills and promised adventure. Every time I brought a horse back I had a good talk with Tim while I was rubbing down.

"You don't need to do that, miss."

"I like to. It soothes the nerves and let's a horse know you appreciate the ride he's given you. It's something I want the children to do after every ride."

"You'll be saving me some work."

"I guess you've got enough."

"You'll be stiff tomorrow."

"I never have been. I've ridden since I was three."

"Where do you plan to take your lot tomorrow?"

"No farther than the paddock rail. I want the children to get to know their horses; then we'll hoist them up to sit bareback and get the feel. That way I can show them how to keep their seats and grip with their knees. The next day will be soon enough to get them into saddles and give them a feel for the reins. We'll work for a week in the ring before we go out on the trails."

Dusk was beginning to filter out of the woods and over the lake. I put my pencil in the notebook, picked up my paddle and started back to the dock. I began to think about the sermon for next week. A few words seen on a sundial in England gave me an idea. "The days that make us happy make us wise." I'll let my mind run around that and see what may come into words.

August 1, 1925

Summer is half over and things have gone well, without difficulty but with hard work. I think I've proved myself in two spheres—writing in a way new to me and handling children with authority. The days in ring and on trail have been easier than those in the cabin, but telling stories finally gave me the upper hand. I made it clear to the children that unless order was maintained and camp rules obeyed, there would be no story at night. It was as simple as that and it has worked.

Mail time right after luncheon is, as it was at Tegawitha, the boon of the day. I cherish letters from home, Mother's and Bobby's, cards from Winnie, and occasionally news from one of the O.A.O.'s. Last week I had one from Miss Martin, of all people! She said she had always wanted to know about the Language of Flowers and wondered what information I could get for her. When the truck went to Rutland on our free Friday, I spent most of the day at the public library. I got all the data I could and wrote it at night by flashlight, after taps. I printed it so it would make a neat appearance and sent it to Miss Martin. She was pleased enough to send me a check for $10. Next Friday, when we go to Rutland, I'll treat my friend Dixie to a great big meal. Anything tastes better than camp food day after day.

August 29, 1925

At the last Sabbath Eve gathering, I really let myself go in the sermon. Perhaps I was talking more to myself than the ninety children, so I'm copying it in my notebook. They may forget, but I want to remember what these summer days in the mountains have meant.

> During these eight weeks we've learned to live together and that's important. Sometimes we've gotten into disagreements, but we've come out of them by realizing that each was right but in a different way. It's a key to contentedness to learn that there is more than one point of view. As you grow up, you'll find that not many people see things as you do. Some will laugh at the work you're proud of; some may not understand what you're getting at. Try not to be sensitive. Hold up against different opinions, face the world on your merits, and be yourself. You are a very important person, you know. That's not egotism, that's logic. You'll be sure of it when you go up, but don't forget it when you go down. Always, from somewhere deep within, be able to summon your courage, the fighting spirit that doesn't know what defeat is. If you do this, you'll be stronger than Hercules and more adamant than Atlas. With your own work to do and friends you can trust, you've got your life in hand.

Then we went down to the lake for our last campfire. We sang all our camp songs, clasped hands in a ring, and began saying the good-bys that would continue until the last camper leaves in the morning.

When it was all over, Mrs. Brill called me into her office. She gave me an envelope with a check in it and asked if they could count on me for next summer. Much as I wanted to say yes, I told her I would have to see what happens during the intervening months, but that I'd let her know. Then she gave me another check "to show our appreciation." It was a hundred dollars, half as much as I had earned! I was overwhelmed. If I need a waymark to my future, this is it. It will give me courage to remind Father, when the time comes, of our agreement; and that time is very near.

September 8, 1925

Delicious as it is to be home again, it's as if I'd never been away. At camp I was someone; here I am no one. At breakfast this morning, Father soon got behind his newspaper, then left for his office; Mother soon went out to the kitchen to plan meals with Maria; only Bobby kept asking me questions as if he was really interested in what I had been doing. This is the way it always has been, always will be, I told myself.

There was a highlight when Miss Martin telephoned and asked me to have luncheon with her at the Twentieth Century Club. Mother seemed quite willing to have Andy drive me in to Buffalo and wait to bring me back again.

Miss Martin said little about the Language of Flowers, but much about a new flower shop that was to be opened in one of the hotels in Buffalo. "And, my dear, I've talked with your parents about it. They are willing to make an investment in it so you can run that little shop!"

"Me?"

"It will be so nice to have you home this year, so many young people for you to be with. And you do have a business head, your father has always said that. You'll be a real success."

"No."

"You do like flowers, don't you, dear?"

"Yes."

"Then, why not?"

"I want to be on my own and away. In New York. I want to write."

"But you could do so well in a little business here. It may be very difficult in New York."

"I don't care."

"But you don't have to work, dear. Your father can give you anything you want."

"But I do have to, Miss Martin. There are other reasons than money."

"Since that's the case, I shall give you a letter to an old beau of mine. He's been on the *New York Times* for years. An editor, no less! I'm sure he's still alive."

"Would you really, Miss Martin? I'd appreciate that very much. It might—"

"It might just be the open door. Now, don't let me forget. Better still, I'll write the letter immediately."

"Thank you."

"And you will see Mrs. Ogilvy, won't you, dear? Indeed, you might make your home with her. Who knows!"

"Who knows?"

Miss Martin's letter to the editor gave me assurance; even more came in the mail in a letter from Martha. She had found a two-bedroom apartment with a small bathroom and an even smaller kitchen between the two rooms. She had already moved into the front room, as the light was better for painting; the back room would be quieter for writing. How soon could I come down? I had thought vaguely "sometime in September," because life is so lovely at Hillhurst—riding Bluemouse every day, having Brier to love and Bobby to talk with, the fields and the woods, and even my pigeon loft sanctuary. Tempting as it all is, inside me I know that soon must be now, or perhaps the ease of life and the beauty of the countryside will make me want to stay on and on. I shall announce my plan at dinner tonight. It will be up to me to open the subject, for no one else has mentioned it, except perhaps Miss Martin. I can see now that what she got me to do was a very neatly disguised ruse.

And so I did, as soon as we had finished dessert and Lizzie was serving coffee.

"Your father and I would like to have you home with us for a while. You could write here just as well as in New York, and it won't be long before you may be getting married."

"Why is it you could relinquish me to marriage and not to a career?"

"We don't want you to be hurt."

"And you think I will be?"

"You have a position in life. Your birth, your upbringing, your education, have all been equipping you to fill it."

"Have you thought of it this way: Is it right for you to take work away from someone who may need it to live?"

"I just know that I've got to do this, that I've got to be on my own, and try."

"Your mind is made up?"

"It was, a long time ago."

They had all the arguments and all I had was determination, which to them seemed stubbornness and self-will. My heart ached for what I was doing to them, but I had to hold on or lose everything. Bobby shot me a sympathetic glance and asked to be excused from the table. When he left I felt more alone than ever. I reminded Father that we had made a pact more than a year ago and I had kept my part of it. He said he had not forgotten, but he had hoped my intention would change. He asked me if I had really considered what it meant to leave home, to be on my own, to live within my earnings.

"Yes. I've been saving most of my allowance and all the money I've earned. I have $864.17 in my Savings Account."

"That makes you independent?"

"It should be enough to keep me going for a while, at least until my stories start selling."

"You can always come home if it doesn't work out."

"I won't forget home, and I'll look forward to coming back for Christmas."

"And you think to leave soon?"

"By the end of the week."

"I would like to buy your pullman ticket."

And, just as he had done a year ago, he held out his hand to me. Our pact was confirmed.

September 11, 1925

This year has had so much packing and unpacking that I'm getting expert at it. I've been busy sorting out my clothes and the things I'll need for New York. I've been doing another kind of packing, too. In a red cardboard box I've put the mementos of the years—my diaries, a few themes, the copybooks of poems, early pieces like *Called Coward* and later ones. They are the ladders, as Miss Russell would say, that have got me this far but that I don't need to drag around with me. I tied the box with string and glued a card to it:

> *Requiescat in Pace*
> Childhood
> Born Winter 1905
> Died Fall 1925

and pushed it into the farthest corner of my clothes closet. Maybe some unknown person will open it in some distant time; maybe I will open it in the far, far future.

Brier is sleeping on my bed for the last time. By tomorrow he'll be on Bobby's bed. He's showing his years and that is something that makes my heart ache. Why can't we stay the same? Why can't everything go on as it always has? Asking myself that, I can hear Mother saying to me, as she did so often when I was growing up, "We go forward or we go back. There's no standing still." I'm going forward when I go to New York; the trouble is it's not the kind of forward they wanted for me.

I remember, too, what Mother said to me last winter about success justifying me. I've never really thought of success as such. I've thought that if I became a writer, it would follow as a matter of course. It's odd the things that are coming across my mind on this last night.

September 12, 1925

Standing on the station platform, just Mother and Father and Bobby and me, I had a strange feeling as the train approached. The long beam of its light sliced the darkness and I felt for a moment as if it were cutting me in two. We said good-by all over again, and Bobby whispered to me not to forget to write letters. The porter called, "All aboard! Next stop New York City!"

I'm on my way!

Part II

My Widening World

1925

September 20, 1925

Here I am in New York with every intention of becoming a writer. The apartment Martha found is at 147 East 37th Street, in the shadow and rumble of the Third Avenue El. We share the rent, which is fifty dollars a month, and we'll share the food, so it won't cost us much to live. Martha came down from Buffalo three weeks ago and has her room furnished with things she brought from her home—heavy old family furniture, a Chinese desk, an Italian carved chair, a couch and pillows, a Turkish rug and a Russian samovar. The room is on the front and is all set up as a studio. She's already splashing vivid colors on huge canvases.

My room is in the back, looking out on a small garden. It will be quiet, and I don't need the sun for my work. It's a writer's eyrie, and I have it fixed just the right way for me—a small bed and a big plain table. With a stack of paper, a jam jar filled with pencils, and my typewriter, I'm all set. I have three chairs, like Thoreau in his cabin at Walden: "One for solitude, two for friendship, three for society."

In between our two rooms is a bathroom and a tiny kitchen with a two-burner gas range. We each have our own fireplace. It has taken all this week for me to get settled, finding the furniture I needed and unpacking the things I brought from home.

Home! Just writing that word gives me a twinge. I think about the big house in Buffalo where we lived during the winter, and Hill-hurst Farm where the wonderful summers were spent. Those places will always be a part of me, as will the Franklin School. I think of Mother and Father, of Jinny, my brilliant older sister, and of my darling younger brother, Bobby; of Miss Hyde, always there when Mother was away and always there to help Mother; of Maria in the kitchen, and Andy, of Lizzie, of Al in the barn with the horses, and Jim in the garden. I think of Brier, my beloved dog, who isn't much younger than me, and of Bluemouse, my horse. If I think too much, the twinge becomes an ache, but how glad I am for them all.

Tomorrow—that's the challenge! Martha will go to the John Murray Anderson School of Design, where she is studying, and I'll go to *The New York Times* with the letter of introduction that Miss

The Big House
at Hillhurst

May Martin gave me. It's exciting to be here: an ecstatic, pulsing sensation. I feel ready for great things.

September 30, 1925

Finding a job in New York is like being initiated into a secret society, and the password is *experience*. My letter to the *Times* got me nowhere, as Miss Martin's friend had died two years ago. When I asked to see someone else, the first question asked of me was what experience I had had, and the only answer I could honestly give was, "None." So, that was that. Sitting in Bryant Park and looking at the Help Wanted ads in the paper, I saw one from *The New Yorker* and went to their office; but the help they wanted was to sell subscriptions, and I knew I would not be any good at that; besides, it would not get me anywhere from the standpoint of writing. When I got back to 147, there were two short stories in the mailbox, returned from the magazine I had sent them to only last week. I wondered if an editor had even taken time to read them.

After Martha got home, we made tea, sat by her fire and spent hours talking about my future. She has fantastic ideas and some curious contacts. We both agreed that the important thing for me was to keep as much time as possible for writing, but to do anything to make some money until my stories started selling. She knows a commercial photographer who is always in need of models. Tomorrow I'm going to see him. Martha and I are as different as our tastes and talents, but we have a great bond: We have each achieved freedom to pursue our own lives, and we have been able to keep the respect of our families. It's one thing to be free and another to prove ourselves, and that is going to take time.

October 2, 1925

What will the family say when they see a picture of me sitting on a pile of congoleum rugs! But I doubt if they will, because I've never seen any of them reading *The American Magazine*. I made $25 for a morning of posing, and that's a lot. Besides, I'd better get over thinking what people will say about me and get on with what I came to New York to do. An idea for a novel has been burning in me for a long time and now I'll be able to get it written. I'll do whatever I can to tide me over financially and write with all the time that I can command.

October 10, 1925

Mother telephoned to say that Brier had died. "Just old age, dear. He didn't wake up this morning."

I took the night train to Buffalo and we had a little funeral. Al had dug a grave in the orchard and made a box which Bobby and I carried. Jinny joined us. Miss Hyde was there, in the background as always. Maria and Lizzie came from the house, and Andy too. We all wanted to pay our respects. It was the first break in the family circle. Bobby, at fifteen, can't remember a time when Brier wasn't part of the household. Walking back to the house after the ceremony, I felt closer to Mother than ever before. It's like what Miss Hyde once said about death: It makes the ranks of the living draw closer together.

Al brought Bluemouse to the door, saddled and bridled and looking more handsome than ever. "Thought you'd feel better if you did something," he said. It didn't take me long to get into jodhpurs and boots, then off we went down the lane and over the fields. I really let her out and the wind of her splendid speed swept some of the aching away from me. When I got back, Maria and Andy and Lizzie were all having their tea in the kitchen, so I joined them.

I asked Maria to see that lots of leaves went into my cup so Andy could tell my fortune. When the tea was all warm inside me and the leaves were in the bottom of the cup and up one side, I handed the cup to Andy. He studied it for quite a while before he started to read. He always makes a good story, and he often makes it better when he takes the tip of his knife and looks under a leaf, but what he found for me was still a long way off.

"They're there," he said, "all those good things you are after, but they're nowhere near—yet."

In the train going back to New York, I made up a story in my mind about Brier and all that he had meant to our family. Does it take death to help us realize the preciousness, the wonder, of life?

October 28, 1925

I've got a fascinating job! It starts November 1, for six weeks (then it will be time for Christmas). I saw the ad in the *Times*— Walking Governess needed to take care of five-year-old boy from 2:30 to 5:30 weekdays. The address was in the 60's, just off Fifth Avenue and not far from Mrs. Ogilvy, but I won't run into her, as she is spending the winter in the south of France. When I presented myself as an applicant, Mrs. Hastings-Jones, a handsome but rather forbidding-looking woman, looked me over as if I was not a person in my own right but a tool that she could use for her own purpose. She said that she was to be away for six weeks and wanted to make certain arrangements for her son for that time. She asked many questions, which I must have answered satisfactorily, for she then told me my duties.

I would come to the apartment at 2:30 and take Master Arnold to Central Park for a walk, staying out as long as the weather permitted, then entertaining him with games or conversation until it was time for his supper, when her housekeeper would take charge of him and I would depart. It sounded intriguing, the $10 a day was beyond my wildest dreams, and I still would have my mornings and evenings free.

November 18, 1925

They say it takes all kinds to make a world, but I don't know what kind Master Arnold is! He is interested in just one thing, and no matter what I do, it is the only thing for him. As soon as we cross Fifth Avenue and get into the Park, he whips a tape measure out of his pocket and measures the girth of the trees. When he says "42 inches" or "64" or "18," it is with great excitement, but he isn't a bit interested in what kind of tree it is he has measured. I show him the ducks on the lake, point out a bird in a tree, start to tell him a story, but he has no interest.

Rainy, raw days are the most difficult, because we have to be inside. He has measured everything that can be measured in the apartment, so he amuses himself by drawing numbers on huge sheets of paper, numbers in every imaginable combination. His father is a stockbroker. Perhaps he hears figures talked about so much that he has to make his own. He will soon know more about money than I would ever care to know, but when will he know anything about Winnie-the-Pooh, or Robin Hood, or Sir Lancelot? I'm not sure that he knows my name, but he knows what I measure around the middle and from my shoulders to the floor.

I look ahead on the calendar to when Mrs. Hastings-Jones will return and my task will be completed, but I still hope every day that by some magic I may be able to open another door for her son. However, I am making lots of money and I'm getting Christmas presents for everyone. Books mostly, they are what I like to give (and get), but for Jinny it will be something for her new home.

December 6, 1925

Again, I turn a page in the book of my life.

Year's End, 1925

This is the last entry this year, but I intend to go on with journal-keeping, noting significant events and keeping an eye on my life.

It was wonderful to be home for Christmas, but I can't let myself dwell on just how wonderful: ten days when there was nothing to do but enjoy everything—people, parties, food, friends. I tell myself that I have work to do and my goal must ever be before me. Father gave me an extraordinary present—a bottle of fifty-year-old port from his cellar. In these prohibition days that is like a crown jewel. "Keep it for special occasions," he said. His eyes had their twinkle, and he patted me on my shoulder as he used to do when I was little. A Special Occasion for me will be the day, and days, and more days when work of mine is accepted for publication.

So here I sit in my eyrie as one year merges into another. Martha hasn't got back yet from Buffalo, and I'm alone with much to think about. There's a fire in my little fireplace, candles in my two pewter candlesticks. There is warmth and light, and shifting shadows cast by the fire and the candles. The hands of the clock are moving toward midnight. I feel on the edge of something tremendous.

1926

January 21, 1926

Last year at Oaksmere, that boarding school fast fading into memory, there was an exciting experience. Actually there were many, but this one appealed to me. It was the visit made by Mr. Gilbert Simons, an editor on the *New York Sun*. He spoke to us about writing in general and particularly about writing for the press. He read some of our literary efforts, without comment, but he did say that, after we graduated, if any of us were really serious about journalism, he would be glad to talk with us further. I decided to take him up on his offer and wrote a letter to him, reminding him of his visit to Oaksmere and saying that I, for one, was really serious.

Two days later I had an answer from him from the Editorial Department of the *Sun*—

> Dear Miss Yates:
>
> If Saturday afternoon is convenient for you we could meet then. If you could meet me at the Biltmore under the clock and go to tea at one of the Peg Woofington places where it is sure to be quiet, I could tell you what I have thought about your career. Will you call me at this office at two o'clock tomorrow afternoon? I should like to show you the plant here.

I feel fluttery with excitement, but I must try to be calm, at least when we meet.

January 30, 1926

I had a charming time with Mr. Simons, but if I learned anything, it was what I don't want to do, and that is work on a newspaper. I want to write words that last, not that change every day. Everything at "the plant" seemed so noisy and fast-moving. Presses were turning out papers that were being loaded on dollies to be taken to trucks to be rushed to newsstands. It was hard to hear what Mr. Simons said as he described procedures to me. It wasn't much better in his office, which was cluttered. There were sheets of paper everywhere, half-opened books, and no order that I could see. I could understand why he wanted to go to tea where it would be quiet.

He is tall and quite good-looking, but very reserved. I suppose he's shy and that made me feel less shy. We talked about me, and he

Looking east on 34th Street

in New York City

(shown here in the early 1930s)

was kind and sympathetic. I showed him two of my poems. He nodded as he read them, but all he said that I can remember was, "You have time and promise." I doubt if we ever meet again.

February 15, 1926

Life is a whirl and just being in New York is exhilarating. People are pouring into our lives—friends from home, from school visiting the city. Everybody introduces somebody else, and there are so many men! At home they were boys; now they are college men. Martha and I go to concerts at Carnegie Hall when we can afford them. Theaters are our passion. We stand outside the scalpers' offices on Broadway and wait to get cut-rate tickets. The plays this year are exciting—some we have seen, some yet to see: Alfred Lunt and Lynn Fontanne are at the Theater Guild, Katharine Cornell is in *The Green Hat,* and there's a marvelous musical, *The Vagabond King.* Eva Le Gallienne as Hedda Gabler was superb, but I think I'm going to like her even better in *The Cherry Orchard. Joan of Arc* is coming soon, and Martha can hardly wait for Norman Bel Geddes' production of *The Miracle.* Sometimes after a play, and excited by it with much to talk about, we walk through the park, or along the river, and often we go down to Chinatown.

When we ask our friends to 147, we always entertain in Martha's room, as she has much more furniture and the wind-up victrola. We make tea on her samovar and then we talk—we really soar the heights in conversation. Sometimes we go down to John's in the Village. He lets in only the people he recognizes through his peephole, but once in, it is good Italian food and a bottle of Chianti. The evening may be just for ourselves or we may be a party. Martha has some fascinating Russian friends, and I am meeting more people all the time. Whether it's ourselves or several, it's always hilarious. We can easily talk half the night away and walk the other half.

Last week, Martha and I left John's at midnight, then tramped along the wharves until dawn. Mists were rolling in from the river and there was a strange breathless feeling, as if time were standing still. It was so beautiful. I felt perilously near to ecstasy, as if my soul was ready for flight into some vast unknown. Turning away from the river and looking toward the city, we saw gray buildings peering from the mist like dream castles. The river was a slow, forgetful rhythm; the lights still burning were neglected stars. Maybe we felt what we were seeing, what we were part of, in different ways, because we didn't say anything. That's the best thing about friendship: You don't have to have words, you feel safe in silence.

More than anything, I want to finish my novel, *Cinema,* and send it to a publisher. I'd like to read it to Martha but I won't. I don't understand her paintings enough to comment on them in any way, and she may feel the same about my work. When it's published I'll give her a copy. What a difference between an artist and a writer! Whatever she does is there for all the world to see. My words must grow within me until the time comes for them to move into the world.

March 24, 1926

Ben took me out last night. He is the brother of one of my friends at Oaksmere, and when he called to make a date, I liked the sound of his voice, and when we met I liked him. He has been out of college three years and is the oldest man I know. He's slightly corpulent but otherwise very nice. He is in the advertising business and is going to design some notepaper for me to use when I write letters to editors. He says it will help sell my stories.

We went to see *The King's Henchman,* but it is so popular that Ben could get only standing room. However, we scarcely realized we were standing, because it was so beautiful, words and music sublimely blended. From there we went to Paul Whiteman's new night club. It was gorgeous, the jazz making me feel all thrilly and melty as syncopation does. When we left, we tramped over to 147, stopping at an Automat on the way for coffee and crullers. We talked a lot, then around 5 A.M. we set out for one of my pet walks—along the East River to the Queensboro Bridge and over it. Before us lay mists and the trembling shades of dawn; behind us the city—a cluttered jumble of beloved rock. We were free and the world was ours. There was laughter in our hearts, beauty everywhere, and no return until long after the milkmen had made their customary rounds.

April 1, 1926

Now Ben has gotten serious. He said last night, "I'd like to marry you tomorrow, but I'll wait all my life for you." I didn't want to hurt him, he really is so decent, a brotherly sort of creature, but I had to say no. I had to tell him that there were other things I must do first. He made it worse when he said, "I'm sure I can make you happy." But that's not what I want—comfortable, respectable happiness. Accomplishment may be lean and spare, but it's what I must see to be true to myself. I couldn't seem to put it in words to him. After he left I worked harder than ever on *Cinema,* for the way to end it has been tumbling around in my head with a terrible insistency.

April 2, 1926

It's Good Friday. Martha and I wanted to hear *Parsifal* at the Met, though there were no tickets to be had, only standing room. It was so glorious that we never even knew we were standing for almost five hours. After that we went to an Alice Foote MacDougal's and treated ourselves to waffles and coffee. The music and the settings meant most to Martha, the mysticism of the Holy Grail to me. That's the way it is: We complement and enrich each other.

April 10, 1926

Oh, woe! The novel that began so well and then rushed to its conclusion now seems no good at all. I might be holding ashes in my hands as those pages with their many words. I can't write and I can't give up writing. What am I to do? Some days I feel full of poems, some days of prayers, but most days now I feel full of futility. It's as if I were alone in the universe with all doors shut. Happiness seems like a dream; reality is my despair. It would be so easy to slip in front of a bus on Fifth Avenue and end it all, but I know that would solve nothing.

In my worst moments I seek sanctuary in St. Patrick's and I can generally come away feeling better; a few blocks down the Avenue is the Public Library and that, too, is a kind of sanctuary. So I go back to my eyrie with more resolve. When there's an envelope in my mailbox with a short story returned, I need what sanctuary gives me. It is quite hard not to be discouraged. When will things begin to come my way? I have so many thoughts, so much to say, but there are times when the old fire just isn't there. A little success, just a tiny bit, would fan the flame. Is the fire apt to go out? But I have done one thing: *Cinema* is finished and I shall send it to a publisher.

April 25, 1926

Seward was a senior at Williams last year and now he's in a broker's office in Wall Street. He is sandy-haired, freckle-faced, and fun. We walked in Central Park this afternoon. How prosaic that sounds, but it wasn't. The air had spring in it, streaming sunshine, singing wind, and we felt intoxicated with the joy of living. The world was at our fingertips. We sang and laughed and raced each other. Seward is often shy and quiet, but we do have good times together. I hope he won't get serious, because I don't want things to change yet. It would be so easy to go that route. Maybe the only thing that really matters in life is the human equation: some he and some me. I suppose the propagation of the human race is important and that means marriage, but maybe it isn't for everyone. There just may be some people for whom the propagation of ideas—words, sound, color, form—is important. Maybe I'll never marry.

I wanted to tell Seward my news—that I had finished my novel, finished it to the extent that my typing was completed, that the manuscript was wrapped up and ready to be put in the mail tomorrow, but I didn't tell him. The feeling of accomplishment was as vibrant in me as the springness of the day was vibrant around us, but I didn't say anything. I thought he might not understand what this meant to me, or that he might not care.

April 26, 1926

Cinema has gone to Little, Brown, in Boston.

May 25, 1926

Today I received a letter from Little, Brown, and a package.

> Dear Madam:
> Your manuscript, *Cinema*, has now been carefully considered and we are very sorry that our readers do not find it exactly suited to our needs at the present time. Also, it is rather too slight for a full-length book.
> We can do nothing, therefore, but return your material and it is enclosed herewith. We assure you that we greatly appreciate your courtesy in permitting us to consider your work and only regret that our decision must be an unfavorable one.

There was another letter in the mail, from Camp Kinni Kinnic, asking me if I would return for "a summer of equitation"—same salary, same duties as last year. I've read that when one door closes another opens. We'll keep the apartment, and Martha will use my room to sleep in. It will be cooler.

June 28, 1926

Before leaving for camp in Vermont, I had a final fling with Cleve. It's almost like family, being with him, because I've known him so long. He's a college friend of one of my older brothers and has visited at the farm. He treated me then like somebody's little sister, but he seems to have a different kind of interest in me now that I'm on my own and making my way in New York. He writes poetry and does book reviewing. His poems are more sophisticated than mine, but they get published. If I can stand his being so superior with me, I think I can learn things from him that will help me.

He took me to dinner at Longchamps, then to the theater to see

Jane Cowl. We didn't go dancing, but went back to the apartment, because Cleve wanted to read me some of his poems. I liked them, though I didn't always understand them. Everything seemed right for me to read him a short story that I had just finished and want to send out before I leave for Vermont. He listened, and maybe that proves something, for Ben falls asleep when I read to him. After the last page he said, "I'd call you a second Katherine Mansfield."

"But I want to be a first myself."

He started to get sprawly and that made me mad, much as I like him.

"Come on, this is what life is all about, not words on paper."

"No, it isn't. Not yet anyway."

End of Summer, 1926

The work has been good, in the saddle all day, many an evening idling on the lake in a canoe with one of the other counselors. As it's my second year, I've been given more freedom and more responsibility. Except for the Sabbath Sermon and editing the camp paper, there's been no time for writing, but I've jotted ideas down in my notebook, and I'll have plenty to work on and with next winter. It's my fallow time and perhaps that's as good for a mind now and then as it is for a field. I've made many new friends and it seems they'll all be turning up in New York to see me and meet Martha.

From camp I went to Hillhurst Farm to be with the family for a while. The whole way of life there is so beautiful, so ordered, so full that I could almost succumb to it, but I won't. I go along with it, marveling that my old rebellion at the social aspect of the days has faded somewhat. Ben came for a week. The family all like him and hope "something will come of it"; but I find his attention boring. Jinny came out to the farm several times and she positively shines with all she is doing—active in every kind of society event, especially ones that aid charities, winning tennis matches, and talking of horse shows, but not this year. She's getting plump in the middle and that makes Mother look at her adoringly. It must be wonderful to lead the kind of life that pleases the people near you who know you and love you. I may never do that. They may not be pleased with what I do, but I hope that someday they'll be proud of me.

Bobby and I had some long rides together and we talked. He wanted to know all about New York, and, even though I haven't anything to show for my time there, he was interested, maybe not so much in what I am doing as in me. He's beginning to chafe at restrictions: what he'd like to do versus what Father has in mind for him to do. I tried to tell him that he was so young, that he hadn't even finished school yet, then I remembered people used to say that to me. He's so dear; he would never ride roughshod the way I seemed to have to do, but he has an aching need to be recognized for himself.

Life seems to play a kind of hide-and-seek with us, especially when we're growing up. With each of us, our deepest need is to be found, but we continue to feel lost. Whenever we got to a place in our conversation where I thought I might be able to say something to Bobby that would be helpful, he would say, "Come on, let's give them a run," and off we'd canter.

I'm trying to work out something in my mind. We're clay, of course, but not in the hands of another, rather in the forces of life. Clay is molded, wood is shaped, stone is cut, silver refined, but a human being is shaped by influences, forces, tensions. Maybe, and this is a thought that startles me, when we begin to find ourselves we begin to find God. Our search for identity, then, is twofold.

September 10, 1926

New York again, and while life at Hillhurst was satisfying, the city is stimulating. Something in me quickens at possibility. Tomorrow I begin the round of job hunting. It's hard, because often it seems there is so little that I can do, but I must fight off discouragement with all the power that's in me. It's devastating to get discouraged. It breaks down the thin walls of strength within me that have taken so long to build.

September 15, 1926

An intriguing ad took me to the employment office of R. H. Macy, and now I'm one of their corps of Comparison Shoppers. I think it is going to be exciting and very good training for me as a writer. It will call upon all of me and involve my senses totally. We will meet early in the morning, before the store officially opens, and we will be given our instructions for the day. If Gimbel's or Bloomingdale's or some other department store has merchandise similar to Macy's, our job is to see that particular item and report back on it. In may be a fur coat, a refrigerator, or anything at all, but since Macy's policy is to sell 6 percent below its competitors, we have to see the product, study it, and bring back a complete report. Then the decision will be made by Macy's to reduce its price or keep it.

The first day I was sent over to Newark to compare a stove being advertised with Macy's model. I felt like a spy. It was delicious, looking over, into, around, under the stove, remembering its features, every least detail, then going off and writing down a complete report. It's good for observation, memory, right use of words, all that a writer needs. It will help me, and I'm being paid very well with all my expenses—travel, luncheon, and anything out-of-pocket. The important thing is never to get caught, or reveal the reason for the intensity of my interest.

October 10, 1926

We've added to our household! Today when we took our glass milk bottles back to the delicatessen store on Third Avenue to get our nickels for them, we were given a free black kitten. At first we called him Soot, but we soon changed his name to De Profundis. We've been reading and talking about Oscar Wilde lately and that name seemed more appropriate. He's lively and delights in teasing us, messing himself up in Martha's paints, then scampering into my room. He likes to investigate my typewriter. Watching him, I feel there are times when he might write better stories than I do, except that I don't write on the typewriter. A pencil traveling over lined paper is my method. When I have the work as I want it to be, then I type my finished copy. Each story may be what I want it to be, but it doesn't seem to be what an editor wants. Three have just come back in the mail. One rejection slip said, "Try us again." I will.

I'm taking a philosophy course at New York University on Wednesday evenings and it's a great mind opener. The lectures are good, and the books given us to study are challenging, but often my old trouble comes back: wandering! I find myself thinking about the elderly man in the front row, making up a story about him instead of listening to the professor. That's my problem—everything is a story to me. My head teems with ideas. I get excited, and, once back at 147, stay up the rest of the night writing. Martha says that if her luxury is paint, mine is candles. I like to write by candlelight. It's soft, and there's a feeling that the thoughts eluding me may be lurking in the shadows. I've finished two new stories and sent them to magazines.

November 10, 1926

The stories have come back. What is wrong with me? I saw an ad in the paper for a Literary Adviser. Her name is Miss Weil and she lives in Newark. I made an appointment to see her on a day when Macy's gave me an assignment in New Jersey, and I asked for an extra hour, which Macy's allowed me. From the moment I walked into her room, I wished I had not come. It was all so untidy. She wanted me to leave the stories and asked me to return in a week. I said I couldn't be sure of being in Newark next week and would prefer to wait. So she turned the pages of the two stories, made an occasional comment, read the poem without comment, shuffled the pages together and handed them back to me. She said she had no particular advice to give me, that the stories were good and I should work harder.

"But I'm not getting any accepted."

"Acceptance comes in time. Keep sending them out to the different magazine markets."

"What advice do you have for me?"

"I've given you it—work harder."

So I paid $10 to be told what I already knew.

On the way back to New York, my thoughts were of Miss Albertina Russell, my wonderful tutor during the year at Oaksmere. She did not give me advice so much as counsel, and there is a world of difference between those two words.

December 6, 1926

I'm twenty-one now. I can vote.

December 20, 1926

We're going home for Christmas, and De Profundis will travel in a hatbox and Martha will have him with her in her berth. I'll have to give up Macy's and take my chance at finding an equally good or better job when I get back. I've loved the work. It's been exhausting physically, but otherwise stimulating, and I feel as if I had broken out of the terrible wheel of futility. Many times my boss has said, "Your reports are well written. . .extremely well. . .amazingly well." One day the comment was, "You're wasted in a job like this. Have you ever thought of being a writer?"

1927

January 1, 1927

That last night home was a story in itself! After dinner we were all in the living room by the fire. Father settled behind his paper. I picked up a book, but didn't really feel like losing myself in it. The warmth of Christmas was all around, and the knowledge that I would soon be going my separate way made it seem warmer than ever. I must have got caught up in my book, because, before I knew it, the others had drifted from the room and I was alone with Father. The newspaper rattled, then was folded and laid on the table. He wants an accounting, I thought. A businessman always wants that.

"You like what you are doing in New York?"

"Yes. Of course. Very much."

"But what are you doing?"

"I've had some interesting jobs, most of them temporary. Made lots of friends. Gone to the theater and concerts. Had lots of fun."

"You went away to become a writer."

"Yes."

"And what does that mean?"

"I've written one novel."

He didn't look in the least interested, but why should he? He never reads novels.

"Will it be successful?"

I shook my head. "Not yet." How could I tell him of the letter I had received from Little, Brown. "I think I will do better with my next novel." Words hid my heartache but not my hope.

"That was a nice young man who came up to see you when you were home last summer."

"Oh, Ben? Yes, he's a very decent sort of person."

"Anything serious?"

"No." I felt silenced. The respectability of marriage, that's what they want for me, I thought.

His hands were reaching for the newspaper. "Well, you are doing what you want to do." Then he settled back into *The Wall Street Journal.*

I'm doing what I have to do, I wanted to say, but couldn't get the words out.

1927.

the year Elizabeth met Bill

I picked up the book I'd been reading, but it didn't seem to have any more appeal to me, so I left and went up to my room—disgusted with myself because I couldn't seem to explain to Father what I felt, and hurt because when everything here seems so wonderful on the surface the atmosphere of disapproval makes me feel like a stranger. In their eyes my life is going for nothing, but I've got to keep on, and even if it takes me years, I know that my work will prove itself—and me—someday.

Now that I've written all this down I feel better. And that's the way it has always been, the way it will be. I make an entry in my journal, I write a poem or a story, and I feel relieved. When it's out of me and onto paper, I can see the thoughts for what they are. Or may become.

I stretch out my hands to the new year. What will it bring? What will I bring to it? During these hours between midnight and morning, I've replaced the candles and the fire has gone out; but light is beginning to creep into the room and there's a fire in me: to do, to accomplish.

January 27, 1927

I never thought to be a saleslady, but that's what I am, and loving it! The Frankl Gallery is on East 48th Street, so it's an easy walk from the apartment. They have fabrics, small furniture, china, and things that are a joy to handle because they are so beautiful. The customers can be delightful or annoying, but each one must be treated like royalty. The people I work with are such fun, especially Mrs. Howard. She has a friend who is an editor on *The American Magazine*—Mildred Harrington. She wants me to meet her.

March 30, 1927

Father took Bobby and me to Bermuda for a week. It was school vacation for Bobby, and Mr. Frankl was willing to give me a week off. The journey out by ship was thrilling, just the three of us, and there didn't seem to be any troublesome talks or painful silences. We enjoyed each other as people. Oh, the warmth of the sun, the singing of birds, the air so fragrant from the fields of Easter lilies, and back of it all the saltness of the sea. One day we cycled to Elba Beach and spent hours on the pink coral sand or jousting with the surf, then enjoyed a picnic basket packed by the hotel. We were drenched with sunlight, brimful of happiness. And to think that these sands, this water, sunrays and sea winds are mine forever because I've been a part of them and can tuck them away in my mind to relive.

April 17, 1927

Martha had a party tonight, an Easter celebration. There were lots of people, mostly her friends, but friends brought friends, so sometimes we didn't know who different people were, but we knew we were having a good time. The doorbell rang.

"That'll be Bill." Martha said, "We sent him out to get some ice."
I was the nearest one to the door, so I went to open it.
"I'm Bill."

He had the nicest smile and the warmest voice, and his eyes were gray. Had I ever really looked into a man's eyes before? During the evening we were often together, accidentally, in the crush of people in the room that seemed much too small, then deliberately as we found so many things to talk about. Before he left we made a date to go on a hike next Saturday in the Highlands of the Hudson.

April 23, 1927

We took the train to Haverstraw, walked three miles to Tompkins Cove, then followed an Indian trail over the Timp Range back into the Catskills. We were the first over the trail this year and it was gone in many places. Often we lost ourselves. It took thinking and fighting through the brush to find ourselves again. We rested where the sun shone warm on the rocks. We found a spring near which cowslips were growing in golden clumps. We climbed Timp—1,100 feet; and Bockberg—1,500. They were steep, but there were stubby trees to catch hold of. We stood on the summits and saw for miles and miles great rolling seas of russet and green mountains with touches of dogwood coming into bloom among the trees.

When we found the perfect place, Bill made a small fire and we cooked our meal over it—warming a tin of beans and making a pot of coffee. There was a comfortable cranny against a rock wall, and there we stretched ourselves out, the earth firm beneath and the sky so blue above. The valley was far below us and beyond were distant hills. I had *The Gypsy Trail* in a pocket of my rucksack, and I took it out and read some of my favorite poems to Bill. When I told Bill that I wanted to write, he was interested; he even asked if I would read some of my work to him sometime.

When we came down the trail and out of the woods, the setting sun had turned the river to scarlet with cloud reflections, and a star could be seen over a ridge. The birds were singing their last songs. It was late when we got back to the city. We had laughed and talked and been a part of beauty all through a day. I felt strong, as if nothing could ever hurt me. I think this has been the most exhilarating day of my life. The strength of nature seemed to flood through my feet and up out my fingertips. I don't know when we'll meet again. Somehow it doesn't matter. Bill travels a lot for his company and is in New York only for brief times. He said he would telephone me and we would make another date.

May 10, 1927

Jean came down from Smith College for the weekend and it was good to see her, someone with whom I can keep the link forged in childhood. We drank many cups of tea and we talked about everything—work, our families, books, people, God. She says I'm like a wellspring, sensitive and serious. I showed her the copybook in which I've written my poems, and she read them slowly, often commenting, not like a teacher but a friend. She said she could see in my words and their rhythm the kind of life I was living. We fell into long silences, and our talk was never meaningless.

"You have a commitment to goodness, to beauty," she said. "Don't sacrifice it just because you feel you must sell."

While I was pondering her words, she said something else that made me think. "And don't be unwilling to write something tart and caustic. Life has that side, too."

July 5, 1927

A poem of mine has been published in the *New York World*! I submitted it two weeks ago with a stamped, self-addressed envelope enclosed, and it didn't come back to me. It is in "The Conning Tower," a column that appears daily in the paper and is read by everyone. Franklin P. Adams is the columnist, and he keeps as pleasing a balance between prose and verse as he does between his own work and that of others. He is said to have an eye out for new writers, and I'm certainly that on the Literary Scene! One poem out of a year of work, but what a place for it! It means that F.P.A. has recognized me and maybe other editors will, too. Some people may be in the *Blue Book* or the *Social Register*, but I am in "The Conning Tower"!

July 20, 1927

Martha is going to Paris for a year to study, so we are packing up the apartment and I've found a much smaller one at 243 East 36th Street. We've had great times and gained a lot from each other, but probably it's good for us to go our own ways now. "He travels the fastest who travels alone," Kipling says. I want to spend all my spare time on weekends and in the evenings working on my novel, *Clothed with the Sun*. More than anything, it must be finished. It is filled with things I want to say, thoughts I want to give to the world, and somehow writing it helps me to justify my life.

August 15, 1927

An article I did about Bermuda was bought by *The Smokers' Companion*. It was exciting to see my name in print, to receive a check for $25, but best of all was the letter that offered me a job on the magazine. It won't be hard to give up my work at the Frankl Gallery, because this is a real step forward in my chosen world of writing.

Now that the novel is finished and on its way to a publisher, I'll take a couple of weeks off before I begin the new job. I hope something will come of *Clothed with the Sun*. In any case, I'm glad it's written. My head is cleared of those ideas, and I'm ready for more.

Bill gave me a book by Glenn Frank, *Fishers of Men*. In it I read, "Sure as the tide goes out and then comes in again, just so will all we give out come back to us."

End of Summer, 1927

Two weeks at Hillhurst are a beatitude after the hot days in New York. So much is the same, but Bobby isn't here. He's in the Canadian wheatfields, working as a harvester and having tremendous adventures. Jinny is busy with her family, but Bluemouse is still the best horse in the world to ride, and Andy can still find a fortune in a teacup. Yesterday when he read mine he pushed a leaf aside to discover another leaf. "That's a man in a business suit," he said.

"Oh, Andy, it's just another tea leaf."

"There's tea leaves and tea leaves," he answered, "but there's only one looks like that man. He's so close to you that I can't tell for sure whether he is now, or will be, your man."

Maria started to fill my cup again, but I didn't want to drink any more tea. I had fortune enough for one day.

September 15, 1927

Here I am back in New York, settled in at 243 East 36th, reveling in solitude but no longer alone, because I brought a puppy back with me—a Sealyham, Sinna Lezah, and I'm sure he is going to be a dog of character as well as a staunch companion.

As Chief Manuscript Reader at *The Smokers' Companion* I am wildly happy. This is my work, my life. The very smell of the paste, the clip of scissors, the click of typewriters are thrilling to me. I can work tirelessly, and the great thing is that I am in the office only mornings. Most of my work can be done at home, so I don't have to leave Sinna for too long a time. I feel that now I am really started, I've been given a chance to prove myself and I will forge ahead.

Everyland Magazine has accepted a story of mine, but the novel has been returned. I've put it in my bottom drawer with *Cinema*. Yesterday when I was having luncheon with Mildred Harrington, I told her about the novel. I had to tell somebody, because I was so disheartened. She cheered me when she said, "Of course you can and will do things! What is more, you have already done things."

"So few. So little."

"You must remember that in giving you the wonderful gift of verse, the good Lord also endowed you with the capacity for exquisite suffering. That's why discouragement hurts."

"But it's taking me so long to get anywhere."

"Things will break eventually. They do for those who keep faith with themselves, and you are doing that."

October 10, 1927

Bill is in New York for a whole week. We had dinner last night at John's and it was warm enough to sit in the garden. We had bowls of ravioli and a bottle of Chianti. Just to look into his warm, smiling eyes, to listen to the tone of his wise-worded voice, made up for all my recent disappointments. We talk about everything, books and plays and events in the world, but we always seem to end up talking about God. I'm still searching for some reality, which I think Bill has found. He tells me about his work and I tell him about mine. When he looks across the table at me his eyes say he believes in me.

Later

Saturday morning early we were on the first train out of the city. We got on the Timp trail by nine and Sinna was in his element, frolicking around us, rolling in the leaves, rushing off on some excitement, then dashing back and not quite sure to whom he should show his affection first. Last time we came this way, the woods were alive with the thrust of spring; now the green is tired and there are dried leaves to scuff through.

Whenever we found an opening in the forest, we could see flashes of color on the distant hills—copper and scarlet and gold. Sinna began to weary after a few miles, so we shifted some of the things from Bill's pack into mine, and Bill gave him a ride on his back. As soon as we reached our first real height—hot and tired but exhilarated—I flattened out on the sun-warmed rock and, with my arms outstretched, let the sun caress me as the ground held me. Bill asked me what I was thinking. I said I wasn't thinking, I was praying.

"Oh, Earth, flood through me with your great strength—the strength that rears trees into mansions for the winds and sends rivers leaping to the sea."

"Sounds like a poem."

"It will be—my Antaeus poem."

Later we followed a trail down to a small lake. Bill found the right place to make a fire. We broiled steaks, boiled coffee, ate bread and apples. Sinna had his share, too. Then we studied our map and discovered that a woodland road could get us to Arden for a late train back to the city. Darkness overtook us long before we reached the station, but there were stars. The mountains were a dim rim against the night, the grass was dew-soaked, and Sinna, riding in the pack on Bill's shoulders, was asleep.

"We've come a long way," Bill said.

October 20, 1927

Cleve wanted to see me, so I suggested we go out to dinner. I was afraid he might get slushy if we stayed at the apartment. He's thinking more of me since another poem of mine has been in the *Herald Tribune*. He writes for the *Saturday Review* and has actually mentioned me in his column. He asked if I wanted to see what he had written.

"You read it to me."

"In these first poems there is an honesty of emotion and a directness of expression that make the work worthy of attention. They are youthful poems, filled with revolt against the world as it unfolds itself to the author. But even when she is repeating sentiments which are too familiar to us, her intensity of feeling carries us with her. She does have something to say and she says it at any cost to poetic structure. Her future work will bear watching."

There wasn't anything I could say for a long time. Then the words I wanted came to me. "Cleve, for one whose bread has been rejection slips, this is heady wine."

November 5, 1927

Mildred thinks I should show my short stories to someone capable of judging them rather than sending them out, as I've been doing, and in most cases getting them back. She suggested Loyola Sanford, not so much as an agent but as a person who represents authors that appeal to her. In preparation for meeting her next week, I've spent this evening going over the stories and trying to decide which ones merit her time. The El rumbles on through the night, Sinna makes whiffling sounds in his sleep, and I read—sometimes with satisfaction, more often with dismay. Why do I use such fancy words? Why do I persist in writing about things beyond my ken?

Here they are, spread out on the table before me. Some were written as many as three years ago; all have been sent out several times. "Tabloid Serial"—that's about three wives, each one in a different type of setting; the words are all right, but I can see now that there is no story line to keep it moving. "Streak of White"—that's about an elderly dressmaker who wanted love and never found it. "Ties and Tigers"—how did I dare to set a story in India and inject into it a grisly murder? "Lunatic at Large"—on that one an editor wrote "not sufficient characterization." "Le Rouge Gagne"—gambling at Monte Carlo, and I think I must have wanted to show off my French. "News Item"—about a suicide, and I always thought it was one of the best. "Fools in Darkness"—a tale of mixed-up lovers. "Three Steps"—what did I know about the inner thinking of a prostitute? "Leaves from a Notebook"—marrying without love, a favorite subject of mine and the brunt of my second novel. "Blonde Etching"—mystery, murder, suicide, market crash, domestic troubles; no wonder it came back to me! The two most recently done still please me—"Touching Finger Tips," about a day in the country, and "The House of Loving Touch." In each one, the conversation sounds not as if I were making it up, but as if I were really listening to, or overhearing, two people very much in love. Which ones shall I show to the unknown Loyola?

Our first meeting was in her office, a room of her apartment in the Village. I thought I was going to feel scared, but I didn't. The room was small, with a flat desk, a few neat piles of manuscripts, and a bowl of apples, one of which she offered me. There were many books and just two chairs. Whatever visitor she has must feel rather special. She is tall, slender, quiet; her dark hair is drawn back into a simple knot, and her dark dress is of no particular style. Her very plainness is her beauty. She looked at me as if she really saw me, and she asked questions that were easy for me to answer. I had a portfolio with six of my best stories in it, and when I handed it to her, she took it as carefully as if I were giving her something very precious. We agreed to meet in a week's time.

"And talk," she said, with a smile that made me feel I was with the right person.

At our second meeting, she came to my apartment for supper, and we did talk then, half the night. This time I was the listener, for she had much to tell me.

I told her that I thought I wasn't getting anywhere, and she countered by telling me that in my various jobs I had been observing life on many levels.

"Model, governess, comparison shopper, saleslady, teacher at summer camps, magazine editing—they all have had bearing on writing. It's a course you've given yourself, and you've been paid for what most people have to pay for. Your senses are your tools, and these varied experiences have been sharpening your tools."

I put my hand on the pile of stories and said, "These represent years of work."

"And all the time you have been building into yourself something called discipline. You've finished tasks you set yourself, and you rose out of disappointment. Three years? That's not so long when you measure it up to a life."

"Do you think you can sell any of my stories?"

"I have no doubt, perhaps not these, but the ones you will write."

After she left, I went on thinking. She was giving me encouragement as Miss Russell had when I worked with her, yet each one made it clear that I would have to go on, keep on, if achievement was to be mine. Is life ever going to be long enough for me to learn all that I have to learn?

Thanksgiving, 1927

Was there ever such a day or such a dinner! Bobby is back from the wheatfields looking stalwart and handsome. He is overflowing with stories of his adventure, and he has a magnificent big dog with him, Ronno. Mother and Father, Bobby and Ronno, are all staying at the Commodore and that's where we had dinner. It was fun to be a small family, because so often at home it's a big family, and it gets bigger as the older ones marry and add to it. Father wants Bobby to learn the hotel business, and he'll be starting in at the kitchen in the Commodore, so we'll be able to see each other often.

Bobby told us of his adventures—the hard work, the way he had put his boxing experience to good use, and then about how Ronno had saved his life. It was like reading a book or going to a play just to listen to him, but it was all real, and it was my little brother who was the chief actor. Little? He's taller than I am, and he says I'm not to call him Bobby anymore, but Bob.

Late in the afternoon he walked back to 243 with me. Sinna took to Ronno immediately, and it was fun to watch how gentle the big dog was with the little one. Like Bob, I thought, always doing nice things for people. I put the kettle on to make tea, because I didn't want Bob to go. I wanted to hold on to him, keep him talking about his time in the northwest, fill my eyes with the sight of him and my ears with the sound of his voice.

He pulled some papers out of his pocket. They were in his handwriting.

"It was four days coming home on the train, and I spent some of the time scribbling down my experiences. Thought you might like to read them."

I took them from him. There were forty pages in all, written in pencil on both sides of the paper. His handwriting was never the best, and the motion of the train didn't help, but glancing through the pages, I felt that they positively sang with the reality of what he had been through, what he had done.

We talked far into the night. He wants me to help him make the pages into a book.

"Will you have the time?"

"Oh, Bob, that's one of the advantages of being a writer. I can control my time; work in the day, write at night. But you'll be busy down in that big kitchen at the Commodore. Will you have time to talk with me more, because I'll have lots of questions to ask you, and it will take more than these pages to make a book."

Bob had the kind of smile that could say more than words.

After he and Ronno left, I took Sinna for a walk through the dark, quiet streets. I wanted to think about the adventure I would be on, using Bob's forty handwritten pages. Now I'm sitting by my little fire, still thinking. There is so much I'll have to know to give background to the story and to expand it.

December 20, 1927

I do have time, plenty of time. This week the office staff of *The Smokers' Companion* were informed that the magazine was going out of business and that the issue we were working on was the last one. Somehow I'm not sorry. There will be hours and days, maybe months, to work on Bob's book, and I've a chance to do an article for *The American Magazine*. Mildred said if they liked it, it could lead to more articles.

It may not be possible for me to explain it to anyone else but I can to myself—what I am doing right now is serving an apprentice-ship. Seeing my time that way makes me feel like a craftsman of old, working under a master and slowly perfecting the necessary skills. Who is my master? The great ones of English prose, of course, but in the long run it is myself. I go back to what Miss Russell said to me: "Please yourself." The trouble is that I get harder and harder to please, but maybe that is a good thing.

New Year's Eve, 1927

I end the year with a big decision: From now on I am going to sign my work Brett Yates. That is strong-sounding, much more so than Betty, and I hope to do work that will match up to it. Just as I had to get away from Buffalo to find myself in New York, so I have to get away from the person I've been to the one I have every inten-tion of being. What's in a name? More than the sound: a clarion call.

1928

Spring, 1928

> *A March day that feels like spring.*

So much has been happening! I had just started planning Bob's book with him when Mildred called to say that the *American* had accepted my article and that there was a part-time job in the Research Department if I cared to apply for it. Of course I applied the very next day and was given the job. I can do it on my own time, working mostly at the Public Library to gain background information required. It has to do with particular people who have been successful in their lives, often against great odds. These success stories are wonderful. They show the maintenance of single purpose, one objective dominating the mind. Muddled minds never go far. Life has been hard for most of these people, and that is why they forced themselves to forge ahead and hew out their work and so make their names.

When I have finished one assignment for the *American* I can then turn to Saskatchewan and wheat harvesting to learn about all the things that will give background and a sense of place to Bob's story. In both cases, reading and note-taking are done at the library; my actual writing can be done at home. I told Bob I wasn't going to do anything to add to the details about boxing. That was all his and no words of mine were needed. It's too gory for me. In the evening, after I finish my reports for the *American,* I type up Bob's material for the next time we get together.

Ronno is staying on a farm in Mountainville, across the Hudson, and Bob goes over there weekends to be with him. Sometimes I join him with Sinna, and the dogs have as much fun as we do. They romp and wrestle with each other while we walk and wrestle with words. My problem is that every time Bob and I meet to discuss the book, he remembers more things that happened and wants me to fit them in.

April 12, 1928

"Seven Sons," the story that *Everyland Magazine* accepted last fall, has just appeared. It's actually in print, with my name in print just a little smaller than the title. They sent me two copies of the

Younger brother, Bob,

author of

When I Was a Harvester

magazine and a check for $25. A letter from the editor said that it was different from anything they have had, but it carried their message. *Everyland* is published in Boston and it is a magazine of world friendship for boys and girls. The story is as Irish as I could make it, and, when I was writing it, it seemed as if the stories Lizzie used to tell when I was little came back to me. The words lilted as I read them in print and gave me a feeling of being in another world. I sent the extra copy home to Mother, hoping she would enjoy it. Her roots are Irish, and one of our heirlooms is a sampler done by her great-great-grandmother, Eleanor Obeirne, when she was thirteen years old in Ireland.

April 15, 1928

Two letters in my mailbox: one from Mother saying my story filled her with wonder and surprise: "I'm proud of you." The other was from Miss Hyde: "It is a true gift you have been given, and you deserve great praise for the way you are developing your talent." Lovely words; I have framed them in my heart.

April 17, 1928

Bill and I went to John's last night to celebrate the fact that we have known each other for exactly one year. We ate in the garden, and the air was so still that the candle on our table hardly flickered at all. We always have more to talk about than will fit into the time and we often get very philosophical. Bill knows so much more than I do. After all, he's been in the world seventeen years longer than I have and what he knows he is sure of. I'm still searching. I tell him about the different churches I've been going to ever since I've been in New York.

The most unusual was a Russian church Martha took me to, where we stood around, held lighted candles, understood nothing, but savored the atmosphere. I've been to a Jewish synagogue, a Baptist revival, ever so many churches, and often to St. Patrick's or St. Thomas' on Fifth Avenue, for there are times when the music, the fragrance of incense, and the beauty of light through stained-glass windows seem to answer my need. I wonder where and what God is and I come back to answering my own question: as with writing, I have to find the way myself for God to have meaning in my life. So we talk a lot about God. Bill doesn't try to divert me, or direct me, or improve me. He listens, then says something that makes me go into myself to reply.

Tonight I asked Bill if he thought I was an atheist.

"What did you think when we stood on Timp just a year ago and saw all those billowing ranges around us and above us the sky?"

"I think—I think I felt face-to-face with God."

"And where were you?"

"There, too."

Then I saw something so clearly that I wrote it on a piece of paper and handed it to Bill. Am I an atheist? An atheist is one who does not believe in himself. I do believe in myself. Therefore I am not an atheist.

"Look, I've made a theorem, and I was never good with algebra when I was at the Franklin School."

"Don't worry about algebra if you make a Q.E.D. with your life."

Then he asked me if I had finished my Antaeus poem.

"Bill, that was way back in October—to think that you remembered!"

"You didn't forget, did you?"

"No."

"Can you say it to me?"

"I'll try—some of it anyway: 'Antaeus wishing to renew his strength / Embraced the earth with his body's length. . .Follow Antaeus if you wish to find / Sustenance for your body and mind.'"

"You've skipped some."

"Yes, three verses in the middle. Sometime when it's published I'll send it to you."

"What is its title?"

"Remedia Natura."

When we left, we rode on the top deck of a bus, but we didn't get off at 36th Street. We stayed on, and the bus went to the end of its line, way past Central Park, then turned around. The conductor came up for our fares and Bill gave him another two dimes. The lights of the city were beautiful, the air soft; there was laughter from some people still on the bus, silence from others. With my hand resting in Bill's I felt so safe, so sure.

When we said good-by at the door of my apartment, Bill added his familiar phrase, "And the rest you know." Something in me went still, like a clock losing its tick. I felt afraid. Now, as I write about this evening, what is it I am afraid of?

BEFORE DAWN

What does it mean when I say I love you?
It means that my heart is in your keeping for a while.
I think of no tomorrows or uncertain future years,
I see only tonight and the splendor of bared hearts.
This is no fragile thing woven of moonlight hours,
Rather it is the strength of those who know mountains
Brisk with winds, tender with clouds.
I have no bonds to bind your heart to mine,
Only hands to offer all my heart to you
With deep-felt thanks, for, due to you,
I have more love for lovely things, more pity,
And more hours of loneliness.

Never before have I written a letter in my journal; I do it now because it is a letter that will not be sent to the one to whom it is addressed.

May 20, 1928

Next best to talking with Bill are his letters to me when he is away. His flowing handwriting is like the sound of his voice when he is talking. I see it on an envelope with my name in my mailbox and my heart gives a great leap. I keep his letters to reread when we don't see each other for a time, and the box they are in is marked Peruvian Notes. I often call him The Gentleman from Peru because of his far traveling. Some of the letters are the happy words of friendship, casual and lively; some are comments on my writing. These are taken to my heart and mind, for he has become my mentor above all others.

"The idea is great but it seems too long, too wordy. It's a Trivia gem if boiled way down. A few of your sentences convey the idea beautifully; the others are repetitious. You are doing real writing. Your growing is evident in your letters. They've changed a lot—same delightful style and insight, but with more body, more action."

There is one written from Boston on a stormy night when he was lonely. "My thoughts constantly turn toward you and I wonder where you are and what you are doing. What fun this night would be were we together! I realize how strong in me is some strange influence that would throttle the expression of thoughts which often seem as vital as life itself. Why is it hard for me to say that I love you dearly, that the attributes I value most I find combined in you—enthusiasm, intelligence, honesty, spontaneity. When I am with you my thoughts—like pigeons released by a loving hand—soar toward the sun, but a silent man walks beside you. I would not possess you for that is death itself, but I pray that the capacity and the opportunity to experience much of life with you may increasingly be mine."

That was a letter that made me quiver, but a later one puzzled me. "Since our last meeting, minutes are years and miles whole continents, but I have learned that fierce emotion will pitch one from the heights to terrible abysses in spite of a careless forgetfulness, unless we see straight. Man's instinctive, often awkward, search for happiness is actually his reaching for God: the universal desire to unite with one's Creator. I love you and I am happy with you. And in you my search finds its answer. But, for the time being, we must content ourselves with our lighthearted meetings."

I put the letters back in the box and try to understand.

Summer's End, 1928

In the saddle, in the lake, talking around a campfire, getting to know a few people well, and being paid for doing all the things I like best—what a summer it has been! Out of the two months at Camp Kinni Kinnic, two events stand out—one touched me, the other touched me and Bill. Perhaps that is what ever happens: From a landscape blurring into memory there are summits seen in the mind, held in the heart.

On a warm July night we were alerted to the northern lights, and several of us went to the field that slopes down to the lake to watch the display. We lay on our backs in the evening-damp grass, and it was like being under a tent top as streamers of color shifted across the sky and were reflected in the lake. It lasted an hour or more, then dimmed and slowly faded away. When the colors diminished, the moon coming over the ridge to the east gave a steady glow to the night. Dixie, one of the counselors and a good friend, said she supposed I would write about what we had just seen.

"Indeed I will. Everything is grist to a writer's mill, but could I ever do justice to the aurora?"

"You can always try."

"Sometimes I think I could live on beauty."

"You can't, on beauty alone, if you expect to pay your bills."

What a comedown her words were after that hour of wonder!

The other event was the last time I saw Bill, at the end of August. It was the Sabbath, so I would not be teaching, and I was not needed at camp. The Brills gave me the whole day off. "Be back by dark" was my time limit. We had been planning the day for weeks in our letters, and when it finally came it was bright and warm. I felt that we had forever before us, and that's the way I always feel when I'm with Bill—as if we had all the time there was or would be, just as if our knowing each other had nothing to do with time. But after what happened today, I am not so sure.

We had a picnic luncheon, and on the large-scale map we had found a point where the Long Trail crossed the road, and it was there that Bill could leave his car. Up the trail we went, through woodland, up and up to a ridge. Seas of green forests rolled away from us on every side. The air was still, a few clouds traversed the sky. We passed a fire lookout, and there we left our picnic luncheon, the basket tucked away in a coign of rocks. The tower would be a good place to eat, and we would have to return that way in any case. Without the basket we were much freer. On and on we went, meeting occasional hikers and sharing information about the trail and the weather. We passed a spring, where we filled our canteen with delicious water. We talked, but not nearly so much as we generally did. It seemed good to be silent on that high ridge of the world.

A poem of Leonora Speyer's was in my mind, and, when we stopped for a moment to take the expanse of forest land and sky into us, I said it:

> *Measure me, sky! Tell me I reach by a song*
> *Nearer the stars: I have been little so long.*
> *Weigh me, high wind! What will your wild scales record?*
> *Profit of pain, joy by the weight of a word.*
> *Horizon, reach out! Catch at my hands, stretch me taut,*
> *Rim of the world: widen my eyes by a thought.*

How many miles we walked, how many heights we gained, we did not know—only that we reached a time when it seemed good to turn back and retrace our steps. The sky had begun to haze and when we finally reached the fire tower, mist was coming over the distant ranges. We retrieved our picnic basket and climbed up into the tower. It offered shelter, and soon there was no view at all as the mist thickened and rain came pattering down. Sitting on the bare floor, backs against the metal wall, we satisfied our hunger. We were dry and there was plenty of time before the light changed and signified the end to our day. We talked then, and our words were a continuation of all we had been saying to each other for the past year, but something new was added.

"How deep the arrow went," Bill said, and in my mind I saw those two hearts carved into the bark of a tree with an arrow piercing them, linking them.

We knew we were in love, and we could talk about that with a delirious joy, but the next thought—which might have been marriage—was as remote as the mountains now lost in mist and rain. Our friendship which had been growing and deepening every time we saw each other should have fulfillment, but how was that to be? I had been afraid to love, thinking it would upset my life, put me off course; yet, what faced me now was the necessity to be true to love, as true as I was to myself in my insistence to lead my own life.

As for Bill, I knew he had "promises to keep" in the care of his elderly mother in Rochester, New York, whose support he was and whom he visited frequently. As the rain tapped on the metal roof of the fire tower, he told me he was wary of marriage. "Our friendship has been so perfect. You have not wanted to possess me or dominate me, just love me. Let us go on this way." There was a yearning in me that made me wonder if friendship could go on forever, if it must not in time become something else.

It was comforting to nestle in his arms, to say the only words I could say, had never said to anyone else and knew that I never would say to anyone but Bill. Love was my reason for being. I felt safe in Bill's embrace, and yet the future was so unsure. In our bare shelter on the mountaintop I felt in the presence of forces beyond ourselves.

Then he told me about his eyes, about a condition that might in time take his sight. "It would not be fair to you to put this upon you, if it happens."

I would not listen and with lips and words I hushed him. I could not believe that such a thing could happen to Bill, of all people, so I put what he was saying out of my mind. Later, much later, he said something that pierced me as the arrow had the two hearts we had seen on the tree.

"It will be better if we do not see each other for a while."

"But we can still write letters?"

"No, not even letters. We must go our separate ways—to see."

Yet, even as he spoke, his arms were around me. The world about us was all but lost in mist. It was as if we were on a last outpost of time; perhaps, for us, it was just that.

When the rain ceased, the light soon began to dim, and we knew we must leave our shelter. The downward trail back to the place on the road where the car had been left would be slippery and slow-going. We made it all right, and we got back to the camp gate before it was fully dark. When we said good-by, it was as if by mutual consent we added no endearments to the final word. Stumbling alone over the path to my cabin, I clung to the feel of his arms around me, the press of his lips on mine.

Once in the cabin, I moved around in the dark as quietly as I could, but there was little need—the seven children were sleeping soundly, and rain was thrumming gently on the roof. There was no sleep for me, I had so much to think about. How could two fears be resolved: mine of love, his of marriage? As often happens in exaltation or adversity, my thoughts shaped themselves into a poem, scribbled in the darkness to be rewritten in the morning.

October 15, 1928

Cleve came in tonight with a copy of my poem, which he had seen in the *Herald Tribune*. Nothing would do but that he should read it to me, and I listened, almost as if I had not written it.

AFTER PARTING

You did not know—what?
That your heart could be a world of shattered stars
Whirling with a thousand broken bits of memories,
And your throat so full of aching, straining things
That your thoughts could be a travesty of thinking,
Filtering over the bleak dust of your barren mind;
And you would be lost when the light faded
That led you on so long a way.
You were afraid when you heard your soul cry
So terribly, so very terribly all night long.
But oh, poor fumbler after tortuous things,
What you did not know was that you could love.

He didn't say anything for all of five minutes, and what could I say that hadn't already been said? Then his comment came, almost accusingly: "You're in love, but not with me."

"No, not with you."

"This is what your work needs," and his tone was authoritative. "You won't be talking about human emotions anymore, you'll be them. This is without a doubt the best thing you have done."

"Coming from you, Cleve, that means something."

"May I take you out to dinner?"

Of course I said yes. Cleve has been so critical of me, so superior with me; this time he was almost respectful. Something in me basked. Do we all hunger for appreciation, or am I the only one who feels myself growing under it?

How glad I am to have Sinna! He is a real little dog now, sturdier than ever after his summer on the farm at Mountainville. I talk to him and, cocking his head this way and that, he seems to understand. I am trying to see straight about marriage. Perhaps it isn't all that important. To love, to care, to create in some way or another so that one is part of the creativity that is God, these are important. Yet to love another with heart and soul and mind is to make a commitment, and isn't this marriage?

November 10, 1928

Bob's book is nearly finished. He comes in two or three evenings a week and goes over the pages I've typed. Sometimes he makes changes, and that means a whole page has to be retyped, and still he comes up with one more experience that should be in the story.

"Must you have all those ghastly descriptions of fighting? I know you are a skilled boxer, but I didn't think you were such a fighter."

"Oh, sure, that's life in the raw. You have to tell it the way it is."

"If you bring me many more additions, I'll never get it typed by Christmas."

"What's the hurry?"

"I want to get it on to a publisher's desk first thing in the New Year. That seems an auspicious time."

We discussed titles—*In the Wheatfields, My Summer Adventure,* several others, but none seemed exactly right, so Bob suggested that I list them all on the first page and we let the publisher choose. He says my name should be on it, but I say no, that it is his story, but that he can dedicate it to me. When he leaves, I feel lonelier than ever. It's curious, but on the trail that day, when I said Leonora Speyer's poem to Bill, I didn't say the last verse. Perhaps I couldn't remember it; perhaps it didn't seem to fit with the day. I say it often now.

> *Sky, be my depth; wind, be my width and my height;*
> *World, my heart's span: loneliness wings for my flight!*

I try not to think about Bill, not to hunger for the sound of his voice on the phone or for the sight of his handwriting on a letter, but it's hard. He had said "for a while." How long is a while? I wonder that as I do the articles for the *American,* work on Bob's book, and ease my heart with poems.

December 20, 1928

Just as I was packing to go home for Christmas the phone rang. It was Bill, calling from Boston. We talked a long time, but I can remember only three of his words, "I love you." And I repeated them.

From some dim recess of memory comes a lovely line: "Set me as a seal upon thine heart."

1929

January to August

January 20, 1929

Today I had luncheon with an editor!

It seemed a good idea to put Bob's story with The Macmillan Company. They are right here in New York, and it could be delivered by hand. I had heard that Miss Louise Seaman was a fine editor and that books done by her were successful. At the Public Library, when doing my assignments, I read several adventure stories, and those published by Macmillan seemed to stand out above the others. So I left the big package—typed pages and several titles, all neatly wrapped the way we had learned to do at the Franklin School when I never knew how useful it would be, and a note to Miss Seaman. I requested her to get in touch with me, as I could be reached more easily than my brother.

I never expected a phone call, but only a few days later, it came. She asked me to come to her office and said she would like to take me out to luncheon. I wanted to ask her if she liked the book, but I held myself in check. Obviously she did or she wouldn't want to talk with me about it.

She's just like her voice—warm and friendly, and young; she's very good-looking, too. I didn't feel shy with her, just natural. She took me to the Brevoort, almost across the street from her office, and when the waiter came with the menu, she asked me what I would like. Frogs' legs sounded interesting and unusual, so that is what we both had.

She talked and I listened, except when she urged me to tell her more about my brother. That was easy, for I've loved Bob as long as I've known him. She said that his adventure was one of the best stories that had come to her desk in a long time and that she had not had to read it all before she knew she wanted to publish it.

"When I Was a Harvester," she said, and so gave the book its title. We talked about pictures, a map, the jacket, and all sorts of details, but I was so eager to get to a telephone to give Bob the news that I couldn't take in all that she was saying; besides, I found that a certain amount of attention has to be given to frogs' legs if you expect to get anything from them.

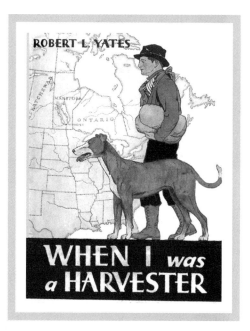

ROBERT L. YATES

WHEN I *was* a HARVESTER

Bob's book

which he dedicated

to the "energetic spirit" of his sister

Bob came over after work and I told him everything.

"If it's that easy to get a book published, maybe I shouldn't be trying to learn the hotel business."

"It has to be written first."

"That's right."

"And before it's written it has to be experienced."

"Right again."

"And you can't disappoint Father."

Bob smiled, the smile I had learned to know so well when we were working on his pages; the smile of sweet agreement.

I told him all that would happen before it became a book and that it would take time. Miss Seaman had said that it would be read by other editors, then it would be copy-edited; after that it would go into galleys, which would be returned to us for checking. It was then that changes could be made if they were necessary, but I warned Bob that we must try not to make any changes, as they would cost us money. She felt the book needed pictures and suggested that many could be found in newspaper files. "She expects that you can supply a good photograph of yourself and Ronno. I asked if my friend, Eunice Stephenson, could submit a design for the jacket, and Miss Seaman said yes, that they are always on the lookout for good artists. Then we got to the contract. She would like to discuss terms with you, Bob."

"Terms! That sounds like a business."

"But of course, a book is a business venture."

"You should be the one to talk terms."

"No, Bob, it's your book."

"You did a lot of work on it."

"You gave me the material to work with."

"It doesn't seem quite right."

"It's right, all right. Don't you remember, when you gave me those forty pages I gave you fifty dollars? You didn't want to take it, but I insisted. It was a business arrangement from the start, not signed and sealed, but just as real."

And then he smiled again.

February 2, 1929

I've just finished an interview for the *American*, my first face-to-face with a person, Edith Keating, an aerial photographer. She found her niche in life and it is in the air, but her work is proportioned between earth and sky, because, when she isn't flying, she is a departmental executive. I asked her where she preferred to be and she said, "In the air. I feel safer up there." She gave me her picture and autographed it for me.

February 4, 1929

And now it looks as if my life will be proportioned between wheels and people, because Father is going on a business trip to the West Coast and has asked me to go with him. I telephoned Bill at his office in Boston to say good-by. We agreed not to write during the month I would be away, but to see each other just as soon as I returned. If love is strong as death, as the Bible says, it must be as strong as distance.

My journal can hold only swift impressions of all that I'll be seeing, and probably none of the conversations I'll be having, but I'll write as much as I can so it will be within these pages when I want to return to it. There will be time for reading when Father is busy or when he gets behind his paper, and I'll have plenty of time to think. The rolling rhythm of train wheels day after day, the distances drawing my eyes will be conducive to long thoughts; and mountains, higher than any I have ever seen before, will stimulate me. Since Bill's telephone call before Christmas I want time to think about us and the possibility that is ahead. Sometime. What a word! What does it mean?

I can remember, when I was little, saying to people, "I love you two bushels"—or ten, or twenty, or however greatly I was inspired, for love then was something that could be measured and dealt out in separate amounts to different persons. Now I am beginning to see that there is no measure to love, no unit of measure, no one or a thousand, for it is all the same. It flows to all alike. It is all around us. It is what keeps us in the heart of God.

This love of mine is not happiness, but it is strong, terribly strong, and yet insecure. So long as I love Bill everything of me is his. I cannot hold more than one star in my hands. Of myself I am sure, but of him I am not sure; yet why do I want to be sure? Where do these thoughts come from? Perhaps from my need to understand. I have just begun to glimpse what love is, and that it is what life is all about.

February 9, 1929

It was overnight to Chicago, then we changed trains and settled in—parlor chairs by day, sleepers at night, and the diner, where we enjoyed everything, especially things that were new and we'd never tasted before. Father is good to travel with; he knows how to leave you alone, because he wants to be left alone to follow his pursuits, mostly the stock reports on those interminable pages of *The Wall Street Journal*. It was cold and gray when we left Chicago and the same as we got farther west, especially through Kansas, where every mile seemed like every other mile. When we came over the Divide and into northern New Mexico in the early morning, I was dazzled, not only by the mountains but by the mesas of glittering snow in the bright sunlight. When we dropped into desert country it was fully as beautiful, but in another way—expansive.

I spend lots of time on the observation platform, and it's easy to get into conversation with other people. Most of them don't want so much to talk as to have me listen to them, but it is all interesting, and I make jottings in my notebook of unusual expressions, situations, names. It may be useful. If I tuck all this away, I'll know where to find it when I need it.

We reached Phoenix late at night and went to our hotel. Oh, to revel in a hot bath after all those days in the train! I finished *The World's Illusion*. It was wonderful to see, within the tight span of a book, how all mankind is really working out of materiality into spirituality.

We are to spend a whole week in Phoenix, and I'll be on my own much of the time. There is glowing sunshine, cool breezes, dawns that skyrocket over distant mountains, and sunsets of splintered gold. A white half moon looks like a lamb on its back, kicking playfully at the stars. Solitary, sentinel cacti in the desert look grotesque and often whimsical. Some of the queer rock formations look like part of a world before time began, and then there is the rich greenness where irrigation has been introduced. I've never seen, or tasted, such fruits and vegetables.

Today we drove with a friend of Father's to Castle Hot Springs, and I swam in a pool where the water was a hundred and twenty degrees, then in another pool it was cooler, and in a third pool the way water generally is. We went to a rodeo at a little frontier town, Wickenburg, then over the Apache Trail to Roosevelt Dam. Painted cliffs! Walls of Bronze! Ends of the Earth! Then we followed the Superior Highway through narrow canyons of glowering red rocks, like a Valhalla of forgotten gods. On our way to Sentinel we saw many mirages across the desert, and my heart ached for the pioneers who had followed mirages in their terrible need for water. Some towns along the way are nothing but names now, and there are rivers with no water in them. We stopped at Yuma, where it never rains, went past miles of sand dunes, and suddenly we were in the voluptuous fertility of the Imperial Valley of California.

February 23, 1929

We left El Centro through the Carrizo Gorge to San Diego, and at Coronado Beach we had a real swim. It's a perfect beach, and the sand has gold leaf in it. The salt smell of the sea was invigorating after the arid breath of the desert, and the water of the Pacific was so cold that we had to swim hard to get warm. San Diego is charming, so many little houses with neat gardens, trees, and a lush tidiness evident. We crossed the border into Mexico and visited the racetrack at Tijuana, a beautiful place, set in a surround of low hills. Father gave me twenty dollars to bet with, and I lost all but two, then I stopped. He had better luck, or perhaps he knows more about horses. I chose them from their names, which they didn't live up to.

Los Angeles seemed a noisy, confused city. Pasadena was beautiful. We saw the Mission Play, and I was stirred, as I always am, by anything having to do with deep truths. Hollywood seemed elegant but vulgar, then there was Mt. Lowe, an ostrich farm, a lion farm, and the train to San Francisco. Much of the route was along the shore—white breakers, sand dunes, great cliffs, fantastic trees on one side, and on the other golden poppies, blue lupin, green fields, and rich vegetation. I gazed far across the ocean in the early evening and it looked truly pacific; the sky was like a scroll of heaven with the first stars telling their stories. San Francisco is hilly and fascinating—the Golden Gate Bridge, the Aquarium, Gumps, Chinatown, the Sky Line Drive, and food such as I had never dreamed of before.

This part of the trip is over; still to be enjoyed are the three days on the train homeward bound. We have had such fun, and I think Father and I know each other better than we ever have before. But when he introduces me to his friends he says, "My daughter"; he never adds, "She's a writer." Will I go on all my life hungering for just that measure of appreciation for what I am as a person in myself?

There's been a story moving in my mind, so I spent much of the time on the train writing it—the impact made on a young girl from the East when she meets the West, and the West to her is a handsome cowboy who can ride bronchos and rope steers. It was the rodeo at Wickenburg that gave me the setting and a rather pallid young woman on the train from Chicago who gave me the other character. Most of the story is what I've done in my imagination, but at least the setting is as true as I can make it.

March 8, 1929

Arrived back in Buffalo in a raging blizzard.

March 10, 1929

Bill met my train at Grand Central Station and we went to Childs' for breakfast. All the news I had for him paled at his news: He is leaving for England in three weeks for a position in his company's office in London. It is a promotion in many ways—salary, responsibility, opportunity; but what does it mean for us?

April 9, 1929

This is the night I shall remember all my life—it is the climax of the past weeks, it wraps up all Bill and I have been saying for the past two years. We went to the theater and saw *Holiday*, then we went to the St. Regis for a late supper and danced. After that we walked up to Central Park and snuggled into one of the horse-drawn carriages. Bill told the driver to go very slowly; we wanted the evening never to end. It was dark and quiet in the Park. Distant lights in tall buildings dimmed, only streetlights glimmered; except for faraway traffic, the only sounds were the clopping of hooves. It was edging toward dawn when Bill left me at 243.

The *Queen Mary* sails at noon, but he does not want me to come down to the dock, nor do I want to. It was better to say good-by here. Is every ending a beginning? We do not know when we will meet again, but we could not feel the way we do about each other if it were not going to be all right sometime. For the time being we have ruled out any thought of marriage. Months ago I had resolved my fear of love, but I sense in our silences that Bill has not yet entirely resolved his fear of marriage. I wanted to write him a bon voyage letter, but knew that if I said anything at all I would say too much, so I made up a riddle, printed it, and sealed it in an envelope for him to open after the ship had sailed.

> *We stood on a river's edge*
> *And saw infinity before us;*
> *We stood on a mountaintop*
> *And felt infinity tower o'er us;*
> *We looked in each other's eyes*
> *And—*
> *What was it there we saw*
> *That made us press close,*
> *Clinging together?*

I keep Bill in the quietness of my mind and talk with him as if we were in the garden at John's or standing on Timp. And there is always Sinna to talk aloud to. He's a wise little fellow and by his presence he helps to fill some of the emptiness I feel. Bill asked me to write him, but he said that except for an occasional letter he would keep in touch with me by cable. It will take him time, and more than time, to establish himself in a new country, with a different approach to his work. I am back at my familiar pattern of work, research for the *American,* assembling pictures for Bob's book, putting into shape the story I wrote on the train. More than ever, I feel an increasing capacity to get on with things.

April 11, 1929

While at the *Herald Tribune,* going through files of pictures, I went past the office of Mrs. Irita Van Doren, who is in charge of book reviewing. That gave me an idea, so I made a telephone call and requested an appointment to see her. When we sat facing each other, I asked her if I might review books for her. She didn't say, "What qualifications have you?" to which I would have had to reply, "None." Instead we went on talking about books, and travel, and dogs, and poetry, all kinds of things, the way people talk when they are comfortable with each other. She is a small, gentle person with the charm of the South in her voice and manner. Half an hour later I left with three of the new spring novels and a promise that she would have more for me when I brought in my reviews in a week's time. "Keep to about two hundred and fifty words," she said, and that was all the direction I had. I like people who give a free rein. Horses always respond better when reins are held lightly.

A cable has just come from the ship. Two words, the answer to my riddle—"Each other." But there were other words that were invisible. So often, perhaps almost always, Bill ended a meeting with "And the rest you know." Those words, and what they meant to me, were in the cable, but only my eyes could see them.

April 25, 1929

Carl, that old darling of my childhood days, telephoned and asked me out for dinner and the evening. He is a senior at Princeton and has just completed his thesis on the Monroe Doctrine. We had a wonderful time—dinner, then the theater, and after that dancing. He has grown to such a fine and handsome man and was happy to talk about God. After graduation next month he and his sister are going to France.

And where will I be next month? With Eunice, my artist friend, at Turn of River near Stamford, Connecticut. How one thing leads to another! Mrs. Howard at the Frankl Gallery introduced me to Mildred on *The American Magazine,* who introduced me to Eunice one day when she brought work in to the *American*. She is a commercial artist, and I liked her from the start. Eunice is one of the few people to whom I have talked about Bill. She knows the emptiness in my life right now, but I think she does not know the uncertainty, and she has asked me to spend the summer with her. It will be as wonderful for Sinna as for me to be out of the city and in the country.

April 28, 1929

[Cable from London]

> HEIGHO DARLING MOVING MODEST HOTEL ENSURING MORE SOLITUDE
> BUSY HAPPY THANKS CABLE LETTER THRILLED SO MUCH LOVE

May 5, 1929

In a matter of days it all became possible. I was able to sublet the apartment until the lease is up in September, and my work can be done anywhere. So now I am part of Eunice's family, which includes her ten-year-old son, Gregg, and her housekeeper, Mrs. Brown. The springtime world is tiptoe with wonder. The Rippowam River, really just an oversized brook, runs through woodland, races through fields, and almost loses itself in marshy places where cowslips grow in clumps of golden color. Buds on the trees are ready to burst into blossom and leaf after a succession of warm days. Birds carol exultantly. There is a feeling of discovery everywhere as growing moves to fruition. I am on the edge of discovery, too. There is so much ahead for Bill and me. It doesn't seem to matter that we have to wait a little while longer. I'm reading Emerson and keep finding thoughts of his that speak for me, like this: "to keep in the midst of the crowd with perfect sweetness the independence of solitude."

May 12, 1929

[Cable from London]

> BUSY DAYS SO MUCH TO DO BUT GETTING ORGANIZED PERSONALLY AND
> ANTICIPATING MORE PLAY FINE HAPPY GRATEFUL ALL LOVE

Eunice has had a portion of the field dug up for a vegetable garden. I made a plan for it the way I used to do at Hillhurst. With Gregg's help I got it all planted. Now, after a morning at my desk, or reading, I go out in the afternoon and work in the garden. What a balanced and beautiful life this is.

May 19, 1929

[Cable from London]

AWFULLY HAPPY THRILLS CONTINUE ALL LOVE THANKS FOR EVERYTHING

May 26, 1929

Our seeds, planted just ten days ago, are showing. I had a telegram from Loyola: *"Romance Magazine* taking "Golden Ocean" at two cents a word. Check next week. Congratulations." Three cheers, and that means the check will be for a hundred and ten dollars. The setting for that story was the wheatfields of Saskatchewan, and I never would have been able to picture it if Bob hadn't made it so vivid and my research had not confirmed it. All the time I was writing it I felt as if I were living in those fields of waving grain.

June 10, 1929

Today we ate the firstfruits of the garden—radishes!

June 11, 1929

[Cable from London]

BRAVO STORY RADISHES LETTERS WONDERFUL GLORIOUS WEATHER COUNTRYSIDE BEAUTIFUL DEEPEST LOVE

My life has resolved itself into great simplicities. I feel as if one hand was held out to Thoreau, who said, "Simplify, simplify," and the other hand to Katherine Mansfield, who said, "Oh, to be simple, as one would be before God." After a morning with words, an afternoon with weeds is in order, then a swim in the pool made by the Rippowam.

June 17, 1929

[Cable from Dublin]

CAN YOU IMAGINE YOU KNOW I REALLY BELIEVE I SAW FAIRIES LAST NIGHT ALL LOVE

A letter came today, marked By Fast Ship. I held it in my hands, realizing that less than a week ago his hands had held it. It was a long letter, so I took it down to sit by the pool and read it alone and quietly, with only Sinna beside me. I'll share some of it with the family at supper tonight, but just for now it is for me.

"The first night, as I walked down Piccadilly, everything seemed familiar to me. I felt as if I had come home." Reading those words brought to me the feeling I had had when I was eighteen and went to England with Mother and Father and Bobby. He went on, drawing pictures with words: "During the peak of early-morning traffic, there was a flock of sheep being skillfully guided across the teeming Strand by an alert dog and a sleepy lad. . . . Men and women around Covent Garden Market before breakfast carry the most amazing loads on their heads. One chap had eleven hampers about the size of ladies' hatboxes, piled to the sky, it seemed. And there were short fat women sitting beside huge crates of fruit. . . . Near Marble Arch there was an old, old lady, with stringy white hair and but a few teeth, standing in the gutter playing on a harp with even fewer strings. It was raining, but she had a twinkle and a smile. . . . Standing on the railway platform at Reading, I heard a screech and a flash, and the Plymouth boat train passed. . . . Some of the old, very old, pubs have such odd names: Ye Old Dive Hotel, The Running Footman, Carryme Inn. . . . I stood by the Sanctuary Stone in Liverpool. It was the bad debtor's retreat, for a man could not be arrested even by law as long as he was on that stone. . . . Railway posters are works of art, showing the beauty spots of England and Scotland. . . . As I walked home from the office to my flat in Bruton Street, thinking of you and hoping there might be a letter from you, my heart leaped because there was one."

June 26, 1929

We are knee-deep in June. Lilacs have given way to rambler roses. Daisies and buttercups brighten the fields. The garden thrives. This morning, when I woke up, a scarlet tanager was swinging and singing on a branch just outside my window. It was a moment of flame and perhaps it was a harbinger, for there was a letter in the mail from Loyola. She has sold "Her Real Debut" to something called *Complete Love Novel Magazine*. That's the story I wrote about the girl who fell in love with the West—the bored young debutante who thought love was a mockery, but out of the dust of the rodeo a new life was born.

[Cable from London]

HEIGHO DEAREST EVERYTHING FINE VERY BUSY ALL LOVE

My bank account is growing and that's good. Whatever is ahead for me, it will help to have funds.

July 13, 1929

[Cable from London]

WELL AND HAPPY ALL LOVE DEAREST

A message from England should be largesse for one day, but there was more—a copy of the magazine with "Golden Ocean." There were no plans that could not easily be changed, so I put a call through to Bob to ask him to have dinner with me to celebrate. Eunice gave me her first rough sketch of the jacket for *When I Was a Harvester*, and I knew Bob would like to see it. "Tell him to make any changes now," Eunice said, "for I can do them easily." Bob liked the jacket design and said it was correct, even to the white tip on Ronno's tail, but he took a dim view of *Romance Magazine*, not of my story. He liked it. "But I think you shouldn't show it to Mother and Father."

"But why, Bob? It means I'm getting somewhere."

"It's sort of lurid."

"You have to start somewhere, Bob, and I'm glad that Loyola is finding magazines willing to pay me two cents for every word."

July 17, 1929

[Cable from London]

GOING LE TOUQUET WEEKEND ALL LOVE DEAREST

August 1, 1929

What a long time without a cable! I tell Eunice that Bill must be away, or very busy. Perhaps there will be a letter tomorrow that will make up for the weeks between.

1929

September to November

September, 1929

Weeks have become a month and summer has passed. I have watched the flowers in the fields change in color and character. The garden has been a continuing harvest, giving us more every day. Now the first leaves fall and winds toss them over the yellowing grass. In the last warmth of a fading season, the air has the scent of drying things. And still, my heart has no answer. Why is there no word in all these weeks? I continue writing letters, but resist cabling. I do not want to bother him if he is very busy.

Three nights of rain, three misty days, and now leaves are falling everywhere. I cannot stand it, so tomorrow I shall go in to Stamford and send a cable.

September 9, 1929

[Cable from Stamford]

WHERE HAS THE GENTLEMAN FROM PERU GONE?

September 10, 1929

[Cable from London]

WROTE YOU LAST WEDNESDAY A MOST DIFFICULT LETTER. HAPPINESS IN A NEW INTEREST HERE HAS SUDDENLY TURNED TO UTTER CONFUSION AND DOUBT. AM PRAYING FOR LIGHT AND SEEK YOUR UNSELFED UNDERSTANDING.

September 11, 1929

[Cable from Liverpool]

AWAY TILL FRIDAY FOG LIFTING PLEASE STAND FAST DEAR

September 11, 1929

[Cable from Stamford]

WHATEVER HAPPENS I KNOW THAT GOD IS GUIDING YOU

Wedding day –

London, November 6, 1929

So, there is a letter on the way, but the second cable makes me feel that when it comes, it may be out of date.

September 14, 1929

The letter is in my hands. I might as well have a stone. I took it down to the pool, the place where the river makes its turn, and held it in my hands, letting my eye travel over that familiar writing—my name, the address, the British stamp. It was a long time before I opened it. Sinna nudged me, then put his head on my knee almost as if he thought I needed him near.

". . .I am deeply in love with a girl I met in Le Touquet. Her name is Rebecca, she is an American, and she has been touring Europe with her mother. We have been seeing a lot of each other since that weekend, and tremendous things have been happening to me. To my amazement, I am finding that all fear of every kind has completely vanished and I am eager and ready for marriage. It is something I have never known before and everything within me tells me it is right. . . . In your last two letters, more beautiful than ever, you remind me of my right to freedom and happiness, and that your dearest prayer is for my good, if not with you then away from you. And, behold, it has happened in this most extraordinary way! . . . I know of your love for me. Your confidence and encouragement have been support and inspiration through many a trying hour. And now—yes, the heart has a way of its own. Nothing can ever erase my memories of our times together—on Timp, over winding roads, by open fires, in wind and rain. But now I pray with all my heart that you will be glad for me in my newfound happiness."

Could this be true? I asked myself. The date of the letter was September 4, and the cable of the 10th said something quite different, as did the one of the 11th.

I went back to the house. Eunice met me at the door. "Is everything all right?" she asked.

"Yes, with Bill," I said, and presumably that was true. Anything I might say otherwise would be betraying him, and that I would not do. I told her I was walking in to Stamford to send a cable, that I might be late and not to wait supper.

Her eyes were moist and warm, her cheeks flushed as they often are after hours of work at her drawing board. I wanted to put my arms around her, to feel hers around me, but I knew that if I did, I would dissolve into weeping. She sensed some strain in me and let me go my way. It was a hard cable to send and yet, in all honor, I felt obliged to send it.

[Cable from Stamford]

LETTER RECEIVED HAPPY IN YOUR HAPPINESS PLEASE UNDERSTAND
CONTINUANCE OF FRIENDSHIP IS IMPOSSIBLE

Midnight

> *There are roads the heart must go over*
> *Before it can learn to forget a lover;*
> *Until sinews know their release*
> *And the nerves find subtle peace*
> *In loss that frees by creating*
> *Voids the soul has had in waiting.*
>
> *The leisured heart shall learn to find*
> *Sustenance of its own kind,*
> *Knowing sometime, some tomorrow*
> *Will lift the lethargy of sorrow.*

September 16, 1929

Back to my work, back to the garden, back to walks in the
woods with my wondering little Sinna, back to living one day after
the other, hoping the futility that beset me during the first years
in New York would not sweep over me again. Thoughtful Eunice
asked no questions, Mrs. Brown made all my favorite foods as if
she felt I needed to be kept eating, and Gregg seemed always
ready to do whatever chore he could for me. No one asked me
what had happened, and for that I ever bless them. How could I
say? What did I know?

A bulky package has come from Macmillan, the galley proofs of
When I Was a Harvester. I'll check them as well as I can, then take
them in to New York for Bob to go over and return to Miss Seaman.

September 21, 1929

[Cable from London]

THIS EXPERIENCE HAS BEEN PRICELESS IN REMOVING ALL FEAR AND
THEN PROVING BEYOND QUESTION THAT YOU ARE THE ONLY ONE
PLEASE HOW SOON CAN YOU COME?

September 22, 1929

[Cable from Stamford]

SOON

Tonight I told them at supper that I would be leaving for England in about a month, or as soon as everything could be arranged, to marry Bill. And glad was I that whatever might have been said before had been locked in my heart. How happy they looked and were in their different ways—Eunice, Mrs. Brown, Gregg. They are very dear to me.

The next mail brought a long letter from Bill—so easy to read, so exciting, and as light a feather in my hands. And within the words I could hear the mellow tone of his voice. "My experience seems like a queer dream. No harm has been done to the other party in any way because of it, so I can only be grateful for the strange working of events which showed me where my affection truly lies. I'll tell you all about it later. There is so much to talk about now." And there is! He said he had written my father asking for my hand "if she will give it." He went on for pages with all kinds of details, and in every few words was a word of endearment.

". . .there are a million things to talk about but I can't think of anything but you, so I'll turn in and lie wide-eyed for hours planning weekends and trips and seeing Scottish mountains and Irish lakes, Yorkshire moors and the Cornish coast, and glorious evenings at home reading in front of a coal fire and talking. Oh, my darling, you are mine and I am forever your Bill."

A writer is generally a curious person, but this time I did not care to know what had happened at Le Touquet and in the weeks following. A designing girl, aided by an equally designing mother, had set her cap for a charming, unattached man. It sounded like a story for *Romance Magazine,* but this was one story that I would not write. The unknown Rebecca had unwittingly done me a good turn, and for this I was grateful. Bill knew now that marriage was something to be faced, that it could not always be avoided in a relationship that went beyond friendship.

September 24, 1929

[Cable from Liverpool]

ECSTATIC COME EARLIEST CONVENIENT SIX MONTHS QUARANTINE
FOREIGN DOGS WRITTEN YOUR FAMILY SURELY LOVE'S FULFILLMENT

I had intended to go into New York within the next few days to see Miss Seaman and deliver Eunice's finished jacket, but after that cable, "soon" could not be soon enough. I took the noon train into the city and got back late. Eunice was waiting for me. We sat at the kitchen table and had a snack, but more important than food was the news I had for her. Proof of how much Miss Seaman liked the jacket was the nice fat check that she would be receiving in a few days, as well as the possibility of more work for Macmillan. Eunice has a motherly way, so she soon hustled me off to bed, saying she knew I was tired after my long day and we could talk tomorrow. I'm not a bit tired, and I want to write everything down, because it has been one of the most impressive days of my life.

On the train going in I made a list of all the things there were to do. If I do that, then check them off one by one, the number doesn't seem so intimidating. First I delivered the picture to Miss Seaman, and she told me the astounding news that the book had been accepted as a selection of the Junior Literary Guild. My news was equally astounding to her, so we made a luncheon date for next week. I went to the American Consul to be sure my passport was in order, to the American Express to see when a sailing would be possible, and then to the owner of the apartment to wind up the lease at 243 and make arrangements with a mover to put my things in storage until I could send for them from London. I phoned the *Herald Tribune* and asked to see Mrs. Van Doren next week. Last thing I did was to send a cable to Bill.

Bob took me out to dinner. It was comforting to sit across a table from him and look into his warm brown eyes. To him, as to no one else, I poured out the whole sequence of the past few weeks and what the next few weeks held. He was amazed and delighted, but when I told him the stupendous news about his book, he leaned across the table and kissed me.

"Think of what that means, Bob. You'll have ready-made readers up and down and across the country."

"Will it mean more money?"

"Yes, quite a lot. Miss Seaman said there would be an advance of a thousand dollars."

"Then that is yours."

"Oh, Bobby—"

"You'll need it in a new country, a new life. You may need it to come home if you don't like it over there."

"Oh, Bobby—"

"When are you going?"

"I sent Bill a cable today that I would be sailing on the *Bremen*, October 25."

"What will happen to Sinna?"

"He's going with me. Bill thought of that even before I did."

"Do Mother and Father know?"

"Not yet from me, but Bill has written to them. I'm going up to Hillhurst the end of next week."

And now, having put down for myself the events of this one day, I must write Bill the letter I promised him.

October 5, 1929

I've been at the farm for a week and it is as always, as if I'd never been away. The pattern of life moves in its orderly fashion—Father goes in to his office in Buffalo every morning, and Mother talks with Maria about the household. Plans are made for the day, and its events may include me and they may not. I can always find Al in the barn, or Jim in the garden, or Andy polishing the Packard. Jinny is often here with her two boys, one a real toddler, the other a small babe. I look at her and think how is it that some people can do everything right—marry a lawyer with a growing practice, produce two fine boys? I watch her with the children, not enviously or with emulation but with the strangest feeling that this will not be for me. I don't know why. It's just that sometimes in life one knows without being told.

So I fit into the pattern more as the young sister home for a few days than the woman with life beckoning ahead, and I remind myself that Emerson said life is a struggle for freedom and the individual must assert himself through moral and intellectual integrity. To Miss Hyde I have always been a person, even when I was little. She has paid me a great compliment. She said, "I shall always think of you as being happy, for that is how I have always thought of you."

One day I went to Rochester to meet Bill's mother. She is very frail and quite old, and in her past there has been much sorrow and illness. She talked about Bill and told me stories of him when he was growing up, of his high standing in school and how, after college, he had planned to go on to law school; then his father died suddenly. Bill was just eighteen, and there was an older sister, who was an invalid, and a much younger brother and sister. There was only one thing for Bill to do—give up his own plans and take over his father's business for the sake of the family. So much she told me that I had not known, and it made me love him more. Over and over she said, "I think you can make him happy and that is what I pray for him. He has done so much for others all through the years. Now he needs a homelife of his own."

She gave me her engagement ring, given to her more than fifty years ago. It's lovely, a small ruby in a crown-like setting of tiny seed pearls, and it fits me as it must have fit her when Lawrence first slipped it on her finger. It seems so right, now, to have an engagement ring.

October 8, 1929

When I came back from a ride with Bluemouse today, Andy and Maria were sitting at the kitchen table having their tea. I joined them because I wanted to talk with them about "the old country." They had left England when they were a young married couple and come to the United States. Now I was going to England to be married. There was so much that I could learn from them. After I had finished my cup of tea, there were quite a few leaves in it, so I swirled them around and handed the cup to Andy to read my fortune. He studied the leaves for a long time, every now and then taking the tip of his penknife to look under a leaf.

"What do you see, Andy?"

"There's a fine man in your cup, taller than you, with dark-brown hair and a spring to his way of walking. See that little leaf? That's him. And there's happiness for the two of you, that's at the rim right down to the bottom. See that small thin leaf? That's your pencil. It's not near the top, but there's nothing between it and the top. That means success."

"When, Andy?"

"Not soon, but sure."

Again he lifted a leaf to look under it.

"What are you trying to find?"

"Something I can't see. It's like a shadow. I don't rightly know where it is or what it means, but it isn't going to interfere with your happiness."

"Andy, you told me what color hair the man in my life—in my cup—has. What color are his eyes?"

Andy studied the leaves that were beginning to dry and shift their positions. He shook his head. "I can't seem to see his eyes."

"They're gray, Andy, and beautiful." Then I asked Andy if he had any advice for me and my life with Bill.

"Just remember that there may come a time when you'll feel contrary, and there may come a time when he'll feel contrary, but don't you both feel contrary at the same time."

I've been going through the things stored away in the R.I.P. box, and I'm destroying a great deal, just keeping a few reminders as waymarks, and the Diaries that cover eleven years of my life. What a trial I must have been to my elders! Such determination for independence! Such fury at convention! Some of the early poems do have a lyrical quality, but I was so extravagant with words. Luxury as a way of life drew my scorn, but I luxuriated in words. And love, what did I know about it then to write about it as I did? My descriptions of nature were really good, and I was always on safe ground when writing about the weather. The poems did serve a purpose: my feelings got out in words on paper; they didn't rankle inside me.

Two cables have punctuated my days. They were telephoned, and I was lucky in being the one to answer the phone both times. I don't dare imagine what some people would have thought at a string of unsigned words whose meaning was only for me.

October 10, 1929

[Cable from London]

HAPPY BUSY THRILLED EAGER LOVE

October 15, 1929

[Cable from London]

GLORIOUS NEWS ROCHESTER SO HAPPY THANKS DEEPEST LOVE

October 16, 1929

Today his letter written on the 9th came—five pages of that beloved handwriting that sings as it flows over the page. ". . .This afternoon your tiny but precious note written from New York in the midst of packing came. . .and the poem, 'O Darling Room,' is lovely. No doubt it speaks a bit for you in leaving East 36th Street. . . . Today I walked home from the office through back streets, thinking sweet thoughts of you and me, not unlike our 'pretending' thoughts of many a time together—of woodsmoke and cool pools and hills and sky and sheep. Can you know how my heart is actually leaping with eagerness these yearlong days?. . .Last evening, after an important meeting, I spent some time with Mr. Mangum. I had just returned from Manchester, where I secured the largest order our company here has yet had. He was in a genial mood and warned me of all the things he is going to tell you about me, especially how I gained the name of Pink Tea Willie. And then he said he was going to give me an interest in the company as a wedding present and put it in your name, by gosh! He has been so fine to me and really thinks I'm great.

"I know how awfully busy you are these last few weeks, dear, and will understand if you don't write—just a cable now and then, please. Soon, soon, you and Sinna will be sailing to me. They tell me I have only to cable the number of Sinna's permit to you. The actual permit should be given here to Van Oppen and Co., the carrying agents, who will meet the *Bremen,* provide a suitable kennel, take care of clearance, etc., and take him to The Dog's Home, Hackbridge, Surrey. That is just a thirty-minute ride from London, where he will be excellently cared for and can be visited any day. . . . Darling, just two weeks from tomorrow—Southampton! Oh, dear God, I am so grateful."

I had need of the letter, for after dinner Father said he would like to have a talk with me. Everyone mysteriously disappeared and we were alone in the living room by the fire. I knew he had heard from Bill more than a week ago; I also knew that he would choose his own time to talk with me. He held the letter in his hand. How well I knew that writing, so legible, so well spaced.

Slowly, carefully, Father read the letter aloud. In it Bill told him, from a man's point of view, all that a man would want to know about his job, his salary, his prospects, his flat in London, the insurance policies he carried, his financial responsibility to his mother, the stocks he held. He even mentioned a Wassermann test, which meant nothing to me, but satisfied Father. Of course, Bill said he loved me.

After the reading was finished, neither of us said anything. It was Father's move. I had long known what I would do, and what Bill had done in words was, after all, only a formality.

"I want you to understand that neither your mother nor I have any objection. We wish you would wait until the spring, when we could be with you."

"To wait would waste time. Bill and I know what we want, and once we are married, we can get on with the business of living."

"You always seem to know what is right for you."

"I know that I love Bill. I have since I met him almost three years ago."

"And you are leaving soon for England?"

"In two weeks."

"Your mother and I will come over in the spring to visit you and to meet Bill."

That was the end of our conversation. When I said good night, he kissed me. The feel of his mustache was not so bristly as when I was a little girl.

Mother was waiting for me upstairs. All her love was in her eyes, in the embrace she folded me in, in her words about wanting me to be happy. She wished that I could have found someone nearer home, that I would not be so far away, but all I could say was that I must marry the one I love. We talked on for a while, but when we said good night I had the feeling that I had from Father, that they understood, as they had four years ago about my being a writer.

And now as I face myself in my own room for the last time—for tomorrow night I'll be on the train to New York—I think of Cleve and Ben and others I have had good times with. It is Bill who loves me not just for what I am now, a person, but for what I may be someday, a writer. This was the key he turned that let him into my life.

October 19, 1929

> *Now I am back at Turn of River*

[Cable from London]

YOUR LETTER SO WONDERFUL OH AM SO HAPPY AND CONFIDENT MY DEAREST SINNA PERMIT NUMBER EYE DEE NINETY ONE THIRTY EIGHT MAILING UNNECESSARY SO MUCH LOVE

October 23, 1929

[Cable from London]

ALL IS WELL INDEED BELOVED BON VOYAGE ALL LOVE MINUTES COUNT NOW

October 25, 1929

S.S. *Bremen*. Just to mark this hour—1 A.M.—this day to remember forever.

October 28, 1929

At sea now for three days, and all around me is space and time, so different from those last days in New York when there was so much to do, so many people to see.

Luncheon with Miss Seaman was exciting, and into my hands she put the biggest check I have ever seen—One Thousand Dollars— the advance from the Junior Literary Guild. *Harvester* is Bob's story, of course, but the shaping and the research, the typing, presentation to an editor, and the proofreading was my part, and Bob had insisted that I take the first payment; all moneys in the future will go to him. After luncheon I went to the bank to close my account, and there I had some of the money converted into English pounds, some into travelers checks, and some into cash. Then I went to Hattie Carnegie's and bought my wedding dress.

I knew what I wanted and when I saw the dress, I knew it was IT. Moss green, with a wide beige collar, like a fichu, that loops into a soft tie. I'll be able to use it for many occasions. I had never been inside Hattie Carnegie's in my life, but I knew it was a very special place. I had never spent such a sum for a dress, three hundred dollars, but I'll be married only once. I showed it to Bob and he approved. When I showed it to Eunice, she wanted to paint a picture of me in it, but I will not put it on until the very day. What the date will be, I do not know, only that it will be soon. Bill is tending to all those details.

Somehow everything did get done. Then, on that last day, in the early evening, Bob took Sinna and me to the *Bremen* for the sailing at midnight. Sinna was put in the charge of the Dog Steward, my trunk disappeared with dozens of others into the hold, an officer took my ticket, checked my passport, and directed us to my cabin. It was like going into a garden—flowers and flowers, as well as a pile of mail, several telegrams, some packages. People kept appearing at the door and squeezing into the room. I never knew I had so many friends. There were the near and dear ones like Eunice and Gregg and Mrs. Brown, fellow Comparison Shoppers from Macy's, Mrs. Howard from the Frankl Gallery, Mildred Harrington from the *American* with her nice husband, Peter. It seemed as if everyone who had had anything to do with my life during the past three years had come to wish me bon voyage. We talked and laughed and they said all the things said to a traveler, but this was no ordinary trip I was going on and coming back from. This was an extraordinary trip, and there was a fringe of sadness to it.

When gongs started to sound and people were told to be off the ship, good-bys were said in earnest, and one by one my friends left. I went to the railing on the top deck to watch them go down the gangplank and take their places in a crowd of people all smiling and waving; then the gangplank was pulled up, and I could feel the great ship slowly edging away from the dock and into the open sea.

Back in my cabin I was suddenly assailed by loneliness. Here was all the evidence of friendship—flowers, fruit, letters—and here was I, myself, alone. I thought of Sinna asleep in his kennel on the boat deck. I thought of Bill waiting beyond the horizon, and then I thought that I had chosen the way in which I must go, and I got hold of myself.

I am enjoying days of quiet thinking and earnest communion with God. Except for a daily walk with Sinna, when the kennels are opened, and going to the dining salon three times a day, I keep to myself. There are many letters to write, and it's fun to use the S.S. *Bremen* stationery. The letter from Loyola I am copying here so that in the midst of my new life I'll be reminded of my pencil. "My only advice is that you keep at your writing, do something every single day, even if it's only a page or two. I'm still convinced that you will someday make a name for yourself, and I want you to keep plugging till you do, even if success seems a long time in coming. I have positive faith in you, and you will always find me encouraging, as, despite the little success we have had so far, I *know* you have talent."

Among the books given me is Stevenson's *Travels with a Donkey*. I like its gentle pace, and it is a good antidote for the excitement that is rushing through me. I sit for long hours in my deck chair, eyes on the far horizon, and I feel a graver assurance and a deeper faith than ever becoming a part of my being. So much has slipped into the past. I am ready for the future.

I have written a Decalogue before Marriage and will keep it here in my Journal as a reminder.

Evening after evening, while sitting in my deck chair, I see the first star appear—sometimes in a clear sky, sometimes through a tumult of clouds—and I wish on it: to make Bill happy and, for myself, to hold on to happiness no matter what. Stevenson says it for me: "There is no duty we underrate so much as the duty of happiness."

[Radiotelegram from London]

HURRAH SOUTHAMPTON WEDNESDAY ON TENDER EXCITED LOVE

October 30, 1929

In my room at the Cadogan Hotel, London

For five days the horizon was my boundary, then land appeared —a faint line at first, then growing more pronounced and green, so green, on the port side. Land's End. The Cornish coast. Devon. Another hour and houses could be distinguished, then cattle and sheep. By midafternoon, as we came into Southampton Harbor, buildings and wharves seemed very near. The throb of the engines that had been like music for days ceased, and the great ship was no longer cleaving her way through the water but resting in it. Out from the wharves came a small boat moving toward the *Bremen*.

There were men in uniform aboard, customs officials, immigration officials in navy dress. Among them was one civilian standing straight and tall, hatless; his dark coat with all the evidence of English tailoring distinguished him from the others in uniform. Dozens of people were leaning against the rail watching the tender as it approached, perhaps wondering who the civilian was who waved his arms.

A ship's officer tapped me on the shoulder and asked me to come below. When the tender touched the *Bremen*, the customs men came aboard through an opening at sea level over a short gangplank. Someone asked to see my passport and stamped it, another said I was to go ashore now, "Captain's orders." With a sailor's arm steadying me I crossed the short distance and was on the tender and Bill's arms were around me. The tender backed away from the *Bremen*, the engine chugged, and Bill and I were headed back to shore in the boat that had held all the officials, alone, save for the sailor at the small engine. What do you say to the man you haven't seen for six months and with whom you are going to spend the rest of your life?

But there were details, there always are, and Bill got through them quickly. Sinna would be met by the carrying agent, my trunk would be passed by the customs and opened in London, because I was coming to take up residence. Mr. Mangum had put his car at Bill's disposal. At the wharf I could see a limousine with a chauffeur standing beside it. As the tender nudged into its berth, we turned to thank the sailor. He gave us a broad smile, touched his cap, and in the first English voice I had heard wished us luck. When we reached the car, the chauffeur murmured a discreet word of welcome as I got in, then the Rolls, purring with a gentler sound than the *Bremen*, took us to the Southampton Hotel.

"Come back in two hours, Pullen," Bill said.

"Very good, sir," Pullen replied.

In the dining room we sat at a small table near a window. There was an electric light with a pink silk shade on the table, and I think I shall see it in my mind always. There was so much we wanted to say to each other, yet somehow nothing mattered for a little while but to look into each other's eyes; and then it was as if there had been no time between, no parting at all.

But we did talk and we did eat.

Bill told me he had received heartening letters from Father and Mother and that all was in order for our wedding a week from today, on November 6, but that I would need a witness to stand up with me. Did I know anyone in England? No one yet, but I would discover someone. Mr. Mangum was loaning us his cottage for the weekend. The furnished flat in Bruton Street was small, but it would do until we found something larger. Bill was eager for my news. Laughter punctuated our talk, and every now and then I reached out to touch his hand, just to assure myself that we were real, that I wasn't in a dream, or pretending.

Then his tone changed, his expression became subdued and, even as his hand rested on mine, he spoke of releasing me. He reminded me of what he had said about his eyes on that mist-shrouded day in the fire tower. "I tried to tell you before, but you wouldn't listen. This time you must listen." I had never seen him so serious.

"Oh, Bill, it doesn't matter."

"It goes back a long way; it could be carried into the future. Look ahead and think of what this may do to your life."

I knew what he meant and I knew that it would not matter. Looking into those gray pools of quiet that were his eyes, I shook my head. There are times when there are no words. There were none for me then.

What I wanted to say was that our marriage—what it would mean to us and might mean, in time, to others—would be the important thing, but the only words I could come out with were those that said I loved him. He smiled, that wonderful smile I had seen so often in memory during the past months, and the pressure of his hand on mine increased. Who knew what the years that stretched ahead might hold, or not hold; we would be traveling them together, strengthening each other, sharing the adventure of life.

Pullen was waiting for us, the door held open. He tucked a lap rug over us as we settled into the backseat, then the car was under way through the streets of Southampton on to the broad road that led to London. It was dark. There were lights in the little towns as we went through them. I held Bill's hand under the lap rug. My head found its place on his shoulder. I knew that I had come home.

It was midnight when Pullen drew up to the Cadogan Hotel. Everything was dark and quiet. A porter came down to take my bag. At the desk Bill was handed a key and was told the room was ready. We went upstairs and Bill seemed to know exactly where to go. When we stood before a door he said, "This is your home in London for a week until you come to 34, Bruton Street"; then he opened the door and we went in. A lamp was on, and what I saw made me wonder if I was a princess in a story. It was a small cozy room, a coal fire was burning cheerily in the grate, there was a table and on it a vase of red roses just opening in the warmth. The bed against one wall had been turned down—linen sheets, and big pillows, and a down comforter. On a stand near the bed was a card in that hand I knew so well with just the word WELCOME. It was so beautiful, so inviting, I'm sure I'll see that room all my life in my mind's eye just as it was at that moment when I stood on the threshold.

November 5, 1929

I've been here almost a week, and London seems so like home I wonder if I have ever lived anyplace else. What a week—so full and yet so different from that last one in New York! I must catch the days up in words now, because after tomorrow I may not write soon again, not because there won't be time but because there won't be need. It will be as if everything had been accomplished. This is the point toward which my life has been tending for the last two and a half years.

We have had breakfast together every morning at the Cadogan, then Bill has gone to his office, and I've had the whole day to myself until we meet for dinner. And I've had much to do. His bachelor flat hardly had enough for even simple housekeeping, so I've been making purchases. I've discovered different stores. As well as buying pots and pans, I've bought some beautiful things, too. Venetia, near Harrod's, had a Venetian amber-glass bowl that will be lovely for fruit or flowers, and to go with it I bought some amber glasses. I cabled a friend in New York who gave me the name of her aunt in Ashtead, Surrey, and when I phoned her and told her of my need for a witness, she invited me to tea. Pullen drove me down and back. My first friend, Mrs. Balmain, will be my ever friend, for we liked each other from the start. She and Mr. Balmain will come to the wedding tomorrow and stand beside me as if they had always known me. They are both quite old, but they made me feel as if I belonged to them.

The days are damp. Twilight begins to settle in at teatime. When we drive through the country, there are still leaves on some of the trees but they are pale gold and russet; the fields are green, and the air has in it the smell of all the coal fires burning for warmth. I like it.

Thanksgiving Day, 1929

34, Bruton Street, London

And now I am Bill's wife.

On the morning of November 6, I dressed in my new green dress with the soft fichu. The porter came for my bag, and I said good-by to the cozy little room that had been my home for a week; then I took a taxi to Bruton Street where Bill was waiting for me. We went to the Piccadilly Hotel for a late breakfast—lamb kidneys and bacon, crisp, dry toast, and tea; we might have preferred coffee but have learned that tea is better. It was a gently rainy day, so we didn't walk but took a taxi to Princes-row Registry Office, almost in the shade of Buckingham Palace. Many were there already—Bill's friends, people from his office, and my dear Balmains. Everyone was smiling and happy.

Just at noon—and I could imagine that I heard Big Ben in the distance—we were ushered into a room where an official sat at a desk. He asked for our names and our intent. We were not called upon for vows, only to repeat after him the words:

"I, William, take you, Elizabeth, for my lawful wedded wife."

"I, Elizabeth, take you, William, for my lawful wedded husband."

The ring of glorious sincerity in Bill's voice was thrilling. We signed some papers, and that was all. Such a chorus of good wishes, such handshaking, and most of them from people I'd never seen before. The embrace that mattered most was back at Bruton Street where we went to change into our country clothes. "All of me to you, darling, forever," Bill said when he put his arms around me.

Pullen arrived to drive us down to the Mangums' cottage at Fer-ring-by-the-Sea, but first he took us to the Royal Court Hotel in Sloane Square, where we had a festive luncheon. On the way out of London we stopped to send cables to my mother and father, and to Bill's mother, then we were off. The drive over quiet roads through a muted countryside, with twilight coming through the rain, was a rare experience. Everything seemed so gentle.

It was dusk when we arrived at Bay Tree Cottage, a small, thatched, fourteenth-century dwelling. There was a light glowing within and a little old woman opened the door to us. "I've put a chicken in the oven for you," she said, "and you'll find other things. What a pile of telegrams you've got! I'll be back in the morning to do for you." She scuttled off into the mist, and Pullen was soon on the road back to London, not to return for us until Sunday afternoon.

There we were with each other, a crackling coal fire making an area of warmth, and a delicious aroma coming from the oven; and there was that stack of telegrams to open. One of them, from Bill's office manager in Scotland, "Lang may your lum reek," had to be translated for me: "Long may your chimney smoke." The one from Dublin was quite clear: "May a wee moose ne'er leave your hoose."

There is so much that I will remember always, but as my inner eye will see things, my inner ear will hear Bill's voice saying "Good night, my wife." There was a solemnity and beauty in his tone that thrilled me, as his promise had in the Registry Office earlier that day.

And it was all real, for the next day in the *London Times* was the statement:

Mr. W. J. McGreal and Miss M. E. Yates

Mr. William James McGreal of Rochester, New York, and Miss Mary Elizabeth Yates of Buffalo, New York, were married on November 6, at noon, at the Princes-row Registry Office, London, S.W., in the presence of a representative from the American Consulate-General and a large body of friends.

Thursday, Friday, Saturday, and most of Sunday we walked—on the pebbly beach with the sea rolling in at our feet, up on the Downs where the wind was sharp, to the next village with tea at the local pub. But, because the days drew in early, we were soon back at the cottage, with a fire burning, a lamp glowing, and a meal that the little old lady had prepared for us. And we talked—sharing ideas, making plans, reading about England and English ways. Bill had an advantage over me, as he had already been there for six months, but I had memories of my time in "the old country" when I was eighteen. Whatever discussion we started on—philosophical or practical, business or literary—there was the marvelous feeling that we could continue it on the next day, or the next; a lifetime of days stretched before us.

On Sunday afternoon Pullen came precisely at five, "so you would have had your tea," he said. Then we were on the way back to London.

On Monday morning we had an early breakfast at Slater's. Bill always wanted to be at the office an hour before anyone else arrived to get things ready for the day. When he left I watched him go down the street to the big red bus that would take him to Holborn. Suddenly I had an utterly blank feeling. An aloneness more total than any I had ever known before swept over me. I sat on at the table and had a conversation with myself. In the midst of so much happiness, with a peace of heart that went beyond my dreams, I seemed compelled to face the thought of death. This was not something I could talk about with Bill. It was a personal problem to which I would have to find my answer. Should I die, it would be simple—a new adventure, a new dimension, the existence of which I had no doubt. If Bill should die, what would happen to me? I faced the stark possibility and told myself that I would go on with life. It would still be our life until the end came for me and I would catch up with Bill, wherever he was, whatever doing.

Now, three weeks later, I can say that we have moved into a smooth pattern of living. The hours with Bill are serene and happy, the hours alone are rich and stimulating; and just to be a part of the life of London is magnificent. Did anyone, anywhere, ever have such an overflowing cup as I on this Thanksgiving Day?

Part III

One Writer's Way — The Creative Years

1930–1931

16, Wythburn Court

January, 1931

Much as I love England and much as it means to both of us, I feel a little uneasy quiver and ask Bill if we will be here all our lives. He assures me that "ninety-nine years" in the lease is a formality, that there is a clause tucked into the wording which says a lease can be assigned any given year.

Four addresses in a little more than a year! On the last lease, for 16, Wythburn Court, the wording is elegant. It sounds like Shakespeare, and there is not a mark of punctuation in the whole two pages. That is the way with a legal document in England. It must be stated in such a manner that the ideas are independent of punctuation and cannot be misunderstood.

Looking Back

Bill McGreal's quarters in Mayfair were right enough for cozy bachelor living, but not "for gracious living," as Mother said when she and Father came to visit us in London early in the year. Bill won their hearts just by being himself, and the time sparkled with dinners at the Savoy, theaters, concerts, shopping. When we saw them off on the boat train for Paris, it was with a relationship secured and sure, and we promised them that we would soon have more of a home to live in.

We heard of a small house in Kensington that could be rented furnished for six months, and soon moved into it. There was little to move but our clothes and books, some china and linen that we had been acquiring. Friends in America, family, and relatives had been sending us checks for wedding presents, so that when the time came for us to furnish our own home we would be able to. What good fortune! We would not have to make do with what people thought we would like, but could get what we really liked, needed, and would use. The exchange from dollars to pounds, with the rate approximately five dollars to the pound, was simple even for my arithmetic.

Number 24, Victoria Grove was a charming little Huguenot

On holiday with Sinna
in Marlow, England

house with a small garden. We had a daily maid, and for the (to me) utterly unfair wage of a pound a week I felt freed to spend a good part of my days exploring London, *Baedeker* in hand. Of course, I did the food shopping, enjoying it immensely once I got accustomed to seeing the great carcasses at the butcher shops and wild birds with their feathers at the poulterer's. At the greengrocer's one day I commented on the high price of beans. "Never you mind, lady," was the comforting reply. "I'm doing a bean at nine-pence tomorrow; come back then."

From Maude I learned to be explicit, to show her, not just to tell her, what was wanted. A certain Sunday morning I had planned a special treat for Bill—lamb kidneys on toast, and breakfast not until nine o'clock. When the kidneys appeared, they resembled little black marbles. I asked Maude about them, and she said she had cooked them when she arrived at seven o'clock. She seemed as surprised as I was annoyed at their appearance. "But, madam," she said, "I did them with love in my heart." Later I shared my woe with Bill. He had an antidote. "God will tell the little girl." It was one of his sayings, and in the face of frustration and vexation it calmed me down.

Spring, 1930

Spring came early, but never too early to leave the damp, shivering days of winter behind, and April meant that Sinna could be part of our life again. Bill's company had loaned him a car for two weeks to visit branches in the southwest, and our first stop was at the kennels in Hackbridge, Surrey. Greeting us, the kennelman said, "That little dog! He's been quiet and good ever since he came here last November, but what did he do last night? He set up such a barking that all the other dogs joined in. It was bedlam for sure; but if you're asking me, he knew you were on your way to fetch him. Good little fellow, and a fine Sealyham he is. He served his time fairly, but when he knew it was near over, he had to tell everyone."

Sinna welcomed us extravagantly, then settled into the car with his eyes ahead and not so much as a backward glance at the kennels.

And we were off.

To drive through the English country in the spring of the year is to see green hillsides dotted with the whitest of lambs and roadsides bright with primroses. Stopping by a little stream for our picnic luncheon, I heard the cuckoo for the first time; and then the skylark, losing itself in the blue above us. It was just like Shelley's poem that I had learned at school:

Higher still and higher
From the earth thou springest
. . . .
And singing still dost soar,
And soaring ever singest.

"Tonight we may hear the nightingale," Bill said.

We did, from a woodland glade, rising like an aria above the accompaniment of waves crashing against the rocks far below us.

We stayed three days and nights at Lee Abbey on the Devon coast, where we had spent our first Christmas. Then it was holly thick and tall, the prickly leaves changing to smooth near the top where the berries grew in abundance, and ivy trailing up old walls—the same holly and ivy that I had sung about in Christmas carols and never dreamed to see actually growing. We took walks along the coast and inland on the moors. The warmth of the sun was balanced by the frequent mists that rolled in from the sea and often turned to rain, but rain was so usual that it never meant any change of plans for us, and Sinna relished all weather. Returning to the inn always meant tea by a fire of great logs.

This is Lorna Doone country, familiar to me from reading about it in the days when I never thought I would be a part of it. On our way into Lynmouth one morning, we watched a hunt gathering at The Blue Ball. The red coats, the handsome horses, the impatient dogs, the sounding of the huntsman's horn were all exciting, like the pages of a book coming to life; but, as I watched them coursing up the Vale of Watersmeet, I hoped with all my heart that the fox would get away. Bill wasn't so agitated as I was, he merely reminded me in that gentle way of his that we must take people as they are. "The English have always gone in for fox hunting, even though there's no nation on earth kinder to animals. Some things you can't change, so don't use yourself up trying to."

At Lee, that lovely old abbey become an inn, I learned how simple it was to travel with a dog in England. At the bottom of our bill, when we came to leave, was Sinna's. It matched him in size.

With the first months of our first year of marriage, I felt that I was drinking in a whole new way of life and people—in London against the backdrop of museums and libraries, plays and antiquity; in the country against the backdrop so well described by Trevelyan as "delicate and fugitive beauty, made up of small touches, a combination of nature with the older arts of man." Impressions came quick and fast, and I jotted them down in my notebook to sort out later. Bill, in love with his camera, was taking pictures, never the usual ones, but scenes that caught his eye and had stories to tell.

Summer, 1930

We spent a week in the New Forest visiting the Paget-Cookes. There we acquired a puppy, Bara, named after our hostess Barbara. He was no more than a little ball of mirth and mischief, but we knew that someday he would grow into being a dignified Scottish terrier. We worked it out logically: We had each other; Sinna needed someone.

There was an unforgettable day when Bob's book arrived. *When I Was a Harvester* is real, and now it will be on its way through stores and libraries into the minds of readers and into their hearts, too. It reminds me of what I hope to achieve someday—but "When?" I keep asking myself. Writing, except in my journal, isn't the focus of life it once was. The days have been so filled with new experiences, and curious things keep happening that take up my time and delight me.

One such happening is the suit Bill wanted me to have made at Bradley's. It meant several appointments, which took up a great deal of time. When it was finished and I wore it for the first time, I felt like royalty. Another happening has been going to Miss Edith Clements for voice lessons, at Bill's insistence.

"But why, Bill? I have no intention of ever becoming a singer."

"You'll be a speaker all your life," he said, and then went on to persuade me of the importance of good enunciation, of deep breathing, and much more.

Until I began to work with Miss Clements, I had not realized how careless I was, how often I slurred a word instead of giving it its due. For years I've been particular about the written word; the spoken word is fully as important. It was through Miss Clements that I met Miss Marguerite Puttick, who has a school for children in Kensington. There was an extra plum when I went to Miss Clements, in that her flat was near Madame Tussaud's. After a lesson, I often visited the waxwork figures and practiced my new techniques in conversation with them. But the real prize was inquiring at Liberty's the price of silk pajamas for Bill and being told in pounds and shillings rather than in dollars and cents.

Autumn, 1930

When our lease ran out at Victoria Grove, we found another furnished house, Number 8, Canning Place. It was a very little house, old and damp, with the only warmth coming from coal fires and a hot towel rail in the bathroom. I knew more than ever how important it was to have a maid, and not only for the fires but to clean the silver weekly, especially the tea service that Bill's company had given us. Fog tarnished it, and when autumn came fog was everywhere, even seeping in through keyholes. I was cold then, trying to write with a hot-water bottle on my lap for my hands and a coal fire at my back. But there was another kind of cold.

One day, getting home in the late afternoon when dusk and chill had taken over the London streets, Elsie opened the door to me with her finger on her lips. "The master is upstairs. Something is wrong. He wanted the curtains drawn—" I did not wait to hear the rest. The door to our room was closed. I opened it and knelt beside the bed. Bill was lying there, a cloth over his eyes. "It's just the pain," he murmured. "Light. Noise. They're like knives."

For two weeks it was like that. Keeping the room as dark as I could, and as quiet, was the only palliative. Even the doctor knew no other way to alleviate this kind of pain. "It will pass," Bill said, and it did. "It may not come again for a long time." But when it came again, he knew—and I had been told—that the price would be a degree of sight. He made light of it: he would—it was his way. The day he went back to his office happened to be our anniversary. That afternoon a box came from the florist, twelve red roses and a card in that exquisite handwriting of his: "Darling, it has been a year of sweetness and joy. You are precious indeed. B."

Twelve red roses. Elsie brought me a tall vase and as I placed them in it I wondered, as I had on other occasions, how a heart could break at the same time with happiness and with anguish. The strength and beauty of the roses filled the room as their fragrance did. I tucked myself into a chair by the fire to read, but when Elsie brought me tea, I put the book away and let my thoughts move with the flames as they circled the shiny chunks of coal.

And I saw that just as the flames released the essence of the coal, so love was doing that to me and to Bill. It was making each one of us something more. I give to Bill and he gives to me—it is an equality—and we each give to life. Determined as I had been to gain my independence when I moved away from the family circle, I did not surrender it through marriage. I gained in finding happiness; and yet I know that happiness doesn't just happen. It is something to be worked at constantly. It may mean hard work, but what doesn't mean that? Growing up was not easy, nor was growing into love.

Elsie came in with the dogs from their usual evening walk.

"Will you be wanting anything more, madam?"

"No, Elsie. Thanks. We're going out to dinner and the theater.

I'll see you in the morning."

And that was my reminder to stop dreaming by the fire and go up to change. It would be evening dress for me, white tie and tails for Bill and that marvelous top hat which worked with a spring and went as flat as a pancake when he got into a taxicab. We were going to celebrate at the Piccadilly Hotel, where we had had breakfast a year ago, and we had seats in the stalls to see Dame Sybil Thorndike in *Saint Joan*.

Winter, 1930

During the next few weeks, much happened. Bill learned of a new block of flats, Wythburn Court, just off Bryanston Square. If we took one, we could have it decorated to our taste. I went to Heal's on Tottenham Court Road and had the joy of choosing what we needed in carpeting and curtains, then essential furniture. All of it was done with the discreet suggestions of a Mr. Warrington, and I learned a great deal from him about colors and fabrics. The flat had central heating. That meant the chill was taken off the air. A coal fire in the living room gave real warmth.

With Mrs. Charles Balmain, my first friend in England, I went shopping in earnest. My guideline was that whatever was purchased must meet our present need, be beautiful, and be sturdy enough to serve for a long time. Bill was firm about that. What we got would not be temporary, but for life. There was a long-established furniture store in Esher, and there we went several times. Mrs. Balmain knew antiques—the makers, the history—and she had a feeling for detail. A piece might look to be in good condition, but her searching fingers could find a defect if there was one; and her eye, like an ear with perfect pitch, knew what was authentic.

We chose a dining room table, mahogany, oval, right for six people, with a leaf to extend it for more. Its date was 1789, and it came from a house in the Midlands where it had served long and been well cared for. The grain was handsome. "Wash it with soap and water, give it a rub of oil now and then, and it will serve you well," we were told. Six chairs went with it, quite as old, and their damask seats were frayed and faded. Their design was in Sheraton's notebook, and it thrilled me to think of all they had witnessed in their lifetime.

To these we added a small tilt-top table for tea, like the kind often seen in Zoffany portraits of the period, a dresser, a desk, a low sofa table that had come from a parsonage. These were the nucleus. Other pieces would be added—beds, comfortable chairs, and a plain table for me to use. Before we left, the clerk made out a sales slip that had not only the prices but the dates.

"You'll need it for the customs when you return to America."

At that time I could not imagine our ever returning, and yet in my heart I knew that sometime we would.

So the checks that had come from friends and family did this for us, exactly to our taste and our need.

By mid-December Elsie's room was finished and the kitchen was equipped. The flat was full of the smell of paint and plaster, and all the furniture had to be cleaned and polished when it arrived from Esher, so we made a lightning decision to go to Spain for Christmas rather than spend the time getting settled. Elsie would take care of the dogs, wash china, put books on shelves, and do a hundred small things. She was as excited about her part as we were about our escapade.

To Málaga was two days and nights on a P. and O. liner, and our cabin was really posh. I learned the meaning of a word often used casually—Port Out, Starboard Home was the comfortable way to travel when people were bound for India. When I had my first sight of Gibraltar, the Gates of Hercules, I felt that I was with Ulysses.

Then Christmas! Last year it had been so very English—holly and ivy, a great tree strung with lights, a Yule log on the fire, roast beef, and a flaming plum pudding, and poppers as part of the table setting. At the proper moment they had been opened, people had snapped them and put the paper hats on their heads. It was all rather ritualistic, as if it were being done that way because it had always been done that way. The huge hotel in Málaga, once a palace, had all the Christmas trimmings and something light-hearted and unpredictable. There was spontaneous laughter and talk in many languages, the least to be heard was English; there was dancing, and it didn't seem to matter who whirled whom about as everyone was there to have fun.

We had a week of warm, sunny days, visiting by foot and sometimes by charabanc much of southern Spain. Then two days home on the S.S. *Viceroy of India,* and the sea in the Bay of Biscay was very rough.

Two weeks away was enough to send Bill to his office impatient to catch up with his work, and me to the small room that had nothing in it but the table, a straight chair, and a shelf for books. There were several letters from America, but two I took very much to heart. Loyola Sanford, editor and friend, said, "Don't fret that you are not writing yet. You are growing into a whole new way of life, and any growing takes time. I know you are not one to lose your dream. It has led you too long." Eunice Stephenson, artist and friend, said, "In spite of all the good things that have filled your letters, I think this year has had some loneliness for you, with Bill away so much of the day and the reserve of the English to counter. Much as I love hearing from you, don't write yourself out in letters. Perhaps it's time now to sharpen your pencil."

Spring, 1931

Springtime comes again, if not always in the air, then with the flower sellers on the street corners—anemones and violets from Cornwall, narcissus and daffodils from the Scilly Isles; and the days are so much longer.

There is a smooth routine now to the pattern of my life. After a morning at home, I take the dogs for a brisk walk around Bryanston Square, then down Wimpole Street, where I pass with a fast-beating heart Number 50, the house from which Elizabeth Barrett slipped secretly one night to be married to Robert Browning in Marylebone Church. Elsie has luncheon for me and then I'm off—often to spend the afternoon in the great circular Reading Room of the British Museum. The buff-colored card that has to be renewed every six months and that gives me entrance is one of my most precious possessions. Evenings are for and with Bill. Sometimes it will be a theater, more often it will be reading aloud and talking by the fire, with the dogs always near.

I had been making needlepoint seats for our dining room chairs. The pattern is beautiful and it follows the Licorne Series of medieval tapestries. In each one there is a royal lady and her attendant, a lion and a unicorn, many small animals, flowers and trees, and each depicts one of the five senses. The sixth, *Mon Seul Désir*, is that which tells of her marriage. In my mind, as I worked, I was writing a story about this. It was slow stitchery, for the colors are many and subtle and they change often. I set myself a year for each piece.

In the British Museum, it wasn't all reading. Sometimes I wandered around the art rooms. One day I was permitted to hold in my hands a folio of William Blake's work, the very drawings he had made! Long have I loved *Glad Day* and when I held it in my hands, it fairly sang to me from the paper and made me echo inwardly Louis Untermeyer's words—

Come day, glad day, day running out of the night
With breast aflame and your generous arms outspread;
With hands that scatter the dawn and fingers busy with
*   light,*
And a rainbow of fire to flicker about your head.

Come soon, glad day, come with the confident stride
Of the sun in its march over mountains, of the wind on its
*   way through the air.*

Recently I'd been deep in books by and about George Eliot, especially her letters and John Walter Cross' biography of her. So real she became, I thought I saw her one day in her long, black cape and with her deep, sad eyes. I felt some poignant kinship and wanted to write about her to bring her ideals and greatheartedness alive again. Bill was away for a week, so I took the train to Coventry to walk in her footsteps. The house where her growing-up years were spent, when she was Mary Ann Evans, can be visited. I was allowed to sit at her desk, to handle and read some of her letters, then to see the school she attended during her "tempestuous teens." She yearned so for perfection and loved those who symbolized it.

March, 1931

Eunice said, "Don't stop dashing off those fascinating letters from the British Museum. Your creativeness and industry are operating through them, and I can see a certain style developing in the more temperate climate of England. You've always been instinctively drawn to the great minds of the ages, and I'm not surprised that you spend so many happy hours in that Reading Room. We all seek the experiences we need in order to grow, any healthy organism does this, and you are taking from people, events, and the life around you what you need for your growing."

I sent Loyola a brief word sketch of George Eliot and she replied, "I am proud of you and the writing you are doing. Your style is improving. You express your ideas with far more clarity and force. Things are moving in you and before long they will move for you. Don't you have the feeling that you can go anyplace in the world, for your career is in you? Your letters are filled with the joy of living. Write out of that."

Now that gave me an idea: Perhaps I should write a story as if it were a letter, and then, when I come to revise it, simply eliminate the salutation and the farewell.

My reading desk at the British Museum gave me the bliss of solitude, a relief after the big gatherings Bill and I had to attend sometimes. They were very formal, and my whole soul seemed to quiver and curl within me at the thought of being among so many people. I kept thinking that if there were just one person with whom I could talk seriously about things that matter, not just cheerless chitchat, everything would be all right. I never have liked big functions. I never will.

When Bill and I entertained at Wythburn Court, the groups were small. There were only six chairs in our dining room, and the table, without the leaf, seated just that number, and six is a right number for conversation. Bill comforted me and told me to be myself, but to remember that no matter how unapproachable a person may seem, there is always some point of contact that can be found. "See it as a challenge," he said.

April, 1931

Mrs. Balmain was earnest about introducing me to the real London, things I should see and know about, not as a tourist, but as a resident. During Holy Week she took me to the Maundy Thursday Service at Westminster Abbey, when King George actually did wash the feet of a dozen poor men. She found a reason to come up to London from Ashtead about once a week, and that meant we met in Green Park for a walk with the dogs, then went to the Army and Navy Stores for tea. In the entry there was a place where dogs could be tied, and each space had its own bowl of water. Then we went in for our tea. It was there that I first met up with a "Bath bun," and I never want to have anything else.

Writing seems to elude me. There are days when I feel as if pursued by a demon. Where is my direction? I pray for a sign. Such great things I have held in thought for myself, and where am I on the road to any accomplishment? Then I think it is no demon but an angel with whom I am wrestling, and I will not let it go until it blesses me. I do seem to be standing still, not doing anything, not realizing the determination I started out with so boldly a few years ago.

In the Reading Room I kept returning to George Eliot as if my salvation were in her, and that led me to an American who wrote about the same time, Louisa May Alcott; that led me to Margaret Fuller and her counterpart in England, Harriet Martineau; that led me to Clara Barton and Florence Nightingale. Each one worked against the odds of convention and mores; each one was determined to make her life count, no matter what the cost. I filled a large notebook with my discoveries and comments about these six women. Perhaps this was the direction I had been praying for; perhaps my work lay not in creation but in interpretation. Talking about this with Bill, I felt a quiver of excitement way down inside me. I was possessed with an idea of biographies of nineteenth-century women on both sides of the Atlantic, women who began a foundation for twentieth-century thinking. The work was a challenge and, as I pursued my people through the stacks of the British Museum, I felt I had not eyes enough to read the books outlined for my study, nor hands enough to get onto paper the words that were flowing.

So I wrote, sometimes at the British Museum, sometimes in my room at Wythburn Court. I would be typing the pages soon. And then, perhaps, before the leaves began to fall from the great trees in the London parks, my leaves would be bundled into a box, to be sent across the Atlantic to Miss Louise Seaman.

A letter came from Loyola: "Two months without any word from you. That can mean only one thing."

May, 1931

"This is the day to go to Kew Gardens," Mrs. Balmain said one morning on the phone.

We agreed to meet at Victoria Station, with the dogs, and set forth in the afternoon. This is something I delighted in about England: Dogs could go anywhere. At the station I bought their two tickets when I bought my own. On their leads they accompanied us into the compartment and behaved as they were expected to. Kew was beautiful. The day was sunny but cool, and the breezes were gentle. Green grass! Spring flowers! Swans going through a mating ritual! I was ecstatic with all that I was seeing.

"But wait," Mrs. Balmain said.

We walked on and approached a wooded area. I stood still. What had happened? Had the sky fallen through the budding beech trees and was it resting just above the ground? There was fragrance on the air, as exquisite as the sight that filled my eyes. Bluebells.

A path led right through them, and with the dogs close at heel we walked down it. What do you do when heaven lies at your feet in bell-like flowers on long, slender stems there in a wood as if they had just happened? Tea was being served outdoors at the pavilion, and we went there, but we talked little. A vision of sheer loveliness was in my mind, and Mrs. Balmain knew what seeing bluebells for the first time meant to me.

July, 1931

Summer in London is different from summer in America. I have worn a cotton dress exactly twice. Tweed skirts and wool jerseys are the rule, as they are through most of the year. However, they have always been my favorite clothes.

September, 1931

In Ireland I am whelmed with its beauty, and something else—a kind of leprechaun quality to life. Bill's Dublin manager, who sent us the wedding telegram about "a wee moose ne'er leaving your hoose" showed us everything. It began in Dublin, and, while Davey and Bill were talking business, I had time to explore the city, see the Book of Kells, watch swans on the Liffey, and adventure to my heart's content. When we went to Blarney Castle, Bill was the adventurer. I got in position to kiss the famous Stone. Davey and a guide held my ankles while I reached up to grasp the bar before they lowered me backward, all the time telling stories of how "they" did occasionally drop a person into the brambles below. I lost my nerve and begged them to pull me up, then they put Bill in position. He wasn't afraid. Perhaps I believed their stories and he didn't. Just as he kissed the Stone, I leaned over the parapet and got a picture of him.

Bill's camera is a part of all our journeys. He's getting more and more expert, using lenses and filters, and measuring the light with a meter. It's all very mathematical, and he has that kind of mind, so it fits together. Next to me, he says, his Leica is his dearest possession. Lakes of Killarney, thatched cottages, people, the village of Adare are not only singing in memory but are captured in pictures to be relived whenever we want. Now it's Bantry Bay, a great sweep of the southwest coast cradling the Atlantic, a tiny town, and an inn that makes us feel we must be living in another time. Last night we went up to bed holding candles in our hands; in the morning we washed in china bowls, pouring the water from a huge pitcher. Right now I am sitting on a rock by the sea, with the Bay so calm it mirrors the sky, and church bells ringing in the distance. Bill is off with his camera, and I am bringing my notes up to date.

October, 1931

Friends had been coming into my life—not the casual kind, but the kind I knew were forever. Marguerite Puttick asked me to write a play for the children in her school, so I started on *The Golden Key*. This would be quite different from the biographies, but they were at a stage when it would be good to set them aside for a while and let them mellow. A play was new for me, but it was just another step in a writing career, and I intended to try every one that came my way.

November, 1931

I was alone when they came. It was Elsie's afternoon off and Bill was not back from the office. Twelve red roses. Oh, Bill! I took them, one by one, and placed them in a tall vase that showed their stems and gave support to the buds that would soon open. The dogs watched me, as they do everything. I wanted to laugh and cry with happiness, but what I did was sit on the floor by the fire, with a dog on each side, and watch the flames, and think. When Bill got home he had a package under his arm from Asprey's, with a note—

> *A softish cashmere rug, my dear,*
> *For the nap you never take,*
> *May it keep you warm and snug, my dear,*
> *Should you doze off by mistake.*

Year's End, 1931

Two years ago, even a year ago, it seemed as if the life we were building together might go on in the same delightful way for a long time, but that was not to be. Events in the world were beginning to make inroads on our world. Mr. Walter Mangum, the president, hinted to Bill that the company might soon be sold, and, if so, Bill might want to start making other plans. But not yet, Mr. Mangum said. Things may change for us all. The shafts of light before the sun goes down are long, often very bright, and not to be ignored. We would continue to live as we had, but we would prepare ourselves for a change. When we talked about that possibility, as we did so often, I used the word "ready" while Bill used the word "willing." There is a difference.

1932

A Mountain View

Winter, 1932

These are trying times for Bill, with decisions to be made, plans to be adjusted. I want to help all I can, and that means giving him my undivided self. I won't lose my interest in the biographies, even though they must be set aside again, nor my impetus, for so much has already been done. Memory is like a little room on which I shut the door for a while, and there the biographies are safely waiting. Evening after evening we sit by the fire in our soft green room, talking. Rosy tulips make shadow shapes on the wall and gleam, reflected, in the polished mahogany of the sofa table. My hands are quietly occupied with my needlepoint. The dogs sleep, oblivious to the changes we are contemplating.

The business that Bill gave so much of himself to for many years had been sold. He was handsomely compensated in sterling, an amount sufficient to see us through a year or more of careful living. The company was being disbanded, the Mangums were returning to America. This did not happen in one day, but on the day that it was made final, we talked far into the night.

We decided to take a period of time to assess our life. Bill had worked hard for more than twenty years, and before turning to some other form of usefulness, he needed a long view, and what better place to have it than in the mountains? By the time we went to bed our decision was made. We would leave London with its grayness and its magic, Wythburn Court with its colorful comfort, the friends that had been slowly but surely made, and we would go to Switzerland.

"But, Bill, you've always been a businessman, an executive."

"Yes, since before I never went to college, but 'there's always a new firing line.'" Quoting one of his favorites, Justice Holmes, he brought our discussion to an end.

March 25, 1932

This stands out as one of the Great Days in our lives. It was an English Quarter Day, when rents are paid, but not for us. The flat

In the Swiss Alps
with Lotte and Bill

was let, the furniture was put into storage, good-bys were said. We were off with the dogs and a miscellaneous collection of luggage to spend Easter Week in Paris, then we would be on our way to Switzerland.

April, 1932

We were wakened at the border by a customs official wanting to see our passports. He asked only one question and it was about the dogs: *"Quelle race?"* Searching my sleepy mind, I came out with the word, *"Écossais."* That seemed to satisfy him completely. Soon the train was on its way again and the gates of beauty opened to us.

At Montreux we found a pension that was near a park where the dogs could run. In it there were bird boxes and trays for seeds and crumbs that carried signs PENSEZ AUX OISEAUX. The air was fresh off the waters of Lake Geneva and from the snow-covered heights of Mont Blanc and the mountains that were near and far. Each one challenged us, but we knew we had to find a place to live first. Every day we took the neat little train that wound its way up into the Bernese Oberland, and every day we got off at a village a little higher up to see if we could find something to rent for the summer. The fields were filled with narcissus, and children were gathering them in great armfuls. Three weeks went by, and I became impatient, but Bill assured me that a chalet existed and we would know it when we saw it.

So we did the day we reached Gstaad and breathed air like none other.

The estate agent in the village referred us to the local guide, Fritz Gempeler. He had built a chalet for himself and his wife to retire into someday but as yet it was not occupied. It was a mile up—everything was always up or down—from the village, and on the Turbach. "Go talk with him," the agent said.

Bill's German was better than my French, but both were needed, as Herr and Frau Gempeler knew no English. They lived in the village, but we were soon on the road with them to Heimeli. With more smiles than words the Gempelers showed the chalet to us. When we saw it, Bill and I simply looked at each other. It was small, snug, new, built into a hillside, with enough space for a terraced garden. From the balcony we saw a mighty line of mountains in which the Wildhorn was centered; in the narrow valley below the chalet, the Turbach ran, its waters adding music to the day. The rent was reasonable, the furnishings adequate, the dogs as delighted as we. In German that was improving by the minute, Bill told Fritz that we would like to have Heimeli until mid-October.

Fritz cared less about the arrangements than that he would be the one to guide us on the slopes as soon and as often as we wished. Perhaps it had taken three weeks, but time slid away in the wonder of Heimeli, and we could not wait to get back to Montreux, collect our belongings and move in. On our way back to Gstaad we stepped aside for some cows going up to high pasture. Their great bells, differing in size and tone, were more than a melodious symphony: to us they were a paean of thanksgiving.

May 20, 1932

The days in Heimeli are falling into a pattern of simple joy and satisfying work. Lotte, a German *au pair* girl whom we had known of in London, has come out to join us. She wants to learn English and do housework in return. In the mornings, in the small room that looks out upon vast mountains, I resume work on the biographies; Bill goes off with his camera; Lotte sings about her housework, starts turning earth for a garden, takes the dogs down to the Turbach. Afternoons we try our feet on the winding paths, little climbs preparing us for big ones. We bask in the glory of sunshine. Oh heaven, oh earth, oh God of both, what treasures are poured around us! Seeds are planted, sprouts appear, and in fields and meadows and along roadsides the pageant of wildflowers is enacted. It is a golden age.

June, 1932

Bill came back from the Saanen Market with a roll full of film that he is eager to have developed and a head full of things he wants to write. He has been working all afternoon on a story of Market Day, intermingling writing with laying a stone walk along our flower-vegetable garden. He wrote with the care and precision he applies to everything, then read his pages through to himself. Even before showing them to me, he tore them into bits. "You're the writer," he said, "I'll be the picture maker."

It takes courage to sit in judgment on yourself. I admired him and almost envied him, because I found it hard to destroy my work. That evening we had the first produce from our garden—turnip tops! Did anything ever taste better?

July, 1932

In this world of shining sun and shimmering mountains, there is rain at times; and there were dark days for Bill when a damp cloth over his eyes and quiet were the only remedy. He came out of every attack with his wonderful smile and more determination than ever to get the most from every good day, every new experience.

Friends from England and America were finding their way to us, and we were glad that, small as Heimeli was, we could make room for them. Visitors with whom we had great fun were the Hill children, whom we had grown to know well in England, as their parents were our good friends. Erskine was thirteen, Margaret was eleven, Barbara was eight. We did many small climbs during the week they were with us and their response to the heights—the joys and the dangers—matched their years.

One day, while we were having luncheon on the balcony and looking toward the mountains, Lotte said, "Tonight the moon is full."

That was enough. Whoever wants to waste a full moon?

We laid our plans, packed rucksacks with necessities, and at five thirty started off. It was hot. We walked steadily, that pace learned from Fritz, up, up, until we reached the first point of the Durreschild two hours later and just as a twilight glow was turning to orange behind the distant rim of mountains. We found a sheltered spot near a rock, gathered sticks and made a fire. We had supper, big bowls of Maggi soup, fresh bread, and fruit, and waited for the moon to rise. The dogs were excited, but never ventured beyond the rim of light cast by the fire; the children were spellbound. I had my beloved anthology, *The Gypsy Trail*, in my sack, and we read aloud in the flickering light. Lotte read some of the German poems, translating as she read; I let William Blake speak for us all—

> *The moon, like a flower*
> *In heaven's high bower,*
> *With silent delight*
> *Sits and smiles on the night.*

A glow began to spread across the sky to the east, then the moon appeared slowly, oh so slowly, washing the valley with silver, lighting up the distant peaks. Barbara whispered

> *Slowly, silently, now the moon*
> *Walks the earth in her silver shoon.*

By midnight it was bright enough to show the downward way. The fire was out. The rucksacks almost empty. We went singing over the path and reached Heimeli an hour later, filled with beauty. "I shall never forget this as long as I live," said Barbara as I tucked her into bed.

August 10, 1932

Fritz feels we are in condition for the Rubli, and that is a real climb, an almost vertical slab of rock towering above the valley. Looking at it has thrilled me and sent a shudder through me at the same time.

August, 1932

We left Heimeli at 3:30 A.M.—no dogs this time, but Frau Gempeler was coming in during the day to see to them. A half hour later we met Fritz on the path to the Rubli. All was hushed and still, the dark just paling into dawn as we set off. Fritz led with that even mountain pace, not fast, not slow, that will carry one for a day if need be. Through the glories of the sunrise we went up, up, past the last alp and the Rubli hut to the base of the ascent. There Fritz uncoiled the rope he had carried over his shoulders and tied us onto it. Our rucksacks were left in a heap—only the leader had his, and that was Fritz. His eyes ran down each one of us to be sure there was nothing loose—no button undone, no shoe unlaced. He would be in the lead, Lotte and I in the middle, Bill at the end of the rope. The smile that was as much a part of Fritz as his sun-bronzed, wind-toughened countenance had disappeared. He was serious. His lively talk had come down to two words, *"Courage. Prenez garde."* Then we were off and up the sheer wall of rock.

We moved with caution, getting holds with fingers, then gaining footholds with the tips of our boots, aware of a pull on the rope only if one of us slackened, yet always aware that in the rope was our safety, not as one, but as a team. It was 8 A.M. when we gained the summit and, suddenly, there was nothing higher.

A thrilling panorama was spread around us—green valleys, little villages, fields where cattle grazed, square-set hay barns, chalets whose small windows blinked under the jutting brows of their great roofs, and all rimmed by distant mountains whose white snows glistened in the sunshine. Fritz beamed at us all as if we had done some great thing, then he shook hands with us and said, "Bravo."

Still on the rope, but with slack between us, we stretched out on the rocks. Fritz opened his rucksack, filled cups with coffee still steaming from the thermos, unwrapped and offered us rolls that were crisp and crunchy. Two hours was the limit of our time, as the Rubli wall would become too hot for the needed holds. Lotte and I flattened out and breathed deeply. Bill wriggled around a boulder and lowered himself to the length of his portion of rope. When he came back he had in his teeth a bunch of edelweiss, which he gave to me. *"Comme le vrai amant!"* Fritz exclaimed. Rope holds were checked carefully before we started down. The descent was more difficult and hazardous than the ascent.

By noon we reached an open meadow where a spring bubbled into a hollowed log, a drinking trough for cows. Near it Fritz built a small fire of sticks, and soon the contents of another rucksack were emptied and he was frying bacon and eggs, buttering slabs of bread, and making coffee. Dessert was a tin of raspberries, the Hero brand, turned into our tin plates which had been mopped clean with bread. Full, happy, and feeling like conquerors, we stretched back on the turf. Cowbells could be heard in the distance, the sun was warm, the breeze off distant peaks was cool.

Turning around suddenly, I dislodged my rucksack and it started down the slope, bouncing and gaining speed. Fritz saw it and raced after it. Passing it, he reached out for it and it came bounding into his arms. He laughed, shrugged his shoulders, and when he handed it back to me it was almost the way Bill had handed me the edelweiss. Fritz had taught me that if something gets away from you, don't try to catch up with it, get ahead of it, outwit it, and let it come into your outstretched hands.

It was late in the afternoon when we finally reached Heimeli. Tired, yes, but so proud of our conquest that exhilaration made a mockery of fatigue.

August 28, 1932

This is an important day in my life. I have finished the biographies. The title *Challenge* was inevitable—what it was to me when I started thinking about it during those long hours at the British Museum, what I hope the lives will be to every girl who reads them. I packed the typed pages in a box and wrapped them securely, addressed it to go *BY FAST SHIP,* then Bill and I ran all the way down to the village to get the package in the Post. Joy and relief for both of us, followed by rolls and coffee at the Bernerhof.

"This calls for celebration," Bill said, and the kind we are taking is a bit of vagrancy.

September, 1932

Leaving Lotte to care for Heimeli and the dogs, we took off by train for two weeks of sheer adventure. Zurich, Lindau, Munich, Salzburg, Innsbruck, Garmisch, Lucerne, all revealed their charm to us. My notebook was crammed. Bill did many pictures.

We waited on the weather to climb the Wildhorn. Fritz had to be assured of two perfect days, and this was a time of year when change is in the air; but the right moment came. Bill, Lotte, and I with our gear in good shape set out with Fritz, taking the train to Lenk. Then we were off and up, walking slowly, climbing all the way, and the last part wearily. We trudged through the snow around the Iffigensee and Bill got a picture of the last rays of sun drawing a band of pure silver over the black water. It was twilight when we reached the Wildhorn hut, a low stone building with green-and-white angle-striped shutters. Inside was a great fireplace, a spring for water, and bunks built against the walls. The hut is a radial point for many mountains and other climbers were there, with different languages vibrating on the air. Food and rest was the order. After a meal that Fritz cooked, we stretched out on the boards of the bunks. Fritz said he would waken us with the first light. The only book I had tucked in my rucksack was our small *Runner's Bible*, but there was no light to read by. We wrote our names in the hut book and stamped our bible with C.A.S. Section Moleson Cabane Wildhorn 2,315 meters, and the date.

By 6 A.M. we were on our way, climbing over a rough rocky area through a crimson and gold sunrise onto the glacier. The snow was deep and crusty, and Fritz had us on the rope. He went first, testing every foot of the way with his pickax, pointing to crevasses whose ice-blue walls made the air colder there than that around us. Going ever more slowly and cautiously, he looked back now and then and mouthed the word *"Courage."* If he said it, the wind took all sound away. It seemed interminable, the plodding through snowfields. There was no stopping to rest. The wind was cruel and it forced us on. Then we gained the domed summit: 3,264 meters! On one side was the long chain of the Alps, snow-covered, crevassed, glacier strewn, from Mont Blanc in France to the tips of the Dolomites in Austria; on the other, the sweep down into the green valleys of the Oberland.

It was worth everything to stand for those few thrilling moments on a crest of the world. Fritz shook hands with us all in turn. "Bravo," he said. "Bravo," he smiled. Then, swinging off his rucksack, he took out the thermos, handed cups to us, and filled them. The tea was steaming when it was poured, but lukewarm when it touched lips. The wind and the cold would not let us stay, nor would Fritz. It was imperative to get across the glacier field before the sun started melting the snow. *"Courage,"* he said as he checked the rope that linked us all.

This time Bill was in the lead, following the footsteps made earlier. The man at the end had more power to hold back if one of us made a misstep. It was high noon when we reached the hut. Fritz made bowls of soup while Bill changed the film in his camera, and soon we were off again, down, down the long kilometers to Lenk. Much of the way was through a bleak area of rock and snow. We saw five chamois, nimble and graceful. We stood still and watched them, scarcely breathing with the wonder, then one by one they trotted up a slope, stood for an instant on the horizon's rim silhouetted against a clear blue sky, and long enough for Bill to catch them on film, then dropped from sight. We walked on through a narrow pass and at last came into green fields where cattle grazed and children played. That night, when we looked on the Wildhorn from Heimeli's balcony, one thought was in our minds: "We have stood where clouds are resting."

September 28, 1932

Today a letter came from Miss Seaman—fast ship has served us well. "It is an interesting idea. . .shows careful research and the writing is thoughtful. . .but you are speaking through these people. When are you going to speak for yourself? I am returning *Challenge* as it is not for us. Your International Money Order more than covered the postage, so I am including one of our new books." She added a P.S. *"Harvester* is doing very well. The reviews have been consistently good and the sales are pleasing us and your brother."

Do I have the courage to do what Bill did with his piece on Saanen Market? No. Because I think the material may be useful sometime, in some way. It's just another challenge, but this time without a capital C.

October, 1932

And now the summer was memory; but living close to great mountains did something for us both. We said good-by to Heimeli and the Gempelers, to Lotte, who was returning to Germany, and to Sinna. A sudden illness just a week before snuffed out that stalwart life; loyal comrade of my lonely years, dear companion during years of bliss. We placed his brave little body in the earth near where our garden had been, and Lotte said, "There is something of you which will always be a part of Switzerland." With Bara beside us and our luggage around us, we took the train down through the Bernese Oberland on a day of gently falling rain. The countryside was a tapestry of color, but the mountains were veiled.

We arrived in Paris as the sun, swimming out of a coral haze, touched the Seine bridges and the towers of Notre Dame with color. Soon we were installed in a charming flat in Passy loaned to us by some friends. Now I had the fun of keeping house in French for a while. Paris was unutterably beautiful. Leaves were falling and slim dark arms of trees were etched against misty vistas. It seemed noisy and rushing as I remembered the restraint in England, the politeness of Switzerland; but it was not for long. A return to America was imminent. We would sail in December, but before that I planned to return to England to make some arrangements, and Bill was to spend that time at an eye clinic where a specialist would help him if anyone could.

December, 1932

Out of Southampton, the channel was rough, but the S.S. *Franconia* took it steadily; and there was Bill on the dock at Cherbourg with other passengers waiting to be picked up. He was easily distinguished by the small black dog standing alertly beside him in the late light of afternoon. Two weeks had been too long and there was so much to talk about. Soon we were in our cabin, Bara too, as this was an English ship. The steward brought tea, and time was before us.

"How was it to be back in England?"

"Oh, Bill, it was going home. The train seemed to be hurrying on its way from Dover to London, and it was almost too dark to see anything, but tea was served and the soft voices were like music. That sense of unchangeableness always sturdies me."

"And did you get everything done?"

"Yes, and I saw so many of our friends, went to the theater, did some shopping. But you?"

Bill was silent, then he smiled. "I have sight. I shall use it while I have it."

"An operation? Did he think that would help?"

Bill shook his head almost imperceptibly. "Only when the pain becomes too great, but that won't be for a long time. Five years or more." Bill said it as if five years might be forever.

There was so much more to talk about, and while the ship floundered its way through heavy seas we made our plans. Sometimes it seemed that we were always making plans with spaces between when we lived the plans.

"That's the best part of life," Bill said, "always looking ahead, but living in the present."

1933–1935

American Interlude

It has been an interlude, a time between, and we have returned to England, settling in as if we had never left. Facing the present fact of our lives, we know that our tastes are simple, our needs few, and that we can make what we have go much farther in England; and we can live at our own pace.

In America there was so much noise and hurry, so much advertising, so much clamoring for attention, and everything was so efficient. But I relished the easy friendliness and the spontaneity. The air sparkled, the sky was so often cloudless, the buildings pointed up and up. Yet, during our first months, the times were trying. It was the depth of the depression. The February day when the banks closed and President Roosevelt spoke to the nation on the radio, people listened anxiously. There was need for a leader to give heart to the country. His words "The only thing we have to fear is fear itself" spoke to us all.

We saw friends and visited families, then we settled in Boston for a while and began making contacts. One led to another. Bill's photographs with my text to accompany them found their places in newspapers, many in the *Christian Science Monitor*. Checks, small though they were, began to come with delightful regularity. Bill followed every lead he could to make a business connection. There were few openings in those days, and none for a man whose sight was limited. This in itself proved to work for him, as his life insurance policy carried a disability clause that could be invoked, relieving him of paying further premiums and entitling him to a monthly check. It was not large, but it could be counted on.

A friend loaned us her car whenever we wanted it, and we made frequent trips throughout New England, staying in old towns, walking the country roads, wondering when—we had dropped the "if"—we would see the perfect place and our dream of a little farm would come true. But for now, the signs pointed to England. Miss Clements wrote that she had produced two of the plays I had written for Miss Puttick's School and when would I be back to write another? Bertha Miller of *The Horn Book Magazine* suggested arti-

Sailing to America
with Donal

cles she would like that could be done only in England. The *Monitor* was ready to schedule a series of interviews with outstanding English individuals; they would continue the illustrated travel essays, and welcome any book reviewing.

One night, adding everything up and considering what England meant to us, we made the decision to return. And at the thought, the windows of heaven seemed to open for us.

We were only on the edge of accomplishment in our separate but often combined fields of writing and picture making. We knew it would be some time before we were really established, but we felt we could make our way more easily in the gentle clime of England. The pace was too swift in America, the pressures too many. It meant a shift, not an uprooting, as we had never put down roots; it would mean quarantine for Bara; but, as far as we could see, it was the better way for a time.

Before we left, we borrowed our friend's car and went up into southern New Hampshire, spending nights in little inns that had history to them, discovering towns that charmed us—Hancock, Peterborough, Francestown, Temple. We spent a day on the big mountain that dominated the countryside—Monadnock—and saw from its height forests and lakes and rivers, clearings and villages. Bill took pictures of old houses and tall church spires, animals, trees, people. "Nothing particular," he said again and again. "Just the way the country is. I want to be able to see it when we're on the other side of the ocean. Remembering may be the sometime magnet."

On the ship that took us back to England, I read one of Mary Ellen Chase's very New England books, *Mary Peters*. A certain passage seemed to be for us, and I read it to Bill:

> Her life that afternoon had been rounded into a perfect circle, completed and fulfilled. She had nothing to regret, everything to remember with gratitude. Most people were wrong about life, she thought. It was not a struggle against temptation as she had been taught in church. Nor was it a search for truth as the philosophers said, or even for happiness, much as humanity craved happiness. It was rather a kind of waiting—a waiting upon the graciousness and the bounty of the things which had been, in order that the things to come might find one free and unafraid.

Bill said, "We've made another circle. Now, to see what the next will be. Didn't Emerson have something to say about circles?"

"Indeed he did, and that essay is one of the most marked in my book." I reached far back into memory and found a few words: "Something about man's life being a self-revolving circle, small at first, then growing larger, always expanding. That's the thought."

What did I notice as the S.S. *Samaria* steamed into Southampton water—the softness in the light and in the air, and moments later in the voices of the people. There seemed to be no clamor or stress. On the train to London I looked out on a countryside that was still green, with the muted colors of autumn just visible. Everything was neat, and there were flowers blooming in the little gardens of cottages along the way. Then it was London, with twilight coming down like a cloak and that feeling of quiet stability. There were no raucous horns or hurrying crowds, but the gray of buildings, the red of buses; and in Victoria Station friends to welcome us.

"In returning and rest shall ye be saved." We have come back to England to accomplish something. As we establish ourselves in our work, we will be making ourselves ready for the next circle.

1936

Long Live the King

January, 1936

"The King is dead! Long live the King!"

King George has died after a long illness, and there is mourning throughout the land. Even I wear a black armband on the left sleeve of my coat. But within moments his son, Edward VIII, was proclaimed king, so England is not without a monarch.

As the funeral procession passed on its way to Westminster Abbey, Bill and I stood in a huge crowd on the edge of Hyde Park. People all around us were snapping pictures of the cortege, the horses, the soldiers. Bill took a picture of the crowd, focusing on two men just ahead of us—one was very tall with a silk top hat, squared shoulders, every inch of him a lord or a duke; the other, a shabby little man, his cap pulled down over his ears and his hair straggling on his collar.

"Nothing in particular," Bill said, but when it was printed, he entered it in a competition the *Daily Express* was holding. They thought it was something in particular, illustrating "the power of the throne to bring all classes together." It won first prize, was printed on the front page, and wherever the *Daily Express* was read and sold Bill's picture was seen.

High Summer, 1936

What wonderful things happen! Bill learned of a house we could rent in Kent in a village named Trottiscliffe; after the damp cold winter in London, it was alluring. We knew the charm of an English spring; here was a chance to live in and into the unfolding year.

So we took White House for six months. The rent was low, because the owners were to be away and wanted to have the place cared for just as it was, with a maid, a gardener, and a cat. White House had a history going back five hundred years, but only its recent years were known about. Joseph Conrad had lived in it and here he wrote his novel *Victory*. There was a picture of him leaning from a window and calling to his wife in the garden. Sir Philip Gibbs had lived in it. It must be a good place for a writer. The rooms are all

London's Hyde Park

small, as once it was three little shops, but the garden is large.

The April night we arrived, Nelly had coal fires burning brightly in the tiny sitting room and in our bedroom. She soon produced a massive tea "to cheer you." I've got used to being called "madam," and I like to hear Bill referred to as "the master." The cat resented Bara at first and then made up to him seductively; gentleman that Bara is, he tolerated either mood.

Back of the house there was a deep and lovely garden, protected on one side by a gray wall, on the other by a beech hedge. The garden was bright with daffodils when we arrived, and there were primroses everywhere. The earth was alight with them; they were peeking out of hedgerows, blooming in unlikely places. Looking from the house up the village street, we could see two oasthouses, a flintstone church with a duck pond close by, the one store—once called the Universal Provider and now known as the Little Wonder—a few houses, their tiled roofs mossy and mellow, and a triangular Green. Beyond are the North Downs, flinging a protective arm across the countryside. This is the way the pilgrims walked to Canterbury, which is not far distant.

It was cold, at first, and there were some light dustings of snow, but by the end of April, warmth came and with it leaves appeared and birds arrived, their chatter a background to our days.

I couldn't get away from the feeling that I was living in a storybook, for things happened just the way I've read about them. The vicar and his sister came to call, and of course Nelly had tea ready. . . . Two men appeared with a basket, saying they were taking an egg collection for the Maidstone Hospital and they hoped to get hundreds. We found six in the larder that Nelly said she could spare. . . . The butcher in West Malling did not mind bringing the fish, as the fishmonger does not come as far as Trosley—that's the way the village name is pronounced here. And he would accommodate the greengrocer, too. . . . My shoes, needing new soles and left at the cobbler a mile away, were delivered by the newspaper boy on his morning round.

Progress had arrived in the shape of electricity, which never got farther than tarred poles left on the Green. "With the sun giving so many hours of light, we'll not want to be connected until end of summer." Very sensible we think, for the lamplit house satisfies. Another evidence of progress was the large bright TCB pillar-box that almost dwarfed the Little Wonder. "It's taking wonderfully," the villagers said. It was a new model, one of the first to be set up anywhere. "And they put it in Trosley! That shows what they think of us."

The walks were lovely in any direction, but especially up on the Downs, where it was high and windy. I went off with my notebook, Bill with his camera. He came back with film to be developed, I with more flowers than I could name. On the Downs one morning I stopped and caught my breath—bluebells! The ground was azure with their bloom. When I first heard the cuckoo, I thought it was in my dreams; but Bill woke me and said "It's true—" So we went for an early walk, and we heard the call across the fields as flight took him. I thought of the old rhyme "—he comes in May, In June he changes his tune, In July he prepares to fly, In August go he must." Blossoms and leaves were fairly leaping into being and the country-side was different each day than it was the day before. The sun was so warm that Nelly had breakfast for us in the garden. Birds were busy all around us.

"It's like living in an aviary," Bill said, "a tapestry of sound."

It was like the needlepoint chair seats I was making, with their birds and their flowers.

Such loveliness! Everything that can blossom blossomed. The beech hedge was softly green, pear and cherry blossoms were pink and white overhead, while bees droned in them and apple blossoms drifted down the winds. Lilacs poured their fragrance. Edward brought the kitchen garden to the table—cress, rhubarb, lettuce, radish. "And there'll be more, all summer there'll be more."

Friends from London, even from America, came to visit us, and we led them on scented walks along the Pilgrim's Way, past the Col-drum Stones, that strange circle that is a relic of primitive man. At night we went to the Downs to hear the nightingale. But White House was a place for work, too. I resisted the temptation to be outside all the time and settled myself at a plain table in the little room that looks up the village street. I was writing short essays to fit Bill's pictures, and every week one went on its way across the ocean. The new pillar-box was just the right size for mailing the envelopes.

One sunny day led to another into the high tide of summer. Lilies now stood tall in the border along the gray wall, with del-phinium and roses and lavender. Fruit was ripening. Of all the peo-ple who came to stay a few days or a week, the most welcome were Bob and his Martha on their honeymoon. They came when we were picking cherries and drying lavender. Bob was a man of busi-ness by then. He was pleased to talk about his book, but nothing would induce him to write another.

"You're the writer in the family," he said with that wonderful smile that always made everything all right.

He was puzzled about what we were doing, or not doing. He liked the house and the garden, the quaintness of the village, the beauty of the countryside, the comfort of having servants. "But what are you doing except having a good time?"

The explanation was too long to make on a radiant day, with flowers and their fragrance around us, birds and their singing. The simplest thing was to tell him that we were establishing ourselves in a new way.

"But you won't be here after the summer, will you?"

"No, we'll be back in London."

"What doing?"

"What we're doing here—writing, making pictures. Being."

Then we dropped the subject. The day was too nice, he was too happy; but in that brief encounter of words, a national difference became clear to me—in America one must be *doing*, in England *being* seemed to have a reason.

Writing mornings, walking afternoons, reading evenings, so the days went by with a modicum of work in house and garden, as Nelly and Edward had their charges. We knew, too, that we would have gone down in their estimation had we done work not fitting for "the gentry." Sometimes I chafed at the restriction, but we were in England and that was the way. "It may not ever be so," Bill said, the gentleness in his tone, like Bob's smile, closing the matter softly.

Some friends made in books are forever. Before I was ten I had read George MacDonald's books. *At the Back of the North Wind* I have read many times, always finding something more in it to stir my thought. This summer I was deep in his novels, especially *Sir Gibbie* and *Donal Grant*. But, much as I longed to read *Sir Gibbie* aloud to Bill, I could not cope with the Scottish dialect. My eyes slid over what my tongue could not twist itself around. I read MacDonald's life, a big rewarding book, and it made me feel wonderfully close to him.

When Marguerite came down to visit us, she brought with her the three volumes of his poetry, out of print for many years. For the most part they were long, didactic, and very Victorian, but jewels were among them and those I could read aloud to Bill and Marguerite as we sat in the garden. Way deep in me something began to stir. How could I bring this aspect of MacDonald to people again—not the storyteller still so well known, or the preacher so long forgotten, but the poet?

"I know his youngest daughter, Winifred, Lady Troup," Marguerite said. "When you get back to London, I'd like you two to meet. She lives in Kensington."

There was a week when we had no visitors. Nelly tiptoed about the house, and even Edward ceased his whistling when he came in with vegetables from the garden. Bara would not leave Bill's darkened room except when I insisted. The attack was one of the shortest, and my heart leaped with hope that perhaps we were winning the battle; but when Bill returned to his camera, he asked me to read the fine print on his light meter.

The Hill children, Erskine, Margaret, and Barbara, came to visit. Three years had not made too much change in them, and this was something that delighted us. In England children seemed to remain children so much longer. We had noticed the way they shot up with such rapidity in America, as if impatient to get on with life. Barbara was still the adventurer, but becoming more careful about spending money. The day we went to visit Knole House, Bill gave her tuppence for the ladies' room. When she returned, "It wasn't worth it," she announced with scorn that would have pleased her Scottish father.

One afternoon, while Erskine was up on a ladder helping Edward gather early apples and Margaret and I were stripping lavender from its stalks, Bill told Barbara a story. It was such a good story that I thought he must be reading it, but he wasn't. It was coming straight from that fertile mind of his. Later I asked if I could type it and send it to a publisher. He demurred and twitted me about my indefatigable optimism. However, I did type it as I had heard him tell it, and when I read to him, *The Frog, the Penny and the Big Black Tree*, he laughed at his own words. Frederick Warne and Company, who had published the Beatrix Potter books, seemed a logical place to send it, so it went to them with postage enclosed for return.

Late Summer, 1936

The days, so long in late June that it was light at ten o'clock, were shortening noticeably. In the flower garden the colors now were the purple of Michaelmas daisies and the burnished gold of chrysanthemums; the vegetables that Edward brought in for the table were cabbages and Brussels sprouts. Our lease was up in September. In April it had seemed impossible to think of ever leaving White House. Now it was becoming quite possible to yearn for London.

The day we went into the Little Wonder to say good-by, the postmistress handed me a long, thin envelope. "That's one you'll like," she said. She knew the difference in weight, and the meaning of a self-addressed envelope. She was right. It was an acceptance of one of my essays, and it held a check. I opened it and peeked in just for the fun of telling her that what she surmised was true. She smiled and handed

Bill a small square envelope with a London postmark. We waited until we got back to White House to read it. Bill couldn't believe what it said, but I could: "We received your story and would like to consider publishing it with illustrations by Mr. Cyrus Hall. Will you come up to London sometime soon to discuss arrangements?"

With one leap, Bill had become a book writer. Now there was every reason to return to London.

October, 1936

The flat at Edwardes Square is small, but it seems good to be surrounded by our own things again—especially our books. The Square itself is our joy. All who live on it have a key for entrance into it—the greenest of lawns, the richest of shrubbery, and the neatest of pebbled paths. Though we are in the heart of Kensington and embraced by London, there are still birds around us, and the clop of hooves as the milkman makes his early rounds, his small horse always knowing exactly where to stop and when to go on.

Marguerite took me to call on Lady Troup, and I felt as if I had yet another friend for life. I think she felt that way too, for it was so easy for us to talk about her father and of what I wanted to do in making a selection of his poems for publication. She said that she would help me, and I knew that I could turn to her. A small and charming person, she had the fragility of age, but the strength that I had found in her father's books.

Bill was busy with "his publishers." How thrilling that sounded! As soon as he went to call on the firm of Frederick Warne, he was informed that the artist had already done the illustrations, that the book would be published in the spring, and did he have another story in mind? "Yes, indeed," Bill said with certainty.

We were never at a loss for children, either those of friends, or those in Marguerite Puttick's School, or those who rolled their hoops or trundled their tricycles on the paths of the Square. Bill had only to take his key, turn it in the iron gate and start into the Square, with Bara beside him, to be surrounded by an assortment of children, happily leaving their nannies for the man with a story to tell. *Dennis the Donkey* grew as much with the help of the children as through Bill's imagination. The firm of Warne was delighted and even improved on the first contract.

These were productive days for me. I was working on a series of stories about a certain Scottish terrier named Kilts, based on Bara's adventures, of course. The *Monitor* took every one I sent. I embarked on the interviews, and somehow it never occurred to me to feel nervous in the presence of Sybil Thorndike, or Elisabeth Bergner, or Vera Brittain, or any others. Before meeting with each one, I found out as much as was available. I knew what questions I wanted to ask. I listened when they talked to me, taking only a few notes in a shorthand of my own.

As often as possible, we saved our weekends for walking. We had a special day of sun and wind in the Chilterns. With our inch-to-a-mile Ordnance Survey map, our rucksacks, and Bara trotting happily beside us, we followed a wide green track that wound slowly up Ivinghoe Beacon. Its top is not a thousand feet, but once gained, there was nothing between us and the sky. Spur after spur of beech-covered hills disappeared into the distance, while near us were box trees and waist-high bracken. We came upon a signpost:

NORTH POLE	2,760 MILES
LONDON	44 MILES
STAR TOP'S END	1 MILE

We chose the one that sounded as if it might be the farthest but was the nearest and came to a small hamlet. There was an inn, once an old house, set in a velvet lawn, lattice windows thrusting ivy aside. Inquiring if we might have tea, we were told we could, in the garden; so we went through a paneled room with sun shining on polished oak and silver to the garden. There were a few leaves falling, a few birds chittering, and soon a tea appeared that was all a high tea should be—hot scones and thin slices of buttered bread, eggs in cups, honey and jam, and a great pot of tea under a tea cozy to keep it warm. We were well fortified for the five-mile walk back to Beaconsfield and the train to London. This is the sort of day I shall always remember, essence of the England we knew and loved.

December 6, 1936

The year always begins to close and open again with my birthday. This year is more than ever special, as so much is opening for both of us. It begins to seem that the plowing and seeding we've done for so long, the watering and weeding, are producing grain. Reaping time is near.

Year's End, 1936

For the past seven years I've kept account of work sent out, marking acceptances and their amounts. Up to this year the acceptances have been few and amounts small, but now the entries in both left and right columns of my little ledger are looking quite respectable.

1937

High Holiday

February, 1937

Audrey and I were having tea at Fortnum and Mason's. We always had much to talk about to catch each other up on.

"You've been busy?"

"Oh, yes, articles and essays, book reviews, some interviews," I enumerated, "plays for a school."

"But you're not going to do that kind of piecework forever?"

It was hard to find words to answer her. "I haven't yet found—" I started, fumbling.

She cut me short. "Isn't there some one thing that you know just a little more about than anyone else? Write that."

She didn't give me time to disagree, to object, but went on talking about a play she had seen the night before, and we never got back to the subject of me.

On the bus from Piccadilly to Kensington, her question returned to me and my inner answer was, "Of course not. I've led a very usual sort of life, nothing spectacular has ever happened to me." Arguments came to me, but her words were persistent, and the wheels of the bus picked them up, droning ". . .something you know. . .more about. . .than anyone else." Ridiculous, I answered the droning. Then something took hold of me. In Switzerland, I had seen the way three children, different in age and temperament, reacted to the high mountains, to the challenge of climbing, to danger, to beauty. And with that memory I was off. My whole being was quivering. But how to make it into a story?

At supper I told Bill I had an idea for a book. I couldn't say much more, for I have learned that an idea calling to be written must not be spent in spoken words.

"Think on," he said.

And I did—walking with Bara in Kensington Gardens, sitting at my desk and looking at the plane tree outside the window. Whatever I was doing, the idea was there in the back of my mind, growing; and there were pages on my desk with writing on them that proved something was happening.

Taking notes
on the Isle of Skye

June, 1937

Once I had found the way to make it into a story—Michael and Meredith Lamb going out to Switzerland with their Uncle Tony—it had started. It grew as the leaves on the plane tree, from an inner surge. The people became real. The background was there in the experiences we had had, all jotted down in those little notebooks I had carried around with me; the stage for the action was in the pictures Bill had taken. Every time I wanted to be in Switzerland, I could be there by looking at his album. The work went fast, but when summer drew near, I was ready to put all those handwritten pages aside and plan with Bill a holiday on the Isle of Skye.

July, 1937

Grace Allen, whom we had known in America, now married and living in London, was with the Oxford University Press. They were doing a new edition of W. W. Tarn's *The Treasure of the Isle of Mist*, and they wanted Bill to do pictures for it. Phyllis, our delightful and dependable daily, would take care of Bara and the flat. We would have three whole weeks Skye-larking!

Bill was making a name for himself. His picture of Iffigensee, the lake near the Wildhorn hut, had won first prize in a photographic exhibition; and his George V picture had been widely seen. Of the comments he was receiving, the one that pleased him most was that "William McGreal, relying on the richness of black and white, can do more than many who depend on color." Bertha Miller, writing from Boston, was glad that the Tarn book was to come back after being out of print for some years. She told us what Anne Carroll Moore had to say about it: "There is a windswept fantasy of youth and autumn which I always reread in September. When I begin to find books of the year lacking in strength of background, in appeal to the imagination, in skill in the choice of words, I turn to *The Treasure of the Isle of Mist*."

Grace warned us that she could give us no clear directions, for when the distinguished scholar wrote *The Treasure* as a fairy tale for his daughter, he had purposefully disguised place-names. We would have to go in the spirit of detectives, tracking down every clue and hoping to come upon those that would lead us rightly. I read the book aloud to Bill, and he made a list of places in the text that called for illustration—the Atlantic half asleep, the great West cave, the big house, the fairy bridge, a pale dawn coming up out of the sea, the jagged gray range of the Cuchullins, and many more. We would be off with an Ordnance Survey Map, plenty of film, stout shoes, clothes that would take any weather and a copy of Samuel Johnson's *A Journey to the Western Islands of Scotland*.

August, 1937

We left London in the evening of an extremely hot day, with a third-class compartment all to ourselves. The wonder of visiting a land new to us and yet so near beggared sleep. The first glimpse from the window the next morning was of wild moors, craggy mountains, dark rivers, tiny burns, and purple patches of heather. The country grew more dramatic as we approached the fishing town of Mallaig, where we took the boat to Skye. Rain came on, but it did not hide the dim majestic line of the Coolins (properly spelled Cuchullins, but I'm spelling it the way the people pronounce it) nor the green lushness of the fields.

It was late afternoon when we reached Portree, a protected harbor and a gray stone village with all its life at that moment centering at the quay. There were lean-faced lads in kilts, bright-cheeked girls, bearded men, women hugging black shawls about their shoulders, and dogs. Broad Scots was in the air, and the skirl of bagpipes to set my blood racing. The sun was shining, but clouds thick and black gathered, and rain fell again, veiling the distant mountains. When next the sun appeared, it was with a rainbow thrown from the thatch of a small cottage to a boat in the harbor.

The weather that first afternoon gave us a hint of what to expect, and I realized what Dr. Johnson meant when he said those islands were often "incommoded by very frequent rains." Such swift changes and shifts of wind created cloud formations that thrilled Bill. Using his light meter and different lenses and filters, he could make sunlight look like moonshine and get whatever effects he wanted.

Our lodgings overlooked the harbor, and the welcome was typical. "If you wait a wee moment, I'll have tea for you."

We went to our room and, while I was unpacking, Bill discovered, "the necessary." He came back to tell me of the sign that hung near—BATHS BY ARRANGEMENT. LIGHTS OUT AT 11 P.M.

Early the next morning we were off on our search. We walked along the harbor, scrambled up the steep hillside to Fingal's Seat, sheltered under a rock with a huddle of sheep during a bout of rain, tramped across a moor with the sun turning it into a purple sea. Skye is a land of eerie enchantment, of wild, weird beauty. Every rock seems to imprison legend, everyone seems to believe in the "wee folk," and every other person has the second sight. It is like no other place in the world, I am sure—bleak and barren, often shrouded with mist. When the sun shines, dazzling colors are revealed, and there is a splendor to the blue sky with its magnificent cloud formations. "It fairs up quickly," we were told, and so we discovered.

Looking always for the clue that would lead us to the site of *The Treasure*, we went by bus to the northern end of the island. We stopped at a small building that said Home Industries, and Bill bought me a Skye-blue scarf. Duntulm Castle was a ruin, but near it was a corrugated tin shack with a sign "Ian Stewart, Tailor." "And that's where I'd like to have a suit made," Bill said. We saw cattle with curved horns and shaggy hair, and we passed many flocks of sheep, three hundred in one flock, our driver said. He stopped the bus until they had gone by, the dogs alert and conscientious, the shepherds leisurely.

Another day we went in a southerly direction. At Sligachan we left the bus and took the path to Glen Brittle. It was rocky, uphill, with the jagged Coolins piercing the sky behind us. Bill took many pictures, knowing they might be useful sometime. A fine mist was in the air, scarcely to be felt until the wind blew it against our faces. At the top of the pass, the view down the Glen was of a great bare scooped-out hollow, with a river winding its way to the sea. It was stark and lonely; we seemed the only evidence of life until three deer came cautiously over a ledge near where we stood. We looked at each other. They were the first to move, but not in flight, simply because it was time to go.

We felt sure now that what we were seeking must be on the west coast. Before leaving Portree we wanted to call on Old Donal, who, we had heard, had the second sight. Grace had warned us not to say anything about the purpose of our visit to anyone, lest word get back to Mr. Tarn.

"You'll find Donal's shieling just a wee walk up the Struan Road," our landlady said.

I wondered just how far "wee" was, for I was learning about understatement. Only the night before I had been describing something to one of our fellow lodgers and was met with the comment: "Would you not think you might be a bit overrating?" And I was learning about time-talking. More than once I had asked a question and thought I had not been heard, for nothing seemed to happen; but the answer came, in time, and always in the soft voice of the Gael, which was music to my ears.

The sun was strong and warm, the breeze full, and most of the morning gone, when we saw the shieling we knew must be Old

Donal's. He was in a nearby bog, tossing peat.

"Are you Donal?" Bill asked.

"There's more than one Donal hereabouts. Which one are you seeking?"

"The one who has the second sight."

"Ah, well," and there was a smile on his face, "there are those who say I have the gift." So he heaved the sack of peat to his shoulder and led us to the shieling, telling us of it the while.

He was the sixth generation to live there. Twelve children had been born to his mother, all but two living to be eighty, and he was near that himself. We had to stoop to enter the dwelling. Inside, there were two rooms—one where the cow lived, accompanied by a duck and her family of ducklings and some chickens. In the other room, three cats sat by a peat fire, the smoke finding its way up and out through an opening in the thatch roof. The sun streamed through a small window in a long beam, blue with the peat reek. There was a bench or two, a bed, and some indications of housekeeping, but the piece of importance was the large teapot resting in the warm ash on the edge of the fire.

Donal asked us to sit down while he got tea, adding more leaves to the pot and water from the kettle. Then he found three mugs and poured out the blackest, strongest tea I had ever seen, or tasted. He needed to see the leaves in our cups if we would have him tell us what was ahead, so drink it all we must.

"Turn your cups slowly now, to the north, to the south, to the east, to the west," he said, "all the while making a wish."

It was a ritual that sent me back to the days at Hillhurst when Andy read the teacups.

Donal held my cup to his eye as if it were a spyglass, then he held Bill's. "There's not much difference for the two of you," he said, "and your fortune lies in the west, there's no doubt about that." He kept studying the cups with their leaves entangled at the bottom of each one. "It's good things that I see—a wee worry now and then, a removal. Here's a bargain to be closed, and some money to be made, and the worries will be over."

"When will all this happen?" I asked.

A smile twisted his face mysteriously. "Whoever talks of time when there's fortune ahead?"

Bill wanted to take Donal's picture before we left, and he agreed. "But wait till I get a wee duck in my hands." So Donal went back to his shieling and returned with a small duck cupped tenderly in his hands.

Over the path to the road we went, through heather and bracken. The long light of the afternoon deepened around us. The distant Coolins looked friendly. Portree shone like a jewel in a lapis and emerald setting.

The next morning we left for the west in a bus that rattled over as lonely a stretch of moor as we had yet seen. The few crofts and shielings were set wide apart as if nothing would induce their owners to leave their holdings for the compactness of a village. They looked self-sufficient. A line of Johnson's explained it: "The high hills which by hindering the eye from ranging forced the mind to find entertainment for itself."

Dunvegan, our immediate destination, was a small gray village stretched along a loch where the Atlantic came in rolling and crashing, only a few shades darker than the brooding clouds. We found a comfortable lodging with a peat fire to sit by while tea was in the making. What a tea—herrings, several kinds of bread, the best being scones and "girdle cakes," which we did justice to! We went to bed by candlelight. Rain pattered on the slate roof and wind shook the windows as if it wanted to come in. We read and studied the map, preparing ourselves for exploration.

Weather, no matter what it did, did not keep us from adventuring, but it did keep Bill from taking pictures, and we were glad to be able to sit by a fire at night and give our clothes a chance to dry out for the next day. We would set out early, whether the day was tristful or not, fortified by a breakfast of porridge with great clots of cream. Often, on a moor path, rabbits darted before us, and once a wren seemed to go ahead as if leading us. Seeing smoke rising from a vale, we were sure there was a village, but the smoke was spray "from waterfalls shooting upwards," just as the book had expressed it. A Royal Mail van might pass us on the road, or a farmer on horseback, and often a shepherd with his flock. We asked each one for a place known as "the big house." A man breaking stones gave us a lead that sent us down to the shore of Loch Varkasaig where we met a toothless crone milking her three black cows. She knew what we were talking about.

"When the mist clears off, you'll see it on yon far shore, but it's not a house, it's an inn. If the folks there take a liking to you, they may put you up."

That afternoon the wind shifted and the sun came out with its magical effect. The loch glistened. The countryside came alive with color. Distantly we saw the outline of a big house standing high above the loch. We had a few miles to go to get back to our lodging, but a glowing sunset went with us and there was tea and a warm fire to cheer us. Bill made arrangements by phone and that night, before we went to bed, we looked out on a sky full of stars. The next day would see us at the "big house" where Fiona and her father had once lived.

"It's faired up for certain," we were assured as we left in the morning. The wind was strong from the north. The sun rode high in a cloudless sky. The moor danced with color. There was no question in my mind then but that Skye was the most beautiful place in the world.

When we reached Orbost, we knew that it was the end of our search—everything about the house and the surroundings tied with descriptions in the book. They evidently did take a liking to us, for there was a room "but for two nights only." That was all the time remaining to us, in any case.

"It's a pet day," the man at the desk said, "and tomorrow may be likewise. Make the most of it before the wind backs again."

Bill wanted the far shots first, because of the clarity of the light, so we climbed Heleval, mounting slowly through bracken and heather, crossing many burns and one with a fairy bridge. It was slow going, and the last bit was so steep with rock and scree that we could make it only on all fours, but once at the top—what a view! All of Skye seemed spread below us, its great wings flung far out to sea. There were the Outer Hebrides, Lewis and Harris, perhaps even tiny St. Kilda lying against the horizon. Near were moors and villages and rocky coast with the blue Atlantic sparkling in the sunshine. Bill took pictures and pictures, and finally, when we retraced our downward way, I thought the camera must be shouting with the load of beauty it carried. Sunset drowned the distant Coolins in a plum-colored glow.

The next day Bill concentrated on scenes along the loch. The wind had shifted and clouds were massing, so he had what he longed to get into pictures. We rented a boat and went in search of the cave that figured so in the book. There were several caves on the Atlantic side of a small island, and Bill insisted on rowing in one so he could get a picture looking out of the cave entrance.

"Bill, remember what it said in the book. There may be no exit except to come out on the other side of time," I reminded him.

"And wouldn't that be a wee bit of an adventure," he replied.

So I rowed while he positioned his camera. It was dark inside the cave, the walls were dripping, the water, green and clear, felt like ice. I was relieved when we got back into the sunshine, rowing toward a small strip of white sand. Nothing would do for either of us but that we beach the boat and have a quick swim. The water was too cold to be endured for long, but it was invigorating.

"I think I've got all I need," Bill said as we looked at the stars that night and drank in the northern air.

When we packed our few belongings—Bill's films, my notes, and the old worn copy of *The Treasure*—I felt like Fiona when she is told that she has found the treasure: ". . .the spirit of the island which you love. . . . You can walk now through the crowded city and never know it, for the wind from the heather will be about you where you go; you can stand in the tumult of men and never hear them, for round you will be the silence of your own sea. That is the treasure of the Isle of Mist; the island has given you of its soul."

September, 1937

It was not until we were back in London and the films were developed that we were sure—but, oh, were we sure! Bill went through the pictures very carefully and submitted to Oxford only the best, the absolute best. And Oxford was delighted. When the great W. W. Tarn (whom we never met) was shown them, his comment was a classic of understatement; but the check Bill received was not.

November, 1937

I am at my desk. With the stack of handwritten pages before me, I am as happy as Bill is with his camera. This is the time I like best—when the story is all there and I can go through it slowly, carefully, sure of the words I have used or, if uncertain, sure there can be a better one. And then there's the final phase of typing. With it, I'll endeavor to get as shapely a typescript as ever was placed on a publisher's desk. The title came as part of the whole, *High Holiday.* How could it be anything else? Having satisfied myself that it is the best I can do, I read it to Bill.

"I knew you would do it," he said.

1938

Shadow of War

January, 1938

It was just ten years ago I wrote in my journal that I was serving an apprenticeship, like a craftsman of old, working to gain necessary skills. Now, with *High Holiday* finished, I feel that I have fulfilled my apprenticeship.

March 11, 1938

What a day! I walk out of the office of A. and C. Black with a check and a contract in my pocket, and Hitler walks into Austria. The papers have huge headlines, and the world begins to wonder what the consequences will be. So the ordinary events of our lives go on, but against a darkening curtain.

Familiar with the type of books for young people that the Black firm published, I had sent *High Holiday* to them a few weeks before, never expecting to have a telephone call asking me to come in and talk with Mr. Archie Black. It was a pleasant conversation. He liked the book. Would I accept an outright offer of twenty-five pounds and publication within the year? Would I! It was my opening door. Even before I signed the contract, he said, "With your next book you will be on a royalty basis." Then he asked me if I would like to suggest an artist to do the jacket. "It must be something with the feeling of Switzerland and children, as there will be no illustrations in the book." I could think of no one better than Nora Unwin, a friend I had met recently, a graduate of the Royal College of Art. Mr. Black said he would get in touch with her.

When I told Bill about the arrangement I had come to with Mr. Black, he approved. "You may not like figures, but you have a sound sense of business." Somewhere, in the faraway past, my father had said similar words to me.

Bill is busy with another commission from Oxford, and I have my work on George MacDonald almost complete—the selection of his poems and a story of his life. My frequent teatime visits with his daughter, Lady Troup, have helped me, and through her I have drawn close to her father's vigorous mind, his wit, and his tender-

Climbing over a stone wall

in Cornwall

ness. The publisher to whom I would like to offer the book is W. Heffer and Sons in Cambridge. I write and ask for an appointment to see someone in the firm. A prompt reply gives me a date in less than a week!

March, 1938

We take off for a day in Cambridge. Bill has his camera for company and I have the box with my typescript. I even have a title, *Gathered Grace*. The words are from a passage in *Donal Grant:* "The chosen agonize after the light; stretch out their hands to God; stir up themselves to lay hold upon God! These are they who gather grace, as the mountain-tops the snow, to send down rivers of waters to their fellows."

Spring was in the world. The air was sweet, and the lovely lawns —the "Backs" through which the river Cam flows—were gay with daffodils. We agreed to meet for luncheon at the Bull in Trumpington Street, and I walked on to my appointment, past buildings mellowed by time while I was mellowed by sunshine. Presenting myself at the office, I told Mr. Heffer what I had done and placed the box on his desk, then I added that I hoped he would want to illustrate it with wood engravings by Nora Unwin. He looked at my pages casually, murmured something about "always having had a feeling for that old Scot," and asked if I would come back in the afternoon at three o'clock.

Bill and I had luncheon; then, with time to spare, we hired a boat and went rowing on the Cam between those incredibly green lawns and banks of flowers. Bill's camera was busy, and so was my mind, as I thought about *Gathered Grace* and its possible future.

When I went back to Mr. Heffer's office, he smiled and said, "We have decided to publish this. I will draw up a contract for you and write to Miss Unwin about the illustrations."

April, 1938

Being in the country always set us talking about when we would live in the country. Now, more and more, we thought about the dream we had been nurturing ever since we had tramped in the highlands of the Hudson. But where was that little farm to be? Bill decided to explore the possibilities in southern England while I went to Zurich to visit Father and Mother, who are staying there. Other dreams were coming true, why should not this one. Much as we loved London, we are not really city people, our tastes are too simple, our lives too quiet. Why not do now what we had been talking about—find a little farm, perhaps run a small guesthouse along with it, to draw our friends.

Meantime, it was Switzerland for me. Early in the morning, peering from the window of the train, I saw fields carpeted with flowers, dotted with mouse-colored cows, chalets with great stacks of wood, tidy villages. I could almost smell the air, rich with the manure that was being spread on some of the fields. I got to the Baur au Lac in time to join Mother and Father for breakfast on their balcony: croissants, black cherry jam, and what coffee! This was the day they "Burn the Bogg," and all Zurich was gay with festival.

By noon the streets had filled with people. Children in native dress, processions of Guilds in costume, each with its band, floats of flowers, and all preceded the Bogg, like a huge snowman complete with top hat, pipe, and besom, who was carried to his funeral pyre. They marched up and down the Bahnhofstrasse, then to the square near the lake. The Bogg was placed at the top of the pyre, the wood was set alight, flames licked high, the bells in the Gross Munster tolled, the bands played, and, when the flames touched the Bogg, rockets hidden within him went off. Soon he was all on fire and the crowd shouted "Bravo!" His besom, his pipe, his hat fell forward, and the Bogg himself soon went down to ash. And that was the end of winter!

Bill's letters from the farm where he was staying told of walks taken in buttercup fields, of tea in the garden with four dogs gamboling about him, of air filled with the smell of hawthorne and barnyard, of songs of birds and droning of bees swarming in the eaves of the old house. "Peace fills me as I sit here in the garden quietly purring, and a psalm of gratitude sings in me every morning when the sun comes into my room and announces another day. . . . I have long, practical talks with these people. They feel that if we started small—say twenty-five chickens and a cow or two, with a man to help with the milking, and a good size vegetable garden from which we could sell the surplus—we could make a go of it. With five pounds a week in cash coming in, we would be rich indeed. Then, as we got going, we could specialize in some particular field—sheep, perhaps, or honey. Tomorrow I am going out with a farm agent to see what is available. Yesterday I was helping John build his new bull pen, and he told me of his hopes and plans. I realized what every nail he drove meant to him. I am excited about *our* farm, and the enthusiasm I feel is not impetuous, but patient and deep-rooted."

I talked with Father and he shook his head.

"Don't you realize what is happening in the world? Don't you see the war clouds that are gathering?"

"Perhaps it won't happen."

"Your mother and I wish you would begin to think seriously about returning to America."

May, 1938

Before leaving Zurich, I had time for one climb, not a big mountain, but one big enough to give me the experience of walking backward in the year. Spring with its early flowers I left by the lake. In a few hundred feet the path was edged with snow and there were pussy willows, then tiny white crocuses looking like thimbles in the sod. The lake below me was startlingly blue, the distant mountains white walls reflecting the sun. The only sounds were the dull splits and crashes of avalanches far away. On my way down, the sight of an occasional blue gentian caught my eye, peering out from the rocks as if to test the coming warmth. Back at the lake, I was in spring again. I wondered when I reread my notes, if someday I would feel that I was walking backward in my life.

I told Bill about my talk with Father, and he agreed that we must think seriously, but so much was happening now.

July, 1938

Our holiday was determined by a letter from Bertha Miller of *The Horn Book*. She had long thought that there should be a new edition of the Tregarthen legends of North Cornwall, books published at the turn of the century and made well known by the fact that Queen Mary read them aloud to her children. Could we manage a few days in Cornwall to see what we could find?

"Sleuthing again," Bill said, "but think of the pictures!"

The flat and Bara were left in Phyllis' care, and Nora agreed to come in every afternoon, when Phyllis would have tea for her. It was a day-long train journey through summer-sweet English country to the town of Padstow on the Camel River. There was just enough light when we arrived for Bill to see the picture possibilities—a small quaint town on the edge of Bodmin Moor, a wide sweep of river and glistening sands with the tide out, great towering cliffs where the river emptied into the Atlantic. Beyond our range of sight, but within walking reach, was Tintagel and the country rich in Arthurian lore.

We began our search the next morning, but no one at the inn or the post office remembered anyone of the name we were seeking. Then someone recalled that Enys Tregarthen was Nellie

Sloggett, "the little cripple." We found her stone in the church-yard: *"Nell Age 72 Died 1923,"* and we found our way down Dinas Lane to the house where she had lived and been cared for by her cousin, Maude Rawle. That first tea with Miss Rawle was not the last, but it was memorable, with saffron buns, rolls split and covered with clotted cream, and pasties. She would not tell us what was in them, for she said it was well known that the Devil would not come into Cornwall for fear of being put into a pie. During the days that followed she answered our many questions, told us about her cousin, produced the books we were seeking and, as well, a small trunk filled with unpublished manuscripts, which she insisted upon giving us. Many hours I spent alone with Miss Rawle while Bill roamed with his camera.

Cornwall, the search for Enys Tregarthen, the friendship with Miss Rawle, had given us treasure beyond telling. When we left her, the box of manuscripts carried carefully by Bill, we tried to thank her.

"You're welcome," she said. "I don't need them."

But something more was to crown our Cornish stay. When we got back to the inn, there was a package that had come in the afternoon post. It was from A. and C. Black, my copy of *High Holiday.* I showed Bill the dedication: *"To William—Because we have climbed mountains together."*

Nothing would do but that I start reading it aloud to Bill that night, while a rain-laden wind swept in from the sea and a fire of coals whispered warmth.

"It's like being at Heimeli again," Bill said.

August, 1938

Phyllis might smile when we returned and Bara might wag his tail gleefully, but London was different—rumors of war, headlines in the papers, trenches being dug in Hyde Park for shelters, gas masks being issued, and leaves starting to fall because the summer had been dry and hot.

September, 1938

Gathered Grace commenced its journey into the world. It was a handsome book, rich because of MacDonald, beautiful with Nora's engravings. I took a copy to Lady Troup. We said nothing about the world, for at this moment the book was her world and mine; but the strain of the past weeks had been hard on everyone, and there were tears in her eyes when she kissed me good-by.

Bland, warm, and beautiful was the late September day as I walked back to Edwardes Square; it seemed to belie all else that was going on in the world. Leaves were still falling, and the smoke from many burning piles hung in the air, scenting it. I could not escape the headlines as I walked along Kensington High Street. They screamed and newsmen called: What will the Prime Minister come back with this time? He had gone again to Munich to meet with Hitler, hoping to achieve peace. I felt as if I were walking in a dream, so terrible it all was. The end of the world might be at hand or, if the torch of the spirit was raised a little higher, a little longer, it might mark the beginning of a new world. The tension that had been mounting for the past year was so great. How much longer could it go on without something snapping?

When Bill and I got home from the theater there were crowds poring over newspapers, buses racing. It seemed like a mad world. The midnight news said that unless a miracle happened before morning the tide of events would flow only one way. By 4 A.M. the miracle had happened. Neville Chamberlain had returned, with his umbrella and one more concession.

September 30, 1938

Peace is assured, not only here but everywhere, not only for this day but for all time. That is what I say and Bill shakes his head. Two men have met each other in conference. Today is the hinge on which the progress of the world can turn. The gas masks, the trenches in Hyde Park, the sandbags, the big antiaircraft guns erected so hastily have all become scenery in a play, soon to be shifted. We can look on them with eyes of interest instead of horror. Armageddon came near, but it did not engulf us.

The sun is streaming through the windows. I find I can smile again. Phyllis sings at her work and brings flowers "because you have been so kind to me this week." In my heart—a deepening desire to dedicate myself to peace. I can and will do all possible through my work—instantly and forever—to make sure that where I am there is peace.

That night, after Phyllis had left and we were sitting by the fire with our coffee, Bill started to talk about "our farm."

"Where, Bill? In Kent?"

"No, in New England."

I must have looked surprised.

"If there is war," Bill went on quietly, "and we stay here with England through her agony, we will never go home. Having endured, we would feel we should stay to help rebuild."

"But peace has just been assured. Why do you say 'if'?"

He shook his head. "It is not peace, it is time that has been given. We won't go soon, for we both have commitments to fill, but by next summer we should be making other plans. Our lease will be up then, you will have finished the book Mr. Black wants, and I will have had time to complete my work for Oxford."

October, 1938

Perhaps it was the release from the tension of the days, but Bill had a dark time—the room with curtains drawn, the quiet as nearly as it could be achieved, the pain that nothing could lessen. We had time to talk, much time, after the intensity of the first few days, and I was more and more willing to think of a sometime future in our own country. I was even beginning to feel a little pull of the heart. Perhaps I was seeing with Bill's eyes.

So long as we lived in England, we would be living half a life, for we are Americans. England mellowed us, tempered us, disciplined us. It was like a sheltering garden where the small plants of our lives put down their roots; now we were about ready to be transplanted. The winds might blow stronger in America, the light might be sharper, the heat and cold more intense, but we would return with what England had shown us we could do and were doing, with our joint and separate talents. We would find a place in the country, have that little farm, and carry on with our work. We started to make a list of what we wanted to find.

"You must go to America and make a quick survey," Bill said when the dark time passed and he was himself again.

With that ahead, we made our plans.

November, 1938

I was setting out like Columbus to discover America, but unlike Columbus, I knew it was there. I wanted to discover the answer to a big question looming before us. Could we find the way, not the place yet, but the feeling of a life that we could fit into with what we had and had not? As the S.S. *Normandie* glided on over smooth seas through a moon-full night, I wondered.

Five days later I came on deck at 9 A.M. and cried inwardly with joy—sunshine and a glittering sea dotted with little boats, and the big ship approaching harbor in a slow, majestic way! The city was cloaked in a pearly haze; tugs and ferries were going about their business; and there was Liberty, holding her torch high. It was a thrill to see her, and I felt a surge of loyalty rise up in me. This is my land! The lofty buildings told me to look up as if to be ready to face and accept a challenge. We docked at noon and I was soon through the customs, into a bevy of friends and a world as new and different as any Columbus came upon.

Loyola said, "You've grown up."

Eunice said everything in her embrace.

Three days in New York and how could I ever sort out the swift impressions to take back to Bill! There were so many, they came so quickly and they were so conflicting. Shabbiness in many of the side streets, grandeur along Fifth Avenue, and how could people possibly need or want the things the shops were filled with! Unbelievable comfort in a hotel room, food superb, from pancakes at Child's to the best at Longchamps. People were well-dressed and moved with a sort of precision. But the noise, the restlessness, and the haste! Everything was bigger and better, but was there happiness? I looked at the faces of the people I passed in the street and often there was a harried expression, almost a hunted one. What were they pursuing or being pursued by, and why were they all in such a hurry? Everyone talked, but did anyone listen? There was such bitterness against Roosevelt for what he had done, and such bitterness against England for what she had not done.

People quoted authorities: "Dorothy Thompson says. . ." "Walter Lippmann says. . ." And I cried inwardly, "But what do you say?" The depression had left its mark, evident in despair. I heard of people who had "lost everything" and one day I was introduced to a woman who "has nothing," but her clothes, her manner, and the car she drove said otherwise. Much of the conversation I was involved in or overheard had to do with politics, graft, drink, corruption, disease, and underlying it was rebellion against the present administration. "What we need is a leader" came like a theme song. Germany was saying that and got a Hitler. Perhaps it was not a leader so much as a unifying element that was needed. Independence made this country, but in a bus I was shocked when the driver said, "Move away from the door, please," and the passenger replied, "I will not; I'll stay where I am."

The Ellises, old friends with whom we had kept in touch, took a day off to show me the nearby country. I was amazed at the speed with which we left the city—the motor parkways so safe, swift, unobstructed where the stream of cars moved like a metallic river. There were frequent signs saying that the speed limit was 40 mph, and I murmured once to Charles, "Aren't you going seventy?"

"Oh, nobody pays any attention to those signs," he answered cheerfully.

From the backseat Louise spoke softly, "We've forgotten how to be a law-abiding people."

Once we were off the parkway and onto a lesser road, the difference stunned me—signs, advertising, gas stations, diners, dance places, stores, all adding up to shabby confusion. But we left that road for one that passed through a succession of charming villages where a green was graced by tall trees and bordered by gracious houses. Charles drew up to an unprepossessing little inn, where we stopped for luncheon. The food was delicious, everything was simple, clean, attractive, and served with an engaging friendliness.

After luncheon we strolled around the village green. Charles pointed to a small sign, REAL ESTATE, and suggested that we see what might be available. "Just in case you decide to settle here."

We went in. It was a delightful office and the owner was all smiles at the sight of a prospect. I saw a sign that irked me—Gentile neighborhood.

"What does that mean?" I asked.

He looked me over closely, then said with the kind of smile that comes only from the lips, "Just what it says. Coming from New York, as I see you are, you will appreciate that kind of neighborhood."

It was hard for me to turn slowly enough to leave that office.

Charles and Louise followed me out. "What's the matter, don't you feel well?"

"I'm not looking at any houses here," and I tried to explain. "Don't you know what Hitler is doing in Germany? We're not much better here if we have notices like that."

The villages were lovely with their greens, their stately houses and steepled churches, their public libraries and schools. The air was fresh and the people moved with quieter pace and more serene expressions. This was the America I was seeking, the America to which I belonged and yet there was prejudice here, where all races and peoples are supposed to merge as they will in the Kingdom of Heaven. I was haunted by a question: Has this land a soul, or has it sold its soul to the automobile, to self-gratification, to "progress"?

Always there is another side. I was aware of warmth, spontaneity, and a politeness that charmed me: a perfect stranger would hold a door open for me; in an elevator men with hats on whipped them off when a woman entered, and squeezed themselves together to let her out first. Introduced to new people I felt that I was instantly embraced, taken into their lives; in England it took so long to develop a friendship, but once it happened it was forever.

The efficiency bewildered me. One day in New York and I accomplished what would have taken three in London; even to the way books arrived at the New York Public Library desk almost before my request had gone through. At the British Museum I could settle down and read the *Daily Telegraph* before the books I asked for came to my cubicle. And I was fascinated by the way people championed causes almost before they found out whether they were worth championing.

Before I left for Boston I had dinner with Loyola Sanford. She was unhurried, ready to listen. She knew about *High Holiday.* She knew that once started I would continue. "But life moves so fast here," I said. "Can I ever fit into a world of writing?"

"A book must be good to sell, first to a publisher, then to the public, because a book is a business proposition."

I told her that I was uneasy at the thought of writing for a market that demanded so much realism.

"With many people success must be instant or not at all." She smiled in the way that ten years ago had given me confidence. "You are willing to wait and keep on working. You'll survive, and on your own terms."

Boston was different from New York—the people, the pace—and I began to have a distinct feeling of belonging. I had already had several meetings with editors, generally over luncheon or tea. The sense of hurry had abated. My first appointment was with Bertha Miller, editor of *The Horn Book*. She was delighted at the report I brought her of the Tregarthen legends. When I described Bill's pictures and how they set the scenes, she clapped her hands together. She was gentle and charming, a small person with a quavery voice, but what wisdom! She had the joy of a child in little things, and she made me feel that I could accomplish what I set heart and hand to. She told me of some people to see in New York and said she would write letters to them ahead of my next visit.

"Helen Ferris at Stokes, May Massee at Viking, they are great names, but don't feel intimidated. Your work can stand." She gave me many helpful leads and said there would be much I could do for *The Horn Book* "when you and your husband come back to stay."

Maude Meagher, editor of *World Youth,* was interested in some of my ideas, as was Barbara Nolen of *Story Parade.* Very meaningful was the time spent with Margaret Williamson, Ethel C. Ince, and Roscoe Drummond of the *Christian Science Monitor.* The paper had been carrying a good deal of my work, and they could use more—essays with Bill's pictures for the Home Forum page, the Kilts stories, book reviews, and interviews for the magazine section. I had several long talks with Miss Williamson and I savored every word. She was a large, calm person with an almost impassive face. She gave me the feeling of having quiet command of her thoughts and her life. She put me in mind of Miss Russell, my long-ago mentor, for she was teaching me so much. I told her that when a piece of mine was published on her page, I compared it with the copy I had sent her.

"And you found some changes?"

"Yes, a word here, a mark of punctuation there, even a reconstruction of a sentence. Always you have improved me."

"Then you have not minded, have not felt I took liberties?"

"On the contrary. You're an editor, you know."

"Some people don't trust an editor."

What was I to say except that I'm not that kind of person?

The Atlantic Ocean seemed to be shrinking. Soon I could see that it might not exist at all, as the work opening up for me could be better done here.

Ann, friend from the year at Oaksmere, suggested a day in the country. We left Boston easily and drove through such storied places as Lexington and Concord, then Groton, and into southern New Hampshire. The country was beautiful in its late-fall dress. The fields were brown as a deer's coat, the woods gray, the line of hills before us deeply blue. The villages we went through were neat and self-respecting. It was warm enough for a picnic, so we left the car and walked through a woods in brilliant sunshine, leaves crackling underfoot, wind surging in the treetops. We found a brook racing over stones, and it seemed part of the vigor of the day. Somehow there was a newness, a freshness, a sense of possibility over everything. I felt myself becoming a part of it. To the west, one mountain was like a pyramid against the sky. No other mountain is like that. I did not ask Ann what its name was. I knew. Bill and I had climbed Monadnock and looked from its height on a fine countryside.

Thanksgiving, 1938

Snow had been falling softly all day and the countryside was beautiful in its mantle of white. The air was sharp and deliciously cold, and I was aware of the tremendous vitality all around me. The house at Hillhurst Farm had always been expandable and now it had need to be more so than ever. The assemblage of family at dinner was tremendous. The marrieds had children, and they were all there. Father carved a big roast turkey at his end of the table and Mother a boiled turkey with oyster dressing at her end. So easily I seemed to slip back into my old groove. I listened to the talk, and it was of politics for that was a major concern, the movies, the radio, sports, rackets, and wages—up to five dollars an hour, and where will it end—"Working people are never satisfied." The older generation saw a sort of demoralizing madness in all that was happening; my generation, with Bob as a spokesman, saw an inevitability and felt that good would eventually shape from it. They asked me what I thought. Whatever I said, it was tinged with England, and no one is happy about England. After dinner, the younger ones went out to play in the snow and that gave more opportunity for talk in the living room by a blazing fire.

Bob, always my comfort, spoke of the books, Bill's and mine, and said, "Building a literary reputation must be easier in England."

"Why?"

"You've got to be sensational here, and you'll never be that."

Father said, "In many ways you're better off in England, but I'd like to see you back here."

December, 1938

I had much to do with my remaining two days in New York, but I took my time walking slowly up Fifth Avenue and strolling into the shops with their multitude of lovely things. So much was bright and gay, as if to catch the eye and the moment rather than meet a need. I did go into Sulka's and found a handsome tie for Bill.

Appointments following on Mrs. Miller's letters filled my day. A publisher for the Cornish legends was first on my list, then to find someone interested in *Gathered Grace*. At the New York Public Library, Anne Carroll Moore was positively excited about the legends and felt that once they were in print they would become an important part of folklore. She made me feel that I was bearing precious jewels, but when I talked with her about *Gathered Grace*, her attitude was different; she had always had a frank dislike for Mac-Donald. So I called on Helen Ferris at Stokes to tell her about the Tregarthen tales. Her interest was real, real enough for her to say that she would make an offer as soon as they came to her desk; then I told her about the photographs that set the scenes, and she lost interest. No photographs, they distract. I said no more. To me the whole is greater than its parts and the pictures that linked the Cornish land with the words were an important part of the book.

I made a courtesy call at Oxford University Press, because Grace

Hogarth, with Oxford in London, wanted me to establish a relationship with the New York office, and I talked with Harper's about an American edition of the MacDonald. Perhaps they were just being polite, but they appeared interested. Holiday House was next, but it didn't take me long to realize that not one of the three editors I talked with would feel that anything I might do "would be for them." My last call was at Viking with May Massee. What a noble person she was and what authority she had! But I doubted that I could ever please her. In a curious way I was retracing my steps of ten years ago, and, just as I felt then, I felt as surely now that I would carry my own banner high, no matter who said what.

New York was filled with contradictions—so beautiful, so cruel; so rich, so poor; so filled with possibility, so crushing. A taxi driver that morning couldn't be kind enough. He told me he was always on the lookout for people who needed help. "Like you, when you flagged me down. I've got a bundle of joy at home and I want her to be proud of her daddy when she grows up." Then he went on with more of his life story, and I wished that I could have gone farther with him. I could imagine myself writing about him. I didn't have a chance to tell him, he talked so fast and so much, that the reason I hailed him was because I had asked directions from three people: the first person didn't speak English and merely shrugged his shoulders, the second sent me in the wrong direction, and the third growled such a gruff answer that I trembled for moments afterward. But he made up for all of them.

That last night I had dinner with Mildred and Peter, both so sane and sensible, and their home was all a home should be—a haven of peace and beauty. It was late when they took me to the ship, and as we taxied through the quiet streets there was a white moon in a blue-velvet sky playing hide-and-seek with us between the tall buildings. We said good-by at the dock. Once aboard I stood by the rail a long time until I felt the ship begin to move. When I went down to my cabin it was filled with fragrance from a bowl of flowers, violets and lily of the valley and mignonette.

"They came by cable, madame," the steward said.

So much has been confusing these past weeks, but if there is one thing of which I am sure, it is love.

1939

Climbing Higher

London seems very gray and damp. Even with the modicum of central heating that we have at Edwardes Square I have not felt warm, really warm, since I returned. On threatening days, the weather forecast often says that "a depression is bearing down from Iceland." But it is not entirely from that quarter. The trenches are covered over in the parks; the gas masks have been put away in drawers. People are more reserved than ever. A smile seemed so simple in America, whether you knew a person or not; but not so here, not now. Few use the word, but all know what is impending: war. The tension of last September has returned, and it is sharper. A retort comes more easily than a compliment in conversation. How long can people live under this somber, brooding cloud? How long can people endure uncertainty?

And yet, with us in any case, there was reason for satisfaction. We looked at the tiny portion of the bookcase that held our own books: Bill's two picture books from Warne, *The Frog, the Penny, and the Big Black Tree* and *Dennis the Donkey,* and at the two photographic books he has done for Oxford, *First Friends* and *First Animal Friends,* and the beautiful *Treasure of the Isle of Mist;* beside them stand *High Holiday* and *Gathered Grace.*

The reviews that had been coming to Oxford on the picture books were rewarding, and from sources like *Time and Tide,* the *New Statesman,* the *Observer,* the *Manchester Guardian.* All along I had known that Bill, in his pictures, had an eye for the story, and with that he had caught the wonder of children in the things of their world. About these first books for babies, reviewers said they "tell their own stories in photographs that are direct, simple, uncluttered with distracting detail. . .an original departure from the conventional. . .done by a skillful photographer with artistry and humor but with none of the tricks of modern photography. . .clean, polished, unpretentious with a simplicity that is a mark of high technical dexterity."

Those were words to savor!

*Finding their way
in Iceland*

We knew where the next adventure would take us: Iceland! Nora had just returned from a visit there with her cousin who was married to an Icelander. She was ecstatic about the country—the people, the history, and the possibilities for pictures. Her sketchbooks were full, and when she told Bill about the cloud formations that build up and sweep down low in an embrace of the land, he was ready to get film and leave the next day. I saw Iceland as the setting for the further adventures of Michael and Meredith Lamb. The title had already proclaimed itself—*Climbing Higher.*

April, 1939

Days of wind and sleet were followed by mild days and we realized that the marvel of an English spring was again at hand, and it would be our last, of that we had no doubt. In fact, our thoughts went so often now to the little farm in New Hampshire that we started leaving notes around the flat to each other, "Bulletins from Windrush Farm." "The doe has just brought her fawns to the edge of the pasture." "There's a blueberry pie cooling on the kitchen windowsill." "Bara and Wee Maggie have taken their puppies for a stroll." Phyllis, dusting, found one of Bill's notes and asked me whatever it meant, "The hens are now laying 3⅓ eggs apiece per day."

"However can that be?"

"Anything can happen in a story," I explained, "and these are a story we are telling each other."

In the Square, aconites had replaced snowdrops, and crocuses were opening. Such lovely sights came as an assurance that no matter what is happening with people, nature follows her ordered way.

We were just back from one of our walking weekends, this time in the Cotswolds. Never before had the country seemed so beautiful, poignantly beautiful. The villages, each one a pleasant walking distance from the other, looked tidier than ever. The Windrush River, no more really than an oversize brook, was pursuing its course. The footpaths were Bara's joy, and ours. The dogs we met frequently along the way had interesting confrontations with each other, then responded to their owners' voice or call, as Bara did to Bill's warble. The inn at Broadway was all that an inn should be, as we had learned from previous visits.

The path we decided to follow Saturday morning led through Checkers, the prime minister's residence, and along it spring was everywhere, in primroses and birds, fragrance and melody. How it happened I do not know, but somewhere along the way I had put down Bill's beloved binoculars and failed to pick them up again, for

I realized at some point that we did not have them. And they are essential to Bill, even for very near things. I was contrite, he was philosophical.

That night at the Golden Cockerel, another walker came up to us with the binoculars in his hand. "Could these be yours?" he asked.

With so many things we did now, we said, "This is the last time," and yet the ache of parting was eased, for a "first time" was ahead: the seeking and finding of a permanent home, the settling in, the putting down of roots that have been pulled up many times. And with this journey Bara could cross the ocean with no quarantine ahead. He would be with us as part of the new life, and the "wee wifie" that has figured so in my series of Kilts stories would be a reality, once we found that little white farmhouse on a New Hampshire hillside.

May, 1939

We packed everything away that we could do without for the time being. Up to the moment the movers came to take things to storage, Phyllis was with us, smiling, sturdy, and so reliable. She handled with care the Crown Derby tea service that Bill and I had just bought, wanting to have in our new home something so very English, something that would accompany the silver tea set and remind us always of that hour in English life when tea reigns. We made another purchase, at Story's, a small Persian rug, brick and blue, my favorite colors, almost carrying out in shades, on the floor, what the Crown Derby will add to the tea table. Bill packed the china with careful hands as we looked ahead to the time when it would next be used. Where and when would that be?

The next day was so beautiful, soft and sunny, that we called a halt to our labors, told Phyllis to go to her sister's and forget about dinner. We were going to go to Richmond Park for one last walk in a loved place with a bag of bread crusts to feed the deer. Bara could always sense an adventure and was like a bouncing ball when Bill clipped his lead to his collar and we set out for High Street and the bus that would take us to Richmond. He walked properly beside Bill then, not really needing his lead at all, and was a model of decorum when we bought his ha'penny ticket so he could sit beside us on the bus. In the park there were a few people enjoying the day as we were, a few dogs greeting each other and romping together, then responding to their owners, and a few deer approaching cautiously and accepting daintily the bread offered to them.

I can't bear to write this down and yet somehow I must, for it was a part of our lives and of this tense year we all lived through. We had turned back and were going toward the bus stop because, though the days were lengthening, we felt there was good reason to be home early. There were still books to be packed and many things to be done. Behind us a man was walking with a large dog. I scarcely noticed him, and Bara was completely unaware when, with a medley of throaty sounds, the dog suddenly bore down upon Bara.

Bara wheeled quickly and wagged his tail, lifting his long nose in query; but friendship was not the big dog's intent. He seized Bara by the neck and shook him violently, then dropped him. Bara made some small sounds and, valiant Scot that he was, tried to struggle to his feet. The man came running up, attached a chain to his dog's collar, and said, "Sorry." Sometimes an English voice can make that word sound more like "Soddy." "I hope your dog isn't hurt," then went off.

Bara was bleeding terribly, but his eyes were open, and when Bill reached down to pick him up, he did his best to wag his tail. Bill folded him in his coat and carried him. It was not a bus we took, but a taxi, and to the nearest veterinarian. Bara died in Bill's arms, so we did not go to the vet after all, but to Edwardes Square. That night, wrapping Bara in a canvas sheet, we buried him under some bushes in the Square where he had often buried bones. I thought of what Lotte had said about Sinna in Gstaad. Now there was something of us that would always be a part of England.

The war that was as yet no war had given us a casualty. It was all part of the tension that could break anywhere. "Sometimes animals sense things before humans," Bill said.

June, 1939

We sailed on the midnight tide out of Edinburgh, and the adventures we had I gave to Michael and Merry as the new book grew in me. Four weeks were almost like eight, for, at this time of the year, this far north, there was daylight around the clock. Nora had given us open sesame to her friends. On the ship we read more about Iceland, studied the map, and tried to become familiar with useful phrases from our Icelandic–English book. Bill chuckled when he read one of the phrases to me: "How am I ever going to find this when I need it—'I have fallen off my horse.'"

It was a bare, beautiful land and a friendly people. Daily adventures do not make a book, or the kind I wanted *Climbing Higher* to be, but the day when we were on Hekla something happened and the book began to come together.

We were two days away from Reykjavik, on sturdy ponies, horses to the Icelanders, with a guide. We spent the previous night at a pastor's house and left in the morning to climb Hekla, a mountain not quite five thousand feet high and a volcano, too. It was a misty day and the pastor warned us that Hekla was "shy" and did not welcome visitors. Our guide, with far fewer words of English than we had of Icelandic, became more and more cautious as we drew near the summit. It was hard to tell at that point whether the mist we saw was just that or smoke from the volcano which is not entirely inactive.

The ponies had been left in a corral of stones and the last few hundred feet were to be done on foot. We must have been quite near the summit when our guide suddenly said we would go no farther. It was not safe in the thickening mist. I was so disappointed that I kept asking him if we couldn't take the chance. He shook his head, folded his arms across his chest, and nodded in the direction down the way we had come.

"He knows," Bill said, "and don't you remember from Switzerland, we put our safety in Fritz's hands and had to accept his way?"

Aching with chagrin at being worsted by a mountain, even though it was a volcano with a reputation for being temperamental, I turned with Bill and we followed the guide back to where we had left the ponies. But, and this is the important part, at the foot of Hekla we met an Icelander with whom we talked for a few minutes. He had a story to tell. Had we not turned back when we did, we would have missed him, and he (unwittingly) gave me what I needed: the solution to the problem I had set myself. The book now had a plot! In my little bed in the pastor's tiny house I wrote this down, because out of apparent defeat came victory. Looking out of my window and across the flat green field I could see Hekla, no longer swathed in mist, but clothed in a rosy light from the sun which had just dipped down in the west. Instead of being angry, I thought, "Oh, Hekla, you have given me so much more than the view from your summit!"

The night before we left, we did achieve a summit—and all by ourselves—Esja, the great flat-topped mountain across the bay from Reykjavik. We left about nine o'clock and climbed until midnight, had our thermos of coffee and little cakes, then gazed wide-eyed at the world below and around us. The sun had disappeared and there was a kind of half-light for an hour or so. We started down as dawn began to touch distant heights and far-reaching sea.

July, 1939

"What was Iceland like?" Marguerite asked when I called her on the phone from Edinburgh.

"Space filled with light," I said.

"Didn't you miss trees?"

"No."

Traveling down to London on the Flying Scotsman and looking from the train windows, I wanted to push the great trees out of the way, and yet they are such a part of England.

We settled in at Jordans, a guest house in Buckinghamshire. Oddly enough, some of it is made from the timbers of the *Mayflower* which brought the Pilgrims to our land more than three centuries ago. I had just one month to do a whole book, so I worked busily. Much of it was already in my notebooks. I had a history of Iceland, the maps we used, my friend the dictionary, and what helped most of all, Bill's pictures as he got them developed.

The Quaker Meeting House where William Penn worshiped was across a little space of green from the garden of our hostelry. I liked to go there at times to sit and think, or perhaps just sit and be thought through. The story was writing itself and I was reliving our glorious adventure. The typing would be the hardest part, but my machine was in good order, with a new ribbon, and I had a ream of the best quality paper. In between stints of work we walked.

I think we discovered every footpath, visited every hamlet within ten miles of Jordans, but no joyful little dog capered beside us. I still ached about Bara, and if I thought too much, I grew angry.

Bill said, "Life has its hard times for us all, which we must be able to face."

I think he knew more about this than I, than many of us do.

Time did not quite run out on me, for I delivered *Climbing Higher* to Mr. Archie Black on the promised date, and I left his office with a proper contract in my hand.

August, 1939

A ship was throbbing under me again. The S.S. *Nieuw Amsterdam,* a crowded ship, not tourists this time, but people like ourselves who had lived abroad and were now returning. Our furniture might be in the hold, or it might follow on a cargo ship to be stored in Boston until we found our home.

After Jordans, we had stayed with the Unwins at Manor Wood in Surrey, and Nora drove us to Southampton to meet the *Nieuw Amsterdam.* Saying good-by to her was a big wrench, for we had worked together now on three books and would like to work together on many more. What was ahead no one knew, only that war clouds became more menacing with every day. Nora put a bunch of carnations in my hands and it was not dew that glistened on them. I'll never be able to smell that fragrance without thinking of the time when the tender left to take its freight of people out to the ship standing at sea. Nora stood among the great crowd on the dock, waving to us as we waved back to her. Do we never realize what a person means until a parting comes?

Mother and Father and Bob met us at the dock and the hours with them in New York were warm and real. I kept thinking of Stevenson's lines—

> *Home is the sailor, home from the sea,*
> *And the hunter home from the hill.*

Yes, we are home. Before the family left on the train for Buffalo, Father put in my hands a sealed envelope. "This is for you and Bill when you have found your house."

We took no time to see people in New York, to look up friends, do any business, for every moment now was to count. As soon as we got to Boston, we changed stations and took the train to Peterborough, New Hampshire. We were going home.

September, 1939

After breakfast at the Peterborough Tavern, Bill went to Steele's to get a paper. I waited, for as soon as he returned, the next half hour would be taken up in reading the news to him.

"You won't need to," he said. "I can read this much." He pointed to the two-inch-high headline: WAR.

Why weren't people crying the news on street corners? Why weren't bells tolling? Why weren't—I thought of all the things that would have been happening, probably were happening right then, in London, when I realized—it was not "our war," not yet anyway. I read more of the fine type, and the editorials, which Bill always wanted to hear. The news came as no surprise, perhaps it was a relief, though filled with anguish.

We walked across Main Street and called on a real estate man, Mr. Bishop. We told him what we were seeking, though we had begun to modify our thought of a working farm. At the way Bill's sight was going, we knew now that we could realize only a portion of the dream we had held for so long. Bill took the list we had made from his pocket and showed it to Mr. Bishop—an old farm with a small house and a barn, open fields, woodland, a brook, nearby hills and lakes, walking distance to a village, good road, four-season year. The list was studied carefully, then Mr. Bishop said it should not be too hard to find something that would suit us. He did not mention price, nor did we.

October, 1939

During the gentle days of autumn that became ever more golden, I felt in two worlds—a part of me was in England, the other part was in Peterborough. Mr. Bishop felt that to familiarize us with the countryside was more important, at the moment, than to find a house, so he drove us around almost every afternoon. He did manage to show us property as we looked at distant hills and nearby lakes. Some houses were beyond our means, others beyond our needs. A few were worth thinking about, even a second visit; but the perfect one did not appear. Bill assured me that we would know it when we saw it.

It seemed sensible to rent a furnished house for the winter, and Margaret Perry in Hancock had such a house. When approached, she was blunt and generous. "Have it for a month or a year. We won't bother with a lease, just a check now and then until you find your own place and don't need this anymore."

The house was small, old, charming, a mile or so out from the village. It would give us a chance to settle in to the countryside, to learn about the weather, to have quiet when it was needed. The eye attacks were becoming more frequent and more devastating.

December 31, 1939

I've just performed the ritual I do every year at this time since I started really earning. In my little ledger, the left column lists work sent out; in the right are the amounts paid when work is accepted. The columns now almost match each other, and the total, in dollars, not pounds, begins to look quite respectable.

1940–1942

Shieling in New Hampshire

March, 1940

We were still looking at houses and I was forever falling in love with impossible ones. I could not see the disadvantages in a darling house whose brook had a swimming pool and whose beams spoke of a time when fires smoked; but Bill could. It was too remote and the acreage was more than we would know what to do with. Reluctantly I saw the place through his eyes. There was another, a little white house that lay in the lap of a hill. We made several inspections, even spent a day there on our own, drank water from its well, peered in the windows. I was enamored, but Bill felt it was not the one. I got annoyed and asked "Why?"

"It is on a dirt road that may or may not be improved. Do you know the difficulties that might impose in winter or in March mud season?"

"But—"

"The village over the hill is a small one and that might prove stifling."

"But—"

"The land has been abandoned for a long time. It would be costly to bring it back."

Bill had all the arguments, but to me the house was a dream of beauty. When he explained to Mr. Bishop "our" (I wanted him to say "his") thinking, Mr. Bishop agreed with him.

There was another house high on a hill, on a black road, in good condition but needing some alterations. I was ready to set up housekeeping with a blanket roll and a coffeepot.

"It's a long way from any village or town," Bill said quietly. "That may not mean anything now, but for year-round living and for all our years, it is best to be less remote."

I didn't want to give that house up, but I did, marveling always at how much farther Bill saw than I did. I was impatient. Bill was calm.

"We know what we want. We see it clearly with our inward eyes. Wait until we see it outwardly. We will."

"How can you ever be so sure?"

"Mamie" Yates,

Elizabeth's mother, around 1940

"Because I've seen this happen too many times to doubt."

Writing time was hard to come by, and I longed for the days when I could get back to my chosen work, but I had put the Cornish tales in order and with Bill's pictures they were ready to be presented to a publisher. *Climbing Higher* had come out in England and an American edition with the title *Quest in the Northland* had been taken by Knopf. There was every reason for me to go to New York "on business." Wilda Linderman, a friend we had come to know in Peterborough, gave me a letter to Richard Walsh, president of the John Day Company. He had published books by her father, Frank B. Linderman. I wrote to Mr. Walsh and received an invitation to call on him "when next in New York."

April, 1940

Bill's conviction that when a thing is right we know it happened with Mr. Walsh. I had sent ahead the Cornish tales, now called *Piskey Folk*, with a collection of Bill's pictures. I had no sooner sat down in Mr. Walsh's office than he told me they wanted to do the book. "Those photographs," he exclaimed. "What they do to make the land real!" It was a delightful hour and thoroughly profitable for both Bill and me. Before I left, Mr. Walsh said he would like me to meet his wife, Pearl Buck.

I felt as if I were being introduced to royalty when he took me in to her office. She was beautiful and commanding, like a queen on a throne. I thought I would be tongue-tied in her presence, but I wasn't, because she asked me a question that I could answer.

"You write? Tell me, do you develop your characters so that what happens could happen to them only in the lives they are living, or do you have a strong plot in mind and develop it using your characters? Those are two approaches to writing." She smiled. "Which is yours?"

My mind whirled. What if I said the wrong thing? But I could only say what I did whether it was right or wrong. I thought of Michael and Merry, of the Kilts stories, the people in the plays I had done for Marguerite Puttick, and I said the only words I could say. "I get to know my characters so well that the action is theirs. I don't know anything about plot."

The smile that then spread over her face was like the sun rising. "That's the way I work."

My next call was on Lillian Bragdon, juvenile editor at Knopf. She asked me how soon I could follow *Quest in the Northland* with more adventures of the Lamb children.

May 10, 1940

The world news is shattering. Hitler has invaded France. There are bombings, bloodshed, and stricken people. Under Churchill, Britain is doing her mightiest to rearm, to deal with the blows as they come.

July, 1940

Mr. Bishop had yet another house to show us. It was a long drive to see it and through a part of the country new to us. Passing a group of shacks with every evidence of haphazard living, Mr. Bishop waved his hand and said, "These will all be cleaned out soon." Always he wanted us to see only the best. A wrath rose in me that I managed to stifle. But these are homes, people live in them, I thought to myself.

The house he took us to was not for us, but the sight of the shacks and the airy promise of demolition lodged in my mind. I didn't know what I could do about them, or about the social conditions that caused them, but maybe someday there would be something.

December, 1940

Between Christmas and New Year's we went to Boston. One night at a gathering of friends we met Holden Greene, a contractor who had done much of the work at Sturbridge Village and who had a feeling for old houses. He and Bill spent most of the time talking together, and as we left Holden said, "When you find that house you're seeking, let me know. I'd like to have a hand in restoring it."

"I think things are going to happen soon," Bill said to me.

January, 1941

And they did!

Mr. Bishop phoned early of a cold bright day saying that he had a house he very much wanted to show us. It was not on the market, but he had been in touch with the owner, a farmer who lived near, to see if he would be willing to sell it. The farmer was. Enumerating its features, Mr. Bishop made it sound appealing—one of the first houses in Peterborough, 1789 the approximate date, on a black road, about a mile from the center, no plumbing, no electricity, but sound. "See for yourself."

It was so plain, and to me it was the least likely of all the houses we had seen. It had lost its small, many-paned windows and had only long ones; there was a soapstone sink in the front room and water came in by gravity; the fireplaces had been boarded up. I couldn't see it, but Bill could. The more we talked and went through it room by room, the more certain Bill became that it was what we were seeking.

"It needs the touch of a master to restore it to its original state," Bill said, "and that is Holden Greene."

Then I yielded. We had not seen the house, though we must have passed by it many times, until after we met Holden Greene. The two went together.

When we told Mr. Bishop our search was over and the sooner we could have possession the better, he told us the price. "Five thousand dollars: house, barn, and outbuildings, sixty-seven acres of field and woods, a brook; but you will have to do a good deal to it to bring it up to present-day living."

That night we opened Father's envelope. In it was a letter: ". . .when you find the house that you both like, I will send you five thousand dollars as a down payment."

February, 1941

Events moved fast—the title search, the legalities, the deed, then Holden's survey of what the house needed, and the estimated cost. We secured an FHA loan from the bank and work commenced. Holden had two skilled carpenters who moved in with their camp beds as soon as the people who were renting the house moved out. What a story it was, I thought, everything coming together the way the parts of a book do, one event depending on another.

"Bill, remember Old Donal and what he said about a bargain and the worries being over?"

"I've thought of him often."

March, 1941

When the fireplaces were opened, one revealed the original hearth, built to the famous Rumford design; when the stairs were unsheathed, there was more light; when a dormer was cut into the roof, there was space for two bedrooms and a bath upstairs. Small-paned windows replaced the long ones. Plumbing, heating, and electricity were installed under the watchful eye of Holden Greene. If a hinge needed to be replaced, or even a mantel, he found one that was of the period. Always he knew what should be done to preserve the old, to blend it with the new, and his men worked as if the house were their own.

The earth floor in the summer kitchen which would be our dining room was laid with wide pine boards. The buttery became a modern kitchen. Bill and I helped where we could, stripping layers of paint from paneling to get down to the plain pine, and some of the boards were twenty-two inches wide. The most thrilling moment was when layers of wallpaper came off the room that would be our guest room, beneath them was stenciling. "Done about 1815," Holden said, "by a journeyman stenciler, and done for a bride, or those little hearts would never have been part of the design."

There were days when too much was going on for us to be of any use, so we took time off to explore. The sun was riding high and melting the snow. We could begin to plan where our garden would be. We went to the woods and discovered the brook, the old sugar house, the great trees, the stone walls, the magnificent boulders.

May, 1941

The house was ready for painting. The shutters, which were now in place, gave it the look it must have had in its early days. I imagined a red house, or perhaps a yellow one with gray trim.

Holden was shocked. "But this is an old house. It must be what it always was. White. The best color in this countryside. With dark, very dark, green shutters."

I bowed to the man whose feeling for tradition was so strong and right.

There came a day when the work was finished, even the clearing up. The two workmen invited us to supper, laying a plank over two sawhorses for a table in what would be our living room and drawing up nail kegs to sit on. Color came in the soft green of the walls, the brick of the fireplace, and one red rose the men had put in a milk bottle on the table. The next morning they packed up and were gone.

During the past years Bill and I had lived in lovely places—Wythburn Court, Heimeli, White House, Edwardes Square, and others of lesser duration, but now we were home. We had our shieling, our own croft. When our furniture arrived it would bring something of England to New England. We had had goals through the years and now we had a major one: to be settled by Memorial Day weekend when Mother and Father were coming to be our first guests in the room with the stenciled walls.

They liked the house, feeling that it was the perfect place for Bill and me.

"It's well built," Father said.

"It's friendly," Mother added.

They sensed, as we had, that part of its charm was the way the past lay so lightly upon it. There were no creaking floors, no hint of the supernatural. It had been the home of simple, hard-working farming folk over close to two centuries. We were only the fifth in its line of owners, and we felt we would be true to its tradition.

Mother and Father were accompanied by a young, sleek Scottish terrier whose name was Bonnibel. "We knew you shouldn't be without a dog," Father said as he handed me her AKC papers. Again a canny Scot would have a part in our lives!

July, 1941

There had been little time for writing, but I knew that I must soon establish a routine, and it was Bill who was giving me a gift of time as he took on many household tasks. He brought in the wood, laid the fires, dried the dishes, and never did one slip from his fingers. When it came to housecleaning, he claimed the floors and the porcelain in the bathrooms as his right. In the garden, weeding between the rows and thinning were his specialties. His fingers had a sensitivity that served him well now that he had started to learn braille.

The books were bringing in royalties, even from war-ravaged England, and their numbers were increasing. The Lambs had more adventures in a book called *Haven for the Brave*. A collection of children's stories, written over the years, among them *The Marriage Tapestries* which grew as I worked on the needlepoint seats for our dining room chairs, had been gathered into a book: *Under the Little Fir.* I sent it to several publishers, finally approaching John Day because of *Piskey Folk*. It was not for them, but they suggested their associate firm, Coward-McCann. Rose Dobbs, the juvenile editor, and I seemed to see alike about the book. When I mentioned having the artwork done by Nora Unwin, she agreed, "If she can get the artwork done under wartime conditions." Nora could and did and, to me, the illustrations far outshone the text. John Day was doing one of the Tregarthen stories found in the old trunk, *The Doll Who Came Alive,* and Nora's drawings gave it zest.

Lillian had had enough of the Lambs and asked me to be open to a wholly new idea. I soon discovered it was very near. Out of the house itself came something I longed to write. The stenciled walls began to speak in a language I understood. I found myself going about the pattern of my days—the simple chores of the house, the reading aloud to Bill, the trips in to town, the walks with Bonnie—while another pattern was weaving itself in my mind; the people began to become more real than those I met in the course of a day.

September, 1941

Shieling, our shelter, had become a shelter for Ann, our old friend from Boston. She had been so good to us, and now she had need of the kind of counsel that Bill was deft at giving. She settled into the guest room and was glad to help around and about, but most of her time was spent with Bill. Aside from getting the meals, I was able to be for longer periods of time at my desk in the room that looked out on mountains.

October, 1941

Out of the past came the villain I needed, and what story was ever without a villain? The villain was the weather of 1816, weather that caused the year to be known in the annals of New Hampshire as eighteen hundred and froze-to-death. I went to the State Library at Concord for books of the period. I read newspapers so old they all but crumbled in my hands. The Farmer's Almanac of the time gave me facts I needed for the year that caused havoc for most people, but that made Jared Austin. As soon as I had the journeyman stenciler named, he became real to me, as did Jennet and Mr. Toppan, Corban Cristy, the Dunklees, and all the rest.

November 3, 1941

The idea seems so wonderful that I tremble before it. Way down deep inside me is a feeling that I can never do justice to it, then I remember that I have felt this way before, and it is just the prick I need. But still I am waiting for something. I see parts of the story, but it has not come together as a whole.

November 13, 1941

At supper tonight Ann and Bill were talking together, and suddenly the whole structure of the story became clear to me—a house that had been framework became habitable, ready to be moved into. As I followed events in my mind, I felt in a different world, not knowing or even hearing what Ann and Bill were saying to each other. I wanted to shout for joy, and yet I wanted to keep it close to myself until I got a net of words around the idea.

November 14, 1941

This day actual writing begins. I make a rough plan and start the first chapter. I wonder how long it will be and then realize that it will be exactly as long as it must be for the story. It will tell me as it unfolds; it is not for me to dictate to it. *Beauty Is a Bright Flame* is my working title.

November 21, 1941

First chapter is done and the outline of the whole is shaping up well. Jared has acquired his own character and is taking things into his own hands.

December 3, 1941

I've lingered some days over some reading that has just come to light. It is helping me with the background. Now I begin the second chapter.

December 7, 1941

The United States has entered the war. Pearl Harbor has been bombed with frightful destruction and loss of life. My heart has been so torn for England and the long-loved friends; now I feel closer to them, and somehow the suffering is easier to bear, as we are all in it together. I work harder than ever today. Holding on to something good and beautiful is a line of life.

December 11, 1941

Well launched now, but the waters are deep, and I'm rowing hard. Soon the current will carry me.

December 12, 1941

A letter from Lillian today, "Hoping to get your new manuscript before too long." Three chapters are done.

December 19, 1941

Finished chapter four. Halfway mark, I think.

December 29, 1941

Took time out for Christmas, but glad to be back at my desk with Jared wending his way to New Hampshire. The real part of the story is opening up.

January 14, 1942

On chapter seven now, with the excitement mounting. The end begins to be in sight. I love it and feel a day ill spent if there has been no converse with Jared.

January 15, 1942

Lillian wants the manuscript soon. I think I'll be done in ten days, then for the hard but gratifying part—revision and correction.

January 18, 1942

Nearing fulfillment. Thrilled by it all.

January 23, 1942

DONE!

January 28, 1942

Read the first chapter aloud to Bill. He likes it. So do I. Commenced typing.

February 4, 1942

Only one chapter typed. It is slow going, but it does read well, and Bill continues to like it.

February 15, 1942

Half typed.

February 27, 1942

Finished and off to Knopf. I feel like a mother whose child has put on long trousers and gone away to school. It's not mine any more.

March 12, 1942

Lillian says there is not a word that doesn't ring true. She gives it the title *Patterns on the Wall.* Of course, that is exactly what it is. Now for the long wait for production. Lillian says it will be published in the spring of 1943.

May 10, 1942

One of the small joys is writing essays to go with Bill's pictures. With them we can relive the weekend walks we had, the travels we made, the climbs, the places seen, the people. I'm glad for that clutch of little notebooks, for I always carried one in pocket or rucksack. Bill helps me in remembering. His sense for detail is sharp. There have been no pictures now for some time, but Bill still loves to fondle his Leica. Next to me, he says, it is his dearest possession; but he has made up his mind to part with it. Tomorrow when we go to Boston he is determined to sell it.

May 12, 1942

Bill says it is time I have a new typewriter and so he has got one for me.

June 21, 1942

Rose Dobbs has come for a few days and we talk about a book I am planning. It is based on a true happening. A woman, in our neighboring town of Temple, nursed a stillborn lamb to life. The lamb grew to be a member of the family and the leader of the flock.

"Yes, it can be a good story," Rose agreed. "When will you have it for me?"

"Soon, but it may take a while for Nora to do the illustrations as things are now."

"Do you have a title?"

"Mountain Born."

We talked much more, of course, but it is thrilling to tell an editor about an idea and then be told to go ahead.

October 5, 1942

Now Lillian has just gone after being here three days. She brought the galleys of *Patterns* for me to read and return to her. It is with awe that I see my words in type. They look so important, and only a year ago they were tumbling around in my head. She said they were coming out with an extra page and did I want a dedication. I do: *"To my Mother, with love and gratitude."*

1943–1945

Patterns on the Wall

Winter, 1943

Perhaps we had been readying ourselves, Bill more consciously than I, but on that bitter day when I took him down to Boston for the operation that might preserve some sight, I still hoped. Two weeks later, when we drove back to Shieling, Bill was a man who would not see again. The optic nerves had been severed and the eyes had been removed. "He will have no more pain," the doctor said. Plastic eyes, gray as his own had been, now confronted the world. The doctor said many helpful things to me, but more than all the practical things were the words, "Keep him seeing." He had been amazed that Bill had done as much as he had, got on as well as he had, during the past year.

That Bill had been able to do so much was due in large part to the way he had learned to see intently because of his photography. Composition, focus, quality of light, all that made him skilled in his craft, had built into him some power that helped him to go on seeing. But, persistent in hope as I had been, something had been preparing me, too. Memory bore me back to that last day at Oaksmere when Mrs. Merrill took the seniors to a vaudeville show and one of the acts had been a blind comedian who sang a song with the refrain:

> *My darling, my wife, the light of my life,*
> *Has eyes that can see for me.*

I did not know Bill then, and I certainly knew little about blindness except as a word that indicated misfortune.

Bill was fifty-five, more than a midpoint in life and a point at which many might have given up; but not Bill. To him, losing his sight was another challenge, another beginning. It might take time, but finding a home took time. Finding what he could do might take a little longer.

His pictures were coming into use. The Icelandic ones were made into slides and put in order. Bill gave talks on Iceland to church groups, service clubs, and schools. Few people have been there, and little is known about the land that has such contrasts, such interest-

Nora Unwin,

with paper and pencil at hand

ing people, and such inspiring history. I worked the projector and whispered the number of the slide coming up. Bill's memory had always been exceptional—lack of sight made it more so—and he had always been a good storyteller. The Skye pictures would come next as slides, then Cornwall, and with those we would be able to talk about the Tregarthen books and introduce them to people.

March, 1943

Rose Dobb's interest in the story I told her about the lamb gave me all I needed to start writing, and now pages were piling up on my desk. Several strands, in addition to the tale of the lamb, came together to make the book. One was the longing to own a farm, perhaps a sheep farm, that Bill and I had for years. Another was the sweater a friend made for me from wool spun as it came from the sheep. It had a rich, oily smell and was full of twigs and burrs picked up while the sheep was grazing. I had only to bury my nose in it to feel like a sheep. Most important were the long talks I had with Sydney Stearns in Hancock, who had five hundred sheep in his care. After every story he told me, he added, "Sheep are very intelligent creatures."

I sent to Washington for Government pamphlets on sheep raising, the needs, problems, diseases, rewards. I felt I had to know all those things even though I might use only a small part in the actual book. I went over to Temple to talk with Mrs. Leighton. During my first call, when we were sitting in the kitchen with cups of coffee, I heard a sharp clicking sound as if someone wearing high heels were coming to join us. Someone was—the lamb-grown-sheep, Flickertail. That was what Winnie Leighton called her when she saw the motion of tail that gave evidence of life.

Ten years had gone by, and Flickertail was as much a part of the household as a dog. She went to Grange meetings with the Leightons, even to church, waiting outside. Everyone in the town knew her and, when I got her story written, many more people would know her. In the book her name was Biddy.

When my pages were written, a copy went to Nora in England, for she was working on the illustrations. Fortunately, her war service put her in a home, helping to care for children, instead of in a factory making munitions, so she could get on with her work as she had time available. If the artwork was not delayed and if it all reached New York safely, Rose hoped to have the book ready by the end of the year. It was hard to do, mainly because I had to allow for interruptions in my time, but I gave it my best. However, I can never be really sure until I have a word of "Well done" from the publisher, the editor in this case.

It came, and I was gratified.

April 5, 1943

This day *Patterns on the Wall* is published. I hold it in my hands. It has been given a beautiful format. Warren Chappell's decorations are so exactly right. Tonight I shall start reading it aloud to Bill.

May, 1943

We had been on the "Home Front" ever since the United States entered the war, and so were better able to bear the news of human suffering and material destruction because we were involved and everyone was doing something to help. My time away from Shieling was limited, as there was so much I could do for Bill, but one task I could fulfill was that of plane spotter at the Post on the slope of East Pack, only a few miles from Shieling. Volunteers were instructed in the different types of planes "the enemy" used and we knew how to report them if seen or heard. The observation place was a small hut, manned by two spotters in shifts around the clock. One pair of eyes must always be on the sky, one pair of ears equally alert, especially when clouds rolled down the mountain. We had a telephone to report anything questionable. I was at the Post several afternoons a week. There was no chance to read or write, or even talk, but I could think while my eyes were on the sky and I was already working, in my mind, on a novel.

One day the telephone rang. My companion and I looked at each other in horror and bewilderment. It could only be a ghastly emergency. As I was near the phone, I answered.

"Air Spotter Detail, East Pack Mountain," I said.

A familiar ripple of laughter came over the wire. "I may be court-martialed for doing this, but I had to let you know—you've had a telegram from New York. *Patterns* has just been given the *Herald Tribune* Spring Festival Award." The receiver clicked.

"*Patterns*—" Suddenly I was unloosed. I put my head in my hands and cried.

My companion rushed over to me. "Where are the planes? Is New York being bombed? Washington?"

I shook my head and tried to explain, but it was hard to get her to understand the importance of the news to me.

There was another telephone call that night from Lillian with all the details. "The award is to be presented at the *Herald Tribune* office on Friday. You must be here."

I knew that I could not be. There was a commitment to the Air

Spotter Post, but more than that, Bill needed me. I told Lillian that I could not be there, but that my mother happened to be in New York, staying at the Commodore, and that I would ask her to accept the award for me.

Mother telephoned to say how proud she was to accept the award —a check for two hundred dollars. "The judges said the book merited the award for its beauty and its order." How astonishingly right this all was—that Mother should be the one to hear those words about my book, to be a part of the joy and the triumph.

Summer, 1943

The crabapple tree on the south side of the house has long been a part of the life here. When we first saw it, the bare branches against a snowy landscape made it look like a dancer, reaching up, bending but not bowing. When it blossomed, it made us want to bow to its beauty, and when it bore fruit we had to bow many times to fill our baskets with small yellow apples with their pink blush. We made jelly, even tried wine, and gave much of the crop away. Bill had asked me about the tree, and, because I wanted him to *see* it this of all years, I wrote a poem about it.

> *The house had just been built the year I first bore fruit—*
> *apples with which a child played in thin September shade.*
> *Cold strengthened me and when spring came round again*
> *white blossoms crowned my head.*
> *"Look!" the little girl cried, "our tiny crab tree is a bride."*
>
> *When she wore bridal dress I had attained my height.*
> *A branch of mine could rest on the wall to the west;*
> *another reached to salute the east with ripening fruit.*
> *Baskets of apples I bore, plenty rode my golden tide,*
> *but with every spring I was a bride.*
>
> *Families changed in the house and my apples were used*
> *for jelly and wine, sliced, put into jars and spiced.*
> *A nest rode me like an ark, woodpeckers drilled my bark.*
> *Years were so many leaves tossed windward and wide,*
> *but with every spring I was a bride.*
>
> *Storms swept over my limbs, ice bent my branches down,*
> *but only the weight of my gold ever broke a bough's hold.*
> *Gnarled now and deep of root, robust bearer of fruit,*
> *I give shade, yield to wind, stand breasting life's tide,*
> *for with every spring I am a bride.*

October, 1943

And now I held in my hands *Mountain Born*.

Nora's illustrations caught so wondrously the feeling and the beauty of the countryside in which the story was set, and yet she had never been in New Hampshire; but she did have Bill's photographs! Most wondrous of all is her depiction of Benj. When writing about him, I had in my mind's eye Mr. Hill, the farmer who, with his one old horse and mowing machine, had done our big field for the past two years. He was so calm, so peaceful, and did the work with a minimum of commotion and a maximum of effectiveness. Mr. Hill might have posed for Nora, so precisely does he come out in her illustrations, and with him the philosophy of a man who has grown old and wise while working with animals and the land.

Winter, 1944

Rose asked me the question that I was beginning to learn is usual with editors: "What next?" I told her what was in my mind, a story that had been growing there for years and that is laid in England. "That sounds like a novel, and you will have to talk with Mr. Coward about it."

I could not possibly talk with Mr. Thomas R. Coward until I had something to show him, so I began to bring my thoughts together. Once the process was started, I was amazed at how much was there. The idea began for me that first year we were living in London, being a part of English life. Even though I often wanted to be taken as English, I was never more grateful that I was an American than when I became aware of social barriers, the class system that prevailed. My feeling was especially for the house servants, who worked for a pound a week and often less, and had little time for themselves. Granted they had their uniforms supplied, their meals provided and their rooms, those rooms were far from comfortable. Looking at houses that first year when we were renting furnished ones made this very clear to me, and the basement kitchens were often dismal except for the big coal range. From different maids we had—Maude, Elsie, Phyllis—hearing them tell of their own experiences, then getting them to have friends write down their experiences, I had plenty of material, some of it dating before the turn of the century; yet parallel with this was my deep love for England.

The story of Susie Minton, who went into service at the age of thirteen in 1883 because it was the "respectable" and often the only work for a girl, came into being for me against the background of

London and the English countryside. Writing the story, I felt that I was repaying a debt to England while revealing something that troubled me. When I started to write, the story flowed easily, for I had so much material at hand and there were memories that were very fresh. My manuscript was about finished when I met an English woman and her daughter, the Buchanans, who were teaching in a school in Connecticut. They came to stay at Shieling for a week, and Mrs. Buchanan read my work line by line, word by word, checking, correcting, even approving. When I had typed *Wind of Spring*, I felt ready to submit it to Mr. Coward.

June, 1944

Something about Susie Minton must have touched his heart, or perhaps Rose put in a good word for me, since *Mountain Born* was doing nicely, because Mr. Coward was not long in accepting *Wind* just as it was. He suggested no change in my title, though he agreed that one might have to read the book to discover what it meant. It came from those lines of Thomas Moore's that foresee changes coming in the social structure:

> *Then shall the reign of mind commence on earth*
> *And starting fresh as from a second birth,*
> *Man in the sunshine of the world's new spring*
> *Shall walk transparent like some holy thing.*

The day I signed the contract in his office, I could not have asked for any greater praise: "You know what you're talking about." He smiled, that shy smile that people saw rarely. "Now, see if you can find something nearer home."

There was something in my mind that went back to the time when Mr. Bishop was showing us the countryside, wanting us to see only what was attractive. I realized later that he often went out of his way to avoid the unattractive, like the day when he went by some tumbledown shacks and with a wave of his hand said they would all be cleaned out soon. Something in me rose up in rebellion. These are homes where people live, I wanted to shout, but I didn't say anything. Some people can let their fury out in spoken words and get it over with. I'm not like that. With me it goes deep into mind and, often, heart and then comes out gradually in written words.

Mr. Coward had stirred up something in me, but I had a lot of thinking to do.

October, 1944

Things began to come together and, as so often, in unexpected ways.

When Bill and I were on our way home from Boston one day, we gave a ride to a young sailor. I stopped at the post office to pick up our mail, and the sailor asked Bill, "Is she a teacher? She walks like one."

Several times last winter I was asked by Marion Hudson, a friend who is a teacher at Keene State College, to talk with her class about children's literature in general and my books in particular. One of Marion's students is now the teacher in a one-room school in a small village a few miles north of Keene. I spent a day with Evelyn Osborn, sitting in the back of the room, and the children thought no more of me than of a piece of furniture. There were seventeen children in six grades, and I was fascinated as I watched how Evelyn led them in what, at their different stages of development, they were capable of doing, drawing out the best, encouraging, loving, disciplining. I made many more visits, listening, observing, writing down what I heard and saw in my notebook.

The school itself, the village, the tar-paper shacks on the edge of the woods from which two of the children came, the people, some so kind, some so unkind, began to give me what I needed. Soon the children accepted me as part of a day, and they began to share themselves with me. Evelyn let me in on a wonderful secret: that the children had asked if I could be the one to present the diplomas when graduation time came in June. Two boys and a girl were graduating and would be going on to high school in Keene.

Bit by bit the story began to weave itself into a fabric in my mind, from the notes I had been making during my visits to that one-room school. I began to feel that Mr. Coward might realize that it was nearer home, so near that suddenly I found myself with a title, *Nearby,* before even a word had been written or a plan made.

February 12, 1945

This morning when I went out to the mailbox I found a package—it is my copy of *Wind of Spring,* and with it a letter from Mr. Coward. He says it has already been bought for publication in England. "Not a large sum, but at least it moves your name into a rising rank of writers who are concerned about how 'the other half lives.'"

It is a small thin book with a notice in the front saying:

IMPORTANT:

> *Government wartime restrictions on materials have
> made it essential that the amount of paper used in each
> book be reduced to a minimum. This volume is printed
> on lighter paper than would have been used before
> material limitations became necessary, and the number
> of words on each page has been substantially increased.
> The smaller bulk in no way indicates that the text has
> been shortened.*

On the facing pace there were just two words that really mattered: *"To William."* We started to read it that night. Bill didn't want me to stop.

February, 1945

Bonnibel was becoming an important part of the life at Shieling, for she was bred to one of Mrs. John Winant's best dogs. This meant several trips to Concord, the state capital, just an hour's drive away. We even went to the State House to meet Governor Winant. While in his office, we were introduced to Mr. Herbert Rainie, apparently a distinguished lawyer. He told Bill of an organization, the New Hampshire Association for the Blind, and said that he was serving as president. In a gruff but kindly way, he added that he would like to come to Peterborough and talk with Bill sometime. He seemed particularly interested that Bill had been learning to read and write braille.

"That's hard work for anyone, but at your age—why do you do it?"

Bill's answer was, "What's the alternative?"

March, 1945

My story of the schoolteacher was quickening in me and I was glad for mornings when I could work without interruptions. I sat at my desk, my jam jar full of sharpened pencils, and contemplated those long yellow legal pages of my pad, blank but soon to be filled with words. I suppose I could write directly on the typewriter, but writing is a craft, and, to me, seeing the words come from my hand onto the paper means a closer connection with my mind and my heart. It's slow, of course, but for me it is the way. The value of the legal pads is that the number of written words on one is close to the number of typed words on an 8½-by-11-inch sheet.

I began writing. Thinking and planning had gone on for so long that I knew my setting and had named my people. Now I could really get going. The first day was slow and halting, but sure. People and situations came to me as if out of a mist. I had to take time to see them clearly.

The story gained momentum so rapidly that I wanted to stay with it all the time. I was writing something like twenty-five hundred words a day—a morning, that is. I stopped at noon. There were other things to be done: meals to get, household tasks, people to see.

April, 1945

There were several demands and I had to be away from my desk for almost three weeks. I picked up the threads and found to my joy that the story itself was carrying me forward. Nothing was lost, perhaps it was even better for having been set aside for a while.

June, 1945

If I can keep my time free, I should be finished by the end of July, then I'll put the manuscript away for two months before I start revision and the final typing.

September, 1945

It did not get finished in July, because such a wonderful opportunity came for Bill. He was asked to go for the school year to Perkins Institution for the Blind in Watertown, just outside Boston. He is to teach business organization, selling techniques, and consumer education and, in return, be taught advanced braille, typing, and woodworking. What an exchange: Bill's thirty years of business experience balanced by the gaining of skills that a blind person needs to get on in life! That chance meeting with Mr. Rainie last winter was what set this all in motion. We were busy getting Bill's things ready. I took him to Perkins and helped him get settled. He would be home weekends, but during the week I would have hours and hours for work, and the story should surge along.

When I got to my desk and confronted all those pages, I had forgotten that I had gone so far. It took me a long time to read up to page 307. It must be good, I thought, for so much of it gives me shivers. When I came to page 308 and it was blank, I could hardly bear it. I prayed, "Heaven help me: What I want to say is so big, can I possibly get it into words?"

In eight days chapter ten was finished, but I had a long way still to go. This book was showing me more than any of the others that I don't invent my characters, I entertain them. Mary Rowen, the teacher, had been close to me from the start, but when Dan first came into my ken it was quite different. He seemed to emerge from the woods, came across the stone wall, over the field, and then into my room. But I saw him only hazily at first, and he was so shy. It was days before I could get him to sit down and really talk with me.

November, 1945

At 7 P.M. November 1 and at the end of a radiant day, the last words were written, and I printed at the bottom of the page "EBENEZER—Hitherto hath the Lord helped me." That was what George Eliot wrote when she had finished a book. I sent Bill a telegram that would be read to him: "Dan got married last night. Expects to live happily ever after."

November 6, 1945

How is it that twelve red roses can say more than any words, especially when we are away from each other?

December 31, 1945

This year has held many marvels—for the world, cessation of the war; for us, events that enrich our lives. The only way I can bring it to a fitting conclusion is by quoting George MacDonald in a letter to a friend: "I do not myself believe in misfortune, anything to which men give the name is merely the shadow-side of a good."

1946

Bonnibel's Family

January, 1946

The great event we now looked forward to was Nora's coming to stay with us for a year! We had acccomplished so much with books against tumult and distance, that to think of being able to work together, with her at Shieling, filled me with happiness. Exit permits and visas were hard to obtain, as restrictions on travel had not lessened with peace, and there seemed to be endless details to arrange. Bill appealed to Governor Winant and he was so helpful. The way was now finally clear. Nora had her exit permit, her visa, and her flight on British Airways for sometime in April. That was as definite as anything could be and more than anything had been.

It was Bonnibel who began all this, for it was her relationship to a Winant dog that began our friendship with the Winants and so enlisted the Governor to do what he could in Nora's case. Bonnie's first puppies were both so fine, two males, and they went to Mrs. Winant as part of our understanding. Bonnie would be bred again and this time we would have first choice.

So we looked ahead. The best thing to do on the first month of a new year. I knew how important it was for Bill to have something always ahead. It might be just going out to dinner the next week, but a date on his calendar meant anticipation, and that meant something good was before us.

Bill went back to Perkins, and I had to work hard with this stretch of alone time. I finished revising *Nearby* and started typing, setting myself a stint of ten pages a day.

February 20, 1946

It's 5 P.M. and the final page is typed. Now to wrap it up in a neat package and send it on its way to New York. How long must I wait before I get a word of "Well done"? A whisper would satisfy me, though I would like a shout.

March 16, 1946

Today a telegram came: BOOK IS FINE.

*Wheeling in vegetables
at Shieling*

March, 1946

I made a quick trip to New York. In Mr. Coward's office I basked —not in sunshine, but in the warmth of his praise. He showed me the jacket for the book—already done! I liked it. He told me of plans he had for English publication, submission to a book club, when publication would be, the few changes they would like me to make "if you agree." If I agree! When have I not been grateful to an editor for seeing something that my eyes and mind had missed? The changes were so slight that I made them that night at the hotel. His words were never many, but he said four to me that I shall hold on to: "Stick to your last." He handed me an envelope and said it was an advance against royalties. I didn't open it in front of him, but when I did, I gasped—$750! He really must believe in the book. So did I, but then I had ever since the idea first took hold of me.

April, 1946

A letter came from Bill April 1, the first in a long time. He was not finding typing easy, so he wrote it in pencil on paper that rested on a pad with raised lines which he could feel. He hoped I could read it, and I could, even though he sometimes went over a line already written and sometimes went off the right edge. I copied it in my notebook for easier reading. If he gets to writing a book someday, he might want to have it to refer to. He said he had been remembering something he saw when he was staying at the farm in Kent while I was in Zurich:

> I had gone to bed early and was lying wide awake, listening to the stillness and slowly sensing the fragrance of garden and meadow. Then I became aware of a pale panel of light on the wall; curving across the light were a few faint lines of shadow. And even as I realized that the lights of a car coming down the Old Mill Road were shining through the branches of a tree standing near my window, the patch grew brighter and the shadows darker and sharper.

> There, on this canvas of yellow light, were three slender branches lifting themselves into the picture from the wide frame of darkness. From each branch, tender young twigs shot off to right and left and from them fat buds curved to a quick point. I thought how like a lovely Chinese painting, with its delicate feeling created by a few swift strokes.

Then a night breeze must have stirred the tree outside, for the shadows began to move gently to and fro across the panel. I was fascinated by the effect and had begun to fit a silent tune to their rhythmic dance when of a sudden, like a Cinderella at the stroke of twelve, they raced across the square of light—and disappeared. The room was again in darkness. I heard the motorcar going up the road toward the village.

It is an answer to the question I was often asked, "But how does Bill see so much?" It isn't *how*, but *what*. His sight might be restricted, but his vision had no limits.

Remembering when we saw holly that first Christmas in Devon— the prickly leaves within reach, the smoother leaves and great bunches of berries so beyond reach—I wrote a poem about it. I planned to send it to Bill, but as I had not mastered braille, someone would have to read it to him.

THE HOLLY SPEAKS

O holly, your berries red
are so high above my head!
Out of my reach, yes quite,
and so temptingly bright!
Jewels set in wintry skies,
but only for my eyes.
O holly, have you no words?
"Yes, I must remember my birds."

O holly, your leaves prick
my fingers when I pick
even one branch, but if I
could only reach up high,
I'd have berries, boughs and all.
Not a prickle however small
is on those branches, but leaves
smooth turned in glistening
   sheaves.
O holly, have you no words?
"Yes, I must remember my birds."

Those hard fruits the birds will shun,
They'll not have them, no not one!

"No, not now while there's food,
but should the winter brood
and the earth freeze to stone
and the hips be all gone,
the birds will flock round
that which hardness has kept sound."

Bitter as wind from the east,
can the birds call that a feast?
"Feasts are made of answered needs.
Forgetting for what it pleads,
a bird is happy to dine
on such berries as mine
from a table of green
by the wind swept clean.
What matter bitter with sweet to
   follow,
Spring on the wing of a swallow?
Spring at the forest's foot,
a-stir in each primrose root?"

O holly, I love your words!
"Yes, I must remember my birds."

April 18 was a day to mark with a white stone—Lewis Carroll's words for any day special beyond all others. At last, after delays and many setbacks, Nora arrived. In these postwar days, flights were so uncertain and so often deferred that a saying was rife: "If you have time to spare, go by air." But she was here; that was what mattered.

I went to New York to meet her. Coming back on the train, we talked so much that we were both hoarse by the time we got to Boston, but there was so much to say, so much to get caught up on. Bill was waiting at Shieling to greet us, as it was his Easter vacation, and we would all have several days together. Nora would be part of our life now, part of the family of Shieling. The visa said for a year, but we knew in our hearts that it would be for much longer.

June, 1946

Rose Dobbs was here for two days to make plans for the Christmas book that would involve both Nora and me. Almost before illustrations and text were put together, we knew to whom it would be dedicated—Bertha Mahoney Miller; her inspiration and encouragement were unfailing. Rose wrote in our guest book:

> *Come up here, O dusty feet!*
> *Here is fairy bread to eat.*

July, 1946

Bertha and William Miller came to tea one Sunday afternoon. I think tea, with thin slices of buttered bread and little cakes, is the meal I like best of all. The mahogany table in the dining room looked so lovely with a bowl of flowers from the garden, the Crown Derby, and the silver tea set. The Millers had a special something to ask Bill and that was that he go on the board of *The Horn Book* magazine. An honor, yes, but what an opportunity for him to put his business skills at the service of others!

Before they left, and as we were standing by the gate, Bertha said in her little quavery voice, "Are we just too old for you to call us by our first names?" We had always been formal with them, but what a question! Bill knew what to do. He took a step toward them, held out both hands, and in ringing tones called each one in turn and forever, "Bertha! William!"

Later, when we were in the kitchen doing the dishes, it brought tears to my heart to see the way Bill handled the Crown Derby teacups and saucers and plates. Phyllis used to say of him, "He is such a gentle man." That gentleness encompassed china as it did people; now it would be felt in editorial decisions.

End of Summer, 1946

Life was humming for us all. The garden was flourishing, both vegetables and flowers. I was able to establish a routine of work. Most mornings during the week I could be at my desk from after breakfast until luncheon. Nora worked busily at her drawing board in her bedroom studio, for many commissions came to her from other publishers, now that she was at hand, and Bill had his projects; then the afternoons were for chores and fun. How good it was to have Bill home! I depended on his help in the house, in the garden, in the woods where we were clearing trails. Bonnibel had her second family, a little female, which we would keep, and two little males which would go to Mrs. Winant.

And there were guests, flowing through the house and through the summer. The most exciting was Alton Hall Blackington, Blackie to his radio audience. He had a program called *Yankee Yarns,* and he liked to get hold of anything that would make a good yarn. My use of the summer of eighteen hundred and froze-to-death was such a yarn. He and his wife came to stay with us so they could see the patterns on the wall in the guest room and talk with us at length about the stencils, the weather, the research. A few weeks later we heard ourselves on his program.

Nora completed the drawings for another of the Tregarthen stories, *The White Ring,* and was working on illustrations for *Once in the Year,* the book of mine that carries the people of *Mountain Born* into the Christmas season. Now she and Bill were planning a story of Bill's, *Andy, the Musical Ant.* It began when Nora and Bill started to make music together in their odd moments, playing recorders. It grew when Bill had occasion to make up a story for some children who were visiting us, and the story was about an ant who did not play a recorder but an accordion. When I typed the story so it could be sent to a publisher, I felt that the keys on my machine would burst out laughing.

Nora had a marvelous time getting her sketches, crawling around the field and lying on her back under a goldenrod to get an ant's eye view of the world, studying an anthill, then getting the sort of book from the library that showed what an anthill was like on the inside. She described everything to Bill with such care that his laughter rippled through the summer days. The story grew from a jingle of Bill's about ants as they went about their busyness:

> *Work, work,*
> *There's nothing else worthwhile;*
> *Work, work,*
> *Don't even stop to smile.*

But Andy had a different idea, and work was not for him as he went around with his accordion:

> *Play, play,*
> *All work is bad for one;*
> *Play, play,*
> *An ant must have some fun.*

The anthill, faced by catastrophe, was saved by Andy's playing, so the National Anthem became:

> *Work, play,*
> *For each is well worthwhile;*
> *Play, work,*
> *Be sure you stop to smile.*

Now of course, we have an unwritten rule at Shieling that no ant must ever be disturbed, no matter what his business in flower or vegetable garden, because it just might be Andy; and an anthill was to be respected.

We sent the story and roughs of the illustrations to Lillian. It did not take her long to say that this would be for her and that next time she came to Shieling she would talk seriously about it with both Bill and Nora.

Reading galley proof on *Nearby* was taking some of my time, and I had the perfect system. I read for two hours, then went out to the garden to weed or hoe for two hours, then back to my desk. The tasks complemented each other, and one made the other easier.

There is another side to writing a book and that is the letters that come because of the book. The mail brought many from children who have read *Mountain Born* and liked it and wanted to be sure that I would write back to them. Sometimes their letters had such similarity that I suspect they had been told in a school class "to write to an author." One writer was honest enough to say, "If you answer this letter, I'll get an extra mark." Most of the time the letters were spontaneous and the children expressed themselves in charming ways. One such writer said, "I liked it all, except the end when it leaves you just sitting there wondering if there's any more." And there was the occasional child who more than anything wanted to have a pen pal. "Will you be mine?" The letters from people who read *Wind of Spring* were thoughtful, and those who wrote about *Patterns on the Wall* had a glow to them. Not yet had I had a negative letter. Perhaps only people who like books take time to write to the authors.

I do answer the letters, but in such a way that it will not encourage correspondence. I used to be amused when I heard a person talk about having to save herself for something. I was finding that I did have to save myself for the stories I wanted to write, the ideas I wanted to explore. Much as I have loved during the years to write letters to my friends, I couldn't afford now to spend myself that way. My best thoughts would go into my books. Perhaps people would get used to finding them there.

November 10, 1946

Lillian has been here for three days. She came to go over the text and illustrations for *Andy* and to start planning the book, though she has no immediate publication in mind. She is no longer with Knopf, but with American Book Company, and the name for her department is Aladdin Books. This happens, she says. It seems to me that a writer is more closely linked with an editor than with a firm. Lillian is superb to work with, so is Rose. So soon they become friends more than editors. I put Mr. Coward in a slightly different category and am still a little in awe of him.

1947

Beloved Bondage

January 6, 1947

What a way to start the year—*Nearby* was published today!

We had a Coming Out Party at the John Hancock House—we being all those who were involved in the book, and that is six: me, of course, and Bill for standing by and giving me courage and counsel, Marion Hudson for starting me off on the idea, Nora who did the sketch of me that is on the jacket. Percy Hudson and Dorris Frost, Marion's sister, were included because they knew about the book's coming into being, though they did not know the book until they saw it. Evelyn Osborn, on whom my Mary Rowen was patterned, should have been with us but she had some other commitment that night. She was there in spirit, and Marion will share it with her when next she sees her. What a party—place cards made by Nora, jingles composed by Bill, and a toast written by me! To honor Bill:

> *With us tonight is one whose wisdom gleams*
> *Like light from windows in kind golden streams,*
> *And linking hands with wit his thoughts engage*
> *The reader, flowing from page to page.*
> *His was the steady hand, the mind's keen eye*
> *That kept a level between earth and sky.*
> *His was the voice that said, "Is this your best?*
> *If it is not, then see you take no rest. . . ."*

To honor Marion:

> *And there is one who, from the start,*
> *Loved as her own and cherished in her heart. . . .*
> *And from her fund of knowledge, from her store*
> *Brought this and that to lift the book from lore*
> *To actuality and sometime power.*
> *This is the one who, in doubt's lone dark hour,*
> *Gave courage to complete the work begun.*

Greetings from Shieling

Christmas 1950,

courtesy of Nora

And Nora toasted me:

> *There is one here who saw a host of words*
> *Reaching to heaven like a flight of birds.*
> *She caught them in a net of love and care,*
> *And nurtured them, then loosed them to the air. . . .*

The dinner was superb and everyone enjoyed everything, I especially. There was a time when Bill liked to analyze handwriting, and he was as much of a master as Old Donal was in reading tea leaves. Bill discovered something in my writing that indicated "likes to eat." Yes, I do, but more in savor than surfeit.

January 7, 1947

Shall I ever be able to get back to work?

January 14, 1947

Mr. Coward telephones to say that *Nearby* has been accepted by the People's Book Club and that a check for $10,000 will shortly be coming to me.

Oh!

What can I say? Thankfulness so immense spills over everything.

January, 1947

There was an idea growing in me. *Nearby* took time, five years really; and this would, too. It had to do with finding freedom within limitations. What started me was standing by the south window in the living room one morning and looking out at the snow whirling across the field. The wind was wild, free one might say. Before me on the table was a pot of white cyclamen, a dozen blooms, like white birds poised and resting, free in another way:

> *Beyond*
> *was a flawless expanse of snow*
> *from which slim trees rose dark and nude.*
> *The wind swept high, the wind swung low,*
> *ecstatic in its solitude.*
> *Scattering drifts in rampaging delight,*
> *the wind roared on in the path of the night.*

Within
was a cyclamen full and white,
flowers poised like birds to wing a world,
buoyantly resting, gay and light.
The pot was only where roots lay curled
for the cyclamen was free. And the wind—
was it more so, being undisciplined?

It was a difficult idea, and it would be a long time before I would be able to talk with Mr. Coward about it.

February 6, 1947

Nearby's first printing, 7,500, went in a month and it is now into a second. I am learning from the reviews. My heart warms to the favorable ones; my mind quickens to the others. Yes, I can see some of the faults in my writing: a tendency to preach, to drive a moral too hard, to tell the reader what to think instead of making a situation so clear that thinking is inevitable. All of this makes me eager to get on to the next book, to see if I can overcome my faults.

The letters were fabulous. One delighted me especially: "That title is wonderful—not only as applied to living democracy but also in living the life that is nearby you now, and not waiting for the right time or better conditions. Just that one word means a tremendous amount." And the letters were coming from the most amazing people and places—from Mrs. Franklin Roosevelt, from the National Education Association, from radio stations asking how available I was for a program, and from teachers all over the country who felt the book spoke for them.

Of all the letters, the most exciting was the one that had the *big* check in it. Bill and I knew exactly what to do with it. We went to the bank and paid off the FHA loan on Shieling.

May, 1947

Mr. Rainie, the lawyer Bill had come to know in Concord, stopped by one afternoon on his way home from Boston. Blunt and always to the point, he wasted no time in telling Bill the purpose of his visit. I went to the kitchen to get tea and before I was back they had settled something. From then on there was nothing but pleasant chat. It wasn't until Mr. Rainie left that Bill told me what they had settled.

"The Directors of the New Hampshire Association for the Blind have decided that the organization should become more active. Mr. Rainie went down to Perkins to ask Dr. Farrell if he knew of anyone sympathetic to blindness, with some business experience, who might take on the work. Dr. Farrell said there was a man in their own backyard who could do it and he told Mr. Rainie about me."

"And you're going to do it?"

"Of course. There's a slight catch. He said I'd have to find my own salary, that the funds were limited."

I had seen Bill face too many challenges not to realize that this to him was like the starting gun for a race.

We were soon asked to be present at a meeting of the board of the N.H.A.B. in Concord. Bill was told that they had voted to employ him as Executive Director, beginning September first. He would be the first paid employee the Association had ever had. He was allowed a budget of five thousand dollars for the first year, which was to include all travel and expenses, his own stipend, and the salary of a secretary. It was not unlike the arrangement I had entered into with A. and C. Black when I sold *High Holiday* outright. It had seemed then highly unbusinesslike; it soon proved otherwise.

Bill said as we were driving home, "It's a start. I have a chance to serve the blind, and my blindness is going to be my greatest asset."

August, 1947

Holden Greene came into our life again. As Nora's work expanded and her longer stay was an accepted fact, it was clear that she needed more than a bedroom-studio. Attached to the barn was a carriage shed, which had no other use than to hold wood, tools, and things that could easily be stored elsewhere. We saw it as a home for Nora. Holden studied it, made plans for it, and soon had his remarkable workmen on the job. The sills were sound, the uprights sturdy, and of the roof-beam Holden said, "You could hang a church on it."

In a few weeks, the shed was transformed into a dwelling for an artist. There was a fireplace, a tiny kitchen unit, a small room down-stairs, and a large room with exposed beams upstairs, and all the facilities. Windows were long and wide, but many-paned, as they would have been in the old days. The view, more sweeping than that from the house itself, looked across barnyard and field to the East Mountains. There was a little porch made by extending the roof, and a flagged path that joined the Studio to Shieling. Holden had thought of everything—big shelves for art papers, drawers for tools, and the pegs that had been used to hold harnesses were soon holding easels and the pieces of equipment that were part of an artist's life. Linda, Bonnibel's daughter, had long ago attached herself to Nora. Now grown to a reliable age, she became Nora's companion. On the very day that the work was finished, Nora moved across the lawn with her books and papers, clothes, tools, work in progress, and Linda's basket.

Getting breakfast on Sunday morning had always been Nora's joyous rite. The kitchen was hers, and Bill and I did not appear until she called to us, and breakfast was always the same—cornbread and scrambled eggs, with the fruit that was at its best at the time; it might be raspberries from our own patch or blueberries from near hill slopes. This Sunday was no different. But even before the first cup of coffee was poured, Nora's Canticle of the Studio was read to us.

> *Praise Thee, Lord, for Brother Studio,*
> *Who is so dear and friendly and quiet.*
> *For the beauty of craftsmanship and skill of mind*
> *That did fashion all his amenities—*

And then it went on to praise Brother Barn and Sister Shieling, Fire and Wood and Stone and Mountain View and Little Lin. Everything was wrapped up in a paean of thanksgiving for

> *Precious hours, long and quiet, spent herein, with*
> *Rich reward of peace and joy and creativity.*

Breakfast itself, when it followed, was a long amen.

September, 1947

Bill was busy all summer making plans for his work. First was to find a secretary, a man who had bookkeeping and secretarial skills, who could drive, and who would be willing to turn himself to tasks around Shieling when a man's hand was needed. Bill would not have time now to carry on with many of the little chores that he had assumed as his. An ad in a Boston paper brought several responses, and one was exactly right, but he was not able to start until October. I did all I could that month to help Bill get going.

Office space was needed and for that, the guest room, with its patterns on the walls, answered. A card table, file boxes, and a braillewriter soon changed its appearance and limited us as to guests, but only for a while. Bill was already visualizing an office in Concord and much time traveling throughout the state. He had mastered braille to the extent that he made his own notes as I read him lists of cities, towns and their populations, and lists of names of people to be approached. Nora constructed for him a map of New Hampshire with raised lines for counties, raised dots for communities, and real humps for mountain ranges. Bill had a small stylus and pad that was pocket size, and at any time of day or night he could makes notes and read them back.

Once he had familiarized himself with the state, he set out making a list of the people he wanted to call on. The lists were of men and women well known for their activities and for their financial support of good causes. First on the list was the name of a former governor, Huntley Spaulding, known for his stature and his generosity. Bill made constant use of the telephone, and his warm voice rippling over the wire said more, and more immediately, than the words of a letter. His intent was to make the work of the N.H.A.B. known, as well as its need for funds. When he phoned Governor Spaulding, he was invited to call the next week.

So we drove to Rye and called on Governor Spaulding. I was very much the background person and kept myself so, for, though I am Bill's wife, I am, in this instance, his driver and his secretary. I listened attentively to their conversation, but took no part in it. Bill had discovered some of Mr. Spaulding's interests and he spoke of them. They both talked about England and of baseball as compared with cricket. Quite casually Bill mentioned the work of the N.H.A.B., but he moved from it to other areas of interest and commented on the view of the ocean that was seen from the Spaulding house. Rye Beach is a lovely part of New Hampshire's brief coastline, and I had admired the expanse and described it to Bill as he and I walked up to the house.

We left after about an hour, and the two men shook hands as if they had known each other for a much longer time. I was amazed that nothing, nothing whatever, had been said about money, and I thought that had been the purpose of our visit. Safely in the car and headed for home, I turned to Bill in exasperation.

"But, Bill, you never told him you needed funds to get the N.H.A.B. going."

"Of course not."

"But that was the whole point of our coming over."

He turned and looked at me. Schooled as I was to keep my eyes on the road ahead when driving, I turned only just enough to see the inscrutable look on his face and the smile behind it.

"You never talk about the money you want, you talk about other things."

"But I don't see—"

"You will."

October, 1947

T.K. had arrived and the first letter Bill dictated to him was one of thanks to Governor Spaulding for a very generous contribution to the work of the N.H.A.B. I learned my lesson.

Things happened rapidly. A small office was set up in Concord, and Bill was there three or four days every week. That ruled out the possibility of his having a Seeing Eye dog. Too much driving was necessitated and walking is requisite for a dog. We had Bonnibel in the house, Linda in the studio, and in their different ways they lavished their love on Bill. He returned it in a manner that delighted them.

November 3, 1947

This day I begin work with the idea that has been teasing my mind for months. I have been reading a great deal about mental illness. I've had time to think. Now that my pencils are sharpened and a pad is under my hand, I hope words will come. I have the title, *Beloved Bondage*. Perhaps that's enough for one day.

November 20, 1947

The work goes slowly these days as I feel my way, seeing the story that is in the idea. The background is all there, and the characters, but I've not been quite sure where it is going. Then suddenly, today, I saw it clearly—the three stories, John's, Althea's, Louisa's, three approaches to the same problem. I have dwelt with it so long that now it is clear in my mind. I seem to be listening and taking down what I hear. In *Nearby*, I wanted to expose and then extinguish prejudice, so in this book I want to let in light that there may be more understanding of people who suffer mental illness.

After talking with a psychiatrist, and with a nurse in a mental hospital, I begin to feel sure of my direction. I look forward to their help when the story is ready for checking. The doctor said an amazing thing, that 90 percent of the people confined to state hospitals have become the way they are because of selfishness. That bears out my feeling about Althea's condition.

December, 1947

I had two days in New York, seeing friends and publishers. Mr. Coward took me to luncheon at the Yale Club. I told him about the story, a bit fearfully and breathlessly, but his interest was keen and kindly. He felt that this book would be a real turning point for me and said that his firm intended to get back of it and do everything to establish it. He liked my three-way approach, but thought I had set myself a hard task. "But novel writing is hard," he said, and smiled as if to comfort me. He asked if I would like an advance and I said no thank you, not until I had a typescript on his desk.

"And when will that be?"

I couldn't say for sure.

December 31, 1947

My year-end task: adding up in my little ledger the moneys received. This time the total is in five figures.

1948

Amos and Violet

January 2, 1948

Back at my desk and hoping for long uninterrupted hours. Mr. Coward would like to have the finished work sometime in April. Can I possibly do it? Part One, John's story, about 35,000 words, is done.

January, 1948

The middle part was the most difficult, but in three weeks that was done and I could swing into Althea's story. The words came so quickly that I could hardly bear to stop writing. It was not easy to sleep; so much that wants to be said kept tumbling through my mind.

To understand Althea better, I took a course in rug hooking at the Sharon Arts Center on Thursday evenings. For three hours I sat at my frame, as did six other people at theirs, with strips of colored wool slowly being drawn into patterns. Our instructor was wise and gentle. She helped me keep the finished design always in mind while I approached it slowly. A murmur of conversation flowed around the room. How different this creativity is from that of a writer, working alone and always in quiet. Doing this made me feel like Althea, growing strong in herself as she worked out of herself.

February 19, 1948

It is 6 P.M. and I've been at my desk all day, since Bill left for Concord after an early breakfast. He has a talk to give tonight in the north country, so he and T.K. will not be back until tomorrow. Now I can say that the last words have been written. I have been tired often during these weeks, but there is no feeling like this, for suddenly there is nothing more to say, and nothing more in me. A pile of manuscript pages, something like 90,000 words, looks up at me from my desk.

March 1, 1948

My goal is to revise twenty chapters in as many days, and some-

With Nora,

and Linda and Bonnibel

on the front stoop, at Shieling

where in the middle of the revising, I'll start typing the first chapters.

March, 1948

The first part, John's story, was revised and typed. A copy went to the psychiatrist for her checking. These were days of unremitting work, nights of broken sleep, as it all kept going over and over in my mind. Sections came back from the doctor and they carried her "approval of your theme and its outcome." The nurse cheered me after her first reading. "It was a difficult assignment you elected for your talents, but I had no fear of the outcome. It took the Yates balance of head and heart—of sensitive discernment and sympathetic writing—to handle well such a subject."

April, 1948

On this perfect spring day when there was a sense of the newborn everywhere, *Beloved Bondage* was finished. All the typed pages went into a box, wrapped and addressed to Mr. Coward. I got it to the post office minutes before the last mail went out. Alleluia!

May, 1948

Mr. Coward phoned me. He liked it, the Althea parts especially. He suggested a few changes which I could easily make and send the new pages down to him.

Two weeks later Mr. Coward had another feeling. He thought the three approaches were not good and that the whole story should be rewritten. I gave his comment deep and earnest thought, then explained my feeling in a letter to him. To change so radically would be to write a whole new book, and this I could not do.

How easily editors use the telephone! In ten days Mr. Coward called. Astonishingly he agreed with me. The book was to go through as I wrote it, as I saw it. A contract would be in the mail within the next few days. Did I wish to have a dedication? If so, it was to be sent soon, as they were moving right ahead with production. I sent it, and it was an impersonal dedication but one deeply felt—*"To all librarians; especially to those who have helped me through the years and who, by their own love for books, have guided me into high and happy adventures."*

Dedications are such a meaningful way of repaying indebtedness. Two books were dedicated to Bill, *Patterns* to my mother, and *Mountain Born* to my father.

June, 1948

I had to accept the fact that giving talks is as much a part of a writer's life as answering letters, for requests came to me from schools and clubs and libraries, all sorts of groups. Some want to make dates as much as a year ahead. I accepted what seemed right and reasonable, and what fitted in with the life of Shieling. As with everything, I asked Bill for help. He had done much speaking during his business career, and it was part of his work as he made the N.H.A.B. known throughout the state.

He reminded me of my lessons with Edith Clements during that first year in London: to stand tall and breathe from my toes, to hum frequently and feel the resonance, to loosen my tongue with exercises like "Peter Piper picked a peck of pickled peppers" and "Sister Susie's sewing shirts for soldiers."

"Ten people, or fifty, or five hundred in your audience," he said, "it makes no difference. Find one who appeals to you, preferably in the last row, and direct your words—not your gaze—to that person. Weave your humor in with the whole. Don't tell a story just because it's funny, but because it fits."

He held up his right hand, fingers wide spread. "There are really just five things for you to remember, not like a memory exercise, but build them into you so they become part of you." As he enumerated, he took one off each finger.

"Think what the occasion demands and plan accordingly. Write your talk first, then make a brief outline on three-by-five-inch cards and have them to refer to so you won't wander. Drive into your subject at the start and find a point of contact with your audience. Enjoy the telling; if you do, they will enjoy the listening. And it's like writing, stop when you've said what you had to say."

He dropped his hand. Five fingers had done their work, but he had one more point to make: "Be yourself."

"What if my knees shake?"

"Let them shake. It's your voice that matters."

When people come up to me after a talk, just looking into their smiling faces gives me a feeling that the borders of friendship are constantly widening. Sometimes it's an autograph people want, and here I have my rule: Gladly will I sign one or a dozen books, but not little slips of paper.

July, 1948

Lillian came for three days. I still marvel at the way editors came to visit, but she had reasons—to talk with Nora and Bill about *Andy,* and to bring me up to date on the books I've done for her. We did enjoy each other. She brought with her a copy of *Publishers*

Weekly in which Coward-McCann had a full-page announcement of
Beloved Bondage.

On Friday we took Lillian to the Amos Fortune Forum, a lecture
series given in the old Meeting House in Jaffrey Center and named
after a notable citizen of a century or more ago—a freed slave. We
got there early. It was a lovely evening, and I suggested going out to
the graveyard to see the stone that marks Amos Fortune's grave, but
Lillian and Bill were comfortably settled and already deep in conversation. So I went alone. In the gentle evening, with the light beginning to deepen beyond Monadnock and a late thrush singing, I
read the words on the stones of Amos and his wife, Violet, and
thought what an accounting, lives so simply lived, so complete! And
yet I wanted to know more.

How? Why? What? Pursuing me were the questions that pursue
the mind of a writer and will not let it rest until they are answered.
Eight strokes sounded from the great clock on the spire of the
Meeting House so I went back to join Lillian and Bill, but I didn't
hear a word of the lecture. My mind was full of the man for whom
the lecture series had been named.

Before Lillian left for New York, she asked me if I had anything in
mind. I said yes, but that it might deal with the later years of an old
man. Would young people ever be interested in such a book?

She said, "Young people are interested in character wherever,
whenever, it appears. Age does not matter if the story is a living
one."

Lillian wrote in our guest book, "To come to Shieling is like
coming home."

August, 1948

So. She who walks like a teacher has become a teacher!

Asked to conduct a workshop at the University of New Hampshire's Writers Conference, I was tempted to say no to the director,
Carroll Towle. I wondered if I could ever fulfill such an assignment.
Then I realized that the request wouldn't have come to me if I
couldn't do it, so I accepted. After all, there was no work on my
desk calling for attention, Nora was part of Shieling and would
assume my responsibilities, Bonnibel had no puppies on the way,
and the garden at the midpoint of summer was able to take care of
itself. I arrived in Durham on the first Sunday of August, ready to
take up my duties, but feeling very scared and green. However, I
talked with the poet Rolfe Humphries, who was also lecturing at the
conference, and after that I was a different person.

"Be yourself. Give them what you are. If you find that what they have submitted to you is not of the first order, get them to talk about themselves, draw them out. There is always a potential. Look for and develop it." Then, as if he had not said quite all, he added, "It may surprise you what they reveal and you discover."

After I got to know Rolfe better, and as a colleague, I stirred up my courage to show him some of my poems. He read them slowly, then asked me what I thought of them.

"I suppose they're just jingles, really."

"Oh no, they are like you. They have delicacy and dignity. But how seriously do you take them?"

I had to say not very, that my novels were my main interest and always would be.

He didn't say anything in particular when he handed my papers back to me. If he had, it would have been words like those Mr. Coward used: "Stick to your last."

The two weeks at the conference included morning lectures, reading of manuscripts submitted, individual meetings with the students, and an evening talk. Some work turned in to me was good, some was not, but in each piece and in every person there was always something that could be seriously considered. At the end I was tired, almost beyond refreshing. But Carroll Towle renewed me. "Your sincerity and capacity to inspire have been invaluable," he said. "Will you come back next year?"

September 23, 1948

Beloved Bondage has arrived, the first copy, mine. Two colors predominate and they are my favorites—blue for the binding, brick for the jacket. Nora did the design, and the two heads, John's and Althea's, are beautiful. How the title stands out in Nora's calligraphy! The book, even on the outside, looks like a mature piece of work. It has a feeling of substance. Tonight I have the greatest of all joys: I start reading it aloud to Bill.

October, 1948

A telegram came saying that the People's Book Club had taken *Beloved Bondage*. Mr. Coward said he couldn't be more pleased. Nor could I.

The reviews were good, strong and reassuring. *The New York Times* had said of *Nearby* that I wrote "shining prose warmed by strong conviction and gentle faith." Then the *Boston Herald* was saying of *Beloved Bondage* that it "has a transcendent quality of spiritual values which gives it a deeper meaning and validity." There were some reviews that were acidulous, but I thought they were from people who did not understand it. More important than the reviews were the letters that came, especially those that said, as one did, "This has helped me to live my life."

The family urged me to come to Buffalo, and I did, for two days. The life at Hillhurst was filled with the old joys, and there was, as well, an autographing party at a bookstore, some picture-taking, and a radio interview. Yet so much was the same. On the train back I made this notation in my Think Book: "Remember the wisdom of not going public where family can congregate. They will never see you as the world does, and nothing is gained by taxing their credulity. Meet them on your own ground at Shieling as much as possible; elsewhere only if the need is imperative."

November 6, 1948

A day to remember, and the twelve red roses were more meaningful than ever. Bill said, "Do you realize that you have that many books now bearing your name?"

1949

Imprint of a Man

Winter, 1949

The idea that took hold of me last summer as I stood by the two headstones in the little graveyard in Jaffrey Center would not let me go. There was a story if I could find my way into it. I did the reading available, two chapters in the *Town History*, but there was so much more I wanted to know, needed to know. What had Amos Fortune's life been before he purchased his freedom and came to Jaffrey to establish himself as a tanner? Tanning was a subject about which I knew little, and there would be much reading ahead of me if I were to establish some kind of background.

First, I wanted to make sure that I would not be trespassing on another writer; so I queried many people—citizens of the town, ministers, retired professors living in the area—and always I was given the same answer: "But there's nothing known about him, only those last twenty years of his life that are in the *Town History.*"

I had a persistent feeling that though nothing was known, much could be found out about this man who was "born free in Africa a slave in America. . .purchased liberty professed Christianity lived reputably and died hopefully." He was no ordinary man. His memory had left an imprint, but he himself had left a sum of money "for the school." The modest amount has increased with the years, but the Amos Fortune Fund is still carried in the town books and used in some way from time to time, in Amos Fortune's words, "as the town sees fit to educate its sons and daughters."

The road was mine to follow, and no bird dog on a scent was more determined than was I.

From the public library in Jaffrey and from the State Library in Concord, I gathered books for a winter of reading: *The Negro in Colonial America; Rum, Romance and Rebellion; Social History of New England; From Slavery to Freedom; Negro Musicians and Their Music.* I found a book about early methods of tanning. Old newspapers gave me nothing about the man, but a great deal about the times in which he lived. I knew that his will was on file in the Cheshire County Courthouse in Keene. I knew that the

The Amos Fortune cover

with the

John Newbery Medal

house he built on the bank of Tyler Brook was still lived in.

I commenced a search back to the towns in which he had lived before he had come to Jaffrey. Town clerks were helpful and interested, opening to me the vital statistics of years long past. When I came upon his name, it was like a handclasp across the years. With his will in my hands, I could see what possessions he had and how he disposed of them, and I could run the tip of my finger over his own signature. Among those who helped me was Evelyn Ruffle, the librarian in Jaffrey. She finally discovered the whereabouts of his papers that had been "lost" for half a century: his freedom paper that was his passport to life as his own man; the bills of sale for Lydia and Violet; the indenture paper for his Negro apprentice, Simon Peter; and one for the white boy, Charles Toothaker; the neat receipts he gave to people and requested of them. All these were found and, even more, they could be handled and studied.

I often went by the small house he had built for himself and Violet, but I never asked to go in, for at that time it did not seem quite right. I knew where the pool was in the brook, where he had soaked hides before tanning them. The Meeting House where he had worshiped, though no longer a place of worship, was familiar to me. And, to keep contact, I would go to the graveyard to stand by the stones, classic in their simplicity, equal in height, slim slate stones that had taken the weather since 1801, as he had taken the weather of his ninety-one years and Violet, her seventy-three.

Sometimes a friend would ask me what I was doing with myself, and my reply was the brief one, "Reading." Yes, it was a winter of reading, note taking, thinking.

Bill knew of my search and comforted me, so did Nora, and Lillian was always the prod. When I told her in desperation at the beginning that there was so little to go on, she insisted there was plenty. "What you don't have at hand you can find out."

I was doing exactly that, and the fragments were beginning to fit together like the pieces of a puzzle.

Reading books about the slave trade harrowed my heart, and there were many times when I wondered if I could possibly go on.

"Watch out," Lillian said in her commanding way, "or you'll be writing a tract about man's inhumanity, and where will that get you? You have a story to tell, tell it."

She was right and all my instincts said to me that the story was the account of a man living his life against great odds and triumphing over them. I climbed Monadnock and measured myself against the mountain, as he must have done while living in its shadow: great mass of rock shaped by aeons of time, great man shaped by the events of his life, both looking skyward. And as the weeks went on, I felt that I knew this man.

There was much I could put together from what I read and from the countryside, which is mine as it was his, and from the clues I followed that took me to the wharf at Boston where he was sold as a slave and given his name; but I had to imagine the life in Africa. My first chapter would be built from what I read about the tribal customs, the conditions, the raiders, the journey across the Atlantic. A high pile of books stood on one side of my desk, a small pile of notes on the other. When would I know I had enough background? When would I begin to write?

May, 1949

Spring came slowly, with much cold and grayness, but with a beauty of bud and blossom and birdsong that seemed unlike anything before. The crabapple tree was a fountain of bloom. The swallows filled the air with their exultation, then dove into the barn on family business. And suddenly I was ready to write! The reference books went back to the libraries that secured them for me. I had all I needed in my notes, and perhaps more than I needed in my heart. This had happened to me before. I should trust and know that it will always happen. When a story is ready to be written, the words will be there.

Lillian asked Nora to do the illustrations, and, though Nora was involved in other work, she began some preliminary sketches—the house in Jaffrey, the church, the stones, tanning tools. She climbed Monadnock for views she would need. She could do a great deal even before she had a draft from me to work with.

So I started to write and it all came together. When summer intervened, I would put it away for a while. The time between would give me a perspective.

Summer, 1949

The days are long and light. Bill is home more and we have time to talk. When we first met we so often talked about God—the Being that transcends and enfolds all religions, the Being beyond all churches and creeds. I keep wondering what I believe. Bill makes it all so simple.

"There's only one relationship—ours to God. There's only one Way—living love."

I talk about creeds and their formalities, inwardly resisting them.

"Why do you feel so driven?"

"Because I must be honest with myself." As soon as I say that, I realize that one can impale the spirit on such determination.

"The manner by which the Way is found," Bill reminds me gently, "is not so important as living the Way."

"Creeds help, don't they—shaping, guiding, preparing us?"

"Yes, of course, but they can confine, too, putting limits on that in man which should always keep expanding and growing."

I didn't say anything.

"You'll work things out for yourself, you always do, and then you'll put what you've found into your next book."

How well he knows me!

And so we go on, never wanting to arrive at any conclusion, for that might terminate the search, the reaching. Bill has gone much further along the Way than I have—the tenor of his life shows that. I seem to have to keep finding things out for myself, holding to what is right for me just as I hold to what is right for my books.

The past months I have been so filled with Amos and his search for freedom, the way he was compelled to give it to others after he had secured it for himself. What gave him such persistence? Could it not have been part of his search for the reality of God?

July, 1949

Bill had a project which he hoped to work on sometime. It was a book, of course. He and Nora spent hours talking about it and planning the illustrations. It grew from a hump in the lawn between the house and the barn, the hump is Old Joe. In the days when our Shieling was a working farm, Joe was one of the horses. Every day he delivered milk in the village, becoming so accustomed to the route that, even without words from the man who walked beside him or held the reins, he would stop and go forward again from one house to the next. No doubt he had many rewards: pats, a carrot, a lump of sugar, and the kind of words an animal thrives on.

Joe was only five or six at the time of the Civil War, when the need for horses was great. He was mustered into service, wounded, hospitalized, returned to service. After Appomattox he was honorably discharged, was returned to Peterborough, and resumed his milk route as if he had never been away. He lived to a good age and, always having been a part of the family, was buried between house and barn.

Something about Old Joe appealed to Bill, and Nora, too, and they were confident about getting him into a book. Old Joe became a part of our family philosophy of always having something ahead to look forward to.

August, 1949

After my first week at the University of New Hampshire I could say that the Conference was more exciting than the year before and I felt much more competent. There were many new students, but those from last year had tales of work sold and were eager to show work in progress. The hours were long, the reading voluminous, but I would not have had it otherwise. I recalled something James M. Barrie once said: "Work is never hard unless you'd rather be doing something else." Next to writing myself, there is nothing I would rather do than help people with their writing. It's a challenge to me as much as to them to direct them to the stories that need to be told, the stories that they can tell.

October, 1949

After three months away from my desk, I came back to Amos. There was much to be done, but the work was all there, and it read better than I thought. The time away mellowed it, but it also showed me places where I could tighten, and other places where a thought could be further developed. A small, but to me important, bit of new material came to light about Amos' wife, Violet. It gave more meaning to the words about her on the slate headstone: "By marriage his wife by her fidelity his friend and solace." Nothing could hinder me now until I came to the end, the closing period of his life, and the title was there, the title that says it all, *Amos Fortune, Free Man.*

December 15, 1949

The finished pages went to Lillian today. It has been tremendous to do. I have felt so close to a man whose humility and love for others shone like beacons.

December 20, 1949

Editors have a curious way of showing approval. Lillian telephoned to say that my typescript had already gone into production and that the title was right for the story. Would I be able to read the galleys soon and when would Nora send her finished work?

December, 1949

I told Bill of a dream I had, one of those dreams that are so filled with color and so uncluttered that they do not disperse on waking, but stay with all their clarity into the morning and so into forever. I was an archer with bow in hand and a quiver full of arrows over my shoulder. There was a target—gold, red, blue circles, and, in the center, the bull's-eye was black. I fitted an arrow into my bow, drew the cord, let the arrow fly, and it went to the bull's-eye, to the very center.

"Some dreams are hard to interpret," Bill said. "This one is easy."

"What do you mean?"

"You'll see."

Year's End, 1949

Hungry for a holiday, we went to Williamsburg for Christmas— the Yule log, the wassail bowl, the fragrance of many candles, the warmth of great fires, the sight of cardinals on a lawn dusted with snow, and Nora describing it all to Bill as only an artist can. The week crowned the year for each one of us.

1950–1951

A New Voice

January, 1950

On the grayest of gray days with a cold rain falling I began to write the *Olive*. It had been in the back of my mind ever since I discovered Roxbury Center, a wooded hilltop where all that remains of a once-thriving community are cellar holes. There is a small white church, where dried and faded ropes of ground pine spoke of Christmas services, and there is a well-kept graveyard. On the slate stones the name Freelove appears often. It was clearly a feminine family name, and I speculated on the tenderness of its early meaning. Once I had my setting, and that unusual name, the characters began to form in my mind, gathering their own identities.

I called it *Thou, Being a Wild Olive* from that allusive verse in Romans (ch. 11:24): "For if thou wert cut out of the olive tree which is wild by nature, and wert graffed contrary to nature into a good olive tree; how much more shall these, which be the natural branches, be graffed into their own olive tree?" I had a feeling that Mr. Coward would want a title better suited to a novel, and if he didn't, the trade department would. And that would be all right. After all, I had only to write the book, they would have to sell it, and a title goes a long way in that direction. This was a story that would embrace some of the conflicts and struggles that I'd recently been through within myself, struggles to know what I really believed. But it was also about country things and a deep, pure love.

February, 1950

Back to the *Olive*, but I did have to take some time off to read the galleys on *Amos*. It's exciting when a story is ready to be written, what happens—often unexpectedly. It was becoming Benedict's story—the influence of his life, the riches of its lovingness on one particular person. I'm not always sure, at this point, where I'm going, but I trust the idea to develop itself.

April 3, 1950

Nearing the end. Chapter twenty-five, and now I ask myself is it all

Signing books

for young readers

just words—400 pages, 80,000 words—or have I really said something?

April 5, 1950

On this raw and misty day I write the last lines, now for the hard part—the revision: the part I like best of all.

April, 1950

Lillian telephoned to say that *Amos Fortune* had won the *Herald Tribune* Spring Festival Award as the best book for older children. The presentation would be in New York on May 5, and this time I must come down to receive it and the check myself. When Bill got home from Concord and I told him, he said, "Remember your dream?"

May, 1950

Home again after such a satisfying two days—one given over to Lillian and the *Herald Tribune,* the other to Mr. Coward. When I met Mrs. Van Doren and accepted from her the check, we both recalled the day in 1929 when she had given me some books to review. "I can see you've been broadening your field," she said. I agreed, "But you helped me get started." I felt as grateful for that good memory as I was for the check that I held in my hand.

The next day was with Mr. Coward. I had two chapters of the *Olive* typed and an outline for the rest. He liked it, all but the title, and planned to make it their fall fiction if I could have it all to him by the end of May. The calendar told me I would have twenty-six working days: It almost seemed impossible, but, given a challenge, anything is possible. We discussed titles. The one I used was the scaffolding and its only purpose was to support the story.

"How about *City on a Hill*? Or *A Lantern Only*?"

Suddenly *Guardian Heart* came out of the blue nothing, as titles often do. It says what the book is, and we both liked it. He insisted on giving me an advance, and the check is in four figures.

"But it isn't all typed," I remonstrated.

He smiled. "It will be."

June, 1950

At 1:35 A.M. June 3, I finished the typing and got my box of many pages in the mail when the post office opened. I missed the date agreed on by a few days but had been assured that it would not matter.

October 1, 1950

Guardian Heart was published on the twenty-ninth of September, and today there is a full-page ad and a super review in the *Herald Tribune*. Mr. Coward telephones to say that the *Christian Herald* Family Bookshelf has taken the book for their January selection. My cup runneth over.

October 15, 1950

How is it that I feel at such a low ebb—wondering if I've ever written anything worth reading, wondering if I'll ever write anything again? Everything gets harder to do. Nothing is easy.

"Why, Bill, must this be so?"

"Because your standard keeps going up. You'll never be entirely satisfied. You wouldn't want to be."

We're cutting a new trail in the woods. When I can't get anywhere with words, I put my pencil down, pick up my brush cutter and hatchet and head for the woods. Working hard and being able to see accomplishment helps me get level with myself again.

Perhaps I am in a fallow time. If that is good for the land, it must be good for the mind.

November 6, 1950

Red roses, yes, but a necklace of gold links, too; more than a manifest of twenty-one years, they are a symbol of forever.

December 20, 1950

A Christmas letter from Martha came to fill in the time we've been out of touch with, but never unaware of, each other. "You know of my marriage in Buffalo in 1928 to the handsome Dutchman, Franciscus Visser 't Hooft, a graduate of Delft University with doctor's degrees in Science and Engineering. Presently he is president of a chemical company here in Buffalo. For some years I was a veritable Mother Hen with two daughters and a son, so my descent into the New York Art World was delayed. I now have a big studio outside the house which enables me to spend hours alone and undisturbed to paint, and the family are encouraging and supportive. I've been exhibiting all along, winning numerous awards and feel that I am well on my way as you are. I'm sending you an invitation to my second solo exhibition at Contemporary Arts Gallery, Inc., New York. Being with this gallery has opened the opportunity of being selected for many national exhibitions as well as future ones at the Whitney and other museums, with a possible purchase by the Whitney. Little did we dream, during those early days in New York, where our paths would lead us, but both of us followed a vision: hard work and self-discipline, obtaining some of our goals. You have been painting pictures with words, I with my brush, and we'll continue to tap our creative energies with excitement. And so, back to my easel!"

February, 1951

It was one of the days when Bill worked at home and I was glad, for how could I have stood it if he had not been here? I was in the kitchen making a birthday cake for a young friend of ours who was having her party at Shieling that afternoon, February 16. When the mail came, Bill went out for it. He came into the kitchen with it in his hands.

"Something important for you. I had to sign for it."

It was a letter with the gold of a Special Delivery stamp on it, from an address in Portland, Oregon, and the name of someone in the Children's Library Association. I opened it, wondering why anyone so far away should be in such a hurry. I couldn't believe what I was seeing until I read it aloud to Bill.

"*Amos Fortune* has been given the Newbery Medal as 'the most distinguished contribution to American literature for children.'"

Oh!

We called to Nora, we put the kettle on, and the dogs danced around us in excitement. We moved into the sunny living room, read and reread the letter, poured cup after cup of tea, and rejoiced. The medal belonged to us all: to Bill, whom I had thanked in the acknowledgments "for the confidence he gives me when I assign to myself what seems to be an almost impossible task." To Nora, to whom the book is dedicated, "dear partner in many books and good friend through the years." Her sensitive, careful illustrations brought Amos and his time alive and made the countryside real.

Then the telephone rang. It was Lillian, telling me that, though the news was not to be made public until May 5, and the medal not to be presented until July 10, I must start now writing my acceptance speech. *The Horn Book* would need to have it by April to be printed in the July issue.

"How can I ever do anything so far ahead?"

Her reply was crisp: "You can."

"What do I say?"

"The road you have come by, the way you went about doing *Amos*."

The cake did get finished, the little girl had her party, and when she blew out the candles, no one wished harder than I in my joy that her wish would come true. When I went to bed that night, still almost unbelieving, words of my old friend, George MacDonald, kept coming to me: "It's just so good it must be true."

March, 1951

To New York for the gathering in Mr. Melcher's office with just the few concerned there and several librarians. Katherine Milhous who was to receive the Caldecott Medal for her book *The Egg Tree* was there with her editor; Lillian and I for the Newbery. There were congratulations all around and many kind words were said, pictures were taken, and reporters asked questions that the editors were better able to answer than the medalists.

When Lillian saw me off on the night train for Boston, she said, in that no-nonsense way of hers, "Now, write your speech."

I felt as though the latent fires in me had been kindled, for ideas that had been in the back of my mind were all coming forward, and I wanted to write them. Bill was as firm as Lillian. "Do what you must do first and get that speech done. What you want to do can come later." So I worked on the speech, going way back into my childhood with its desire to write and coming up through the years. I described the search for Amos' story, and inevitably my own philosophy crept in. There was only one possible title: Climbing Some Mountain in the Mind.

Bill, too, had an assignment from *The Horn Book,* and he spent hours on it. T.K. typed it and Bill didn't show it to me until it was all finished.

"Oh, Bill, you've remembered so much about me, about our life."

"Just some important things. I couldn't cover all our years."

"It doesn't have a title."

"Title enough," he said.

So our work was done and the two papers went to *The Horn Book* in good time.

The news was getting around, for letters were crowding the mail-box, and I must take time to answer them. They were from all kinds of readers—young people, of course, but teachers, and ministers, some of my students from the University of New Hampshire, and many friends. One from a twelve-year-old boy in the Midwest gave me utter joy. "Amos Fortune must have been a great guy. Did you know him?"

Did I!

April 1, 1951

Lillian tells me there are three thousand copies of *Amos Fortune, Free Man* at the Colonial Press in Stow, Massachusetts, waiting to be autographed. They have been ordered by libraries all over the country. I am to do them as soon as possible. Writing my name 3,000 times? Why, I could write a whole story with that number of words. It is less than an hour's drive to Stow and through pleasant country. The Press has set up a table for me in a corner where I can work. It is stacked with books; as they are done more books are brought on large dollies.

April, 1951

It took me three days. Stopping for an hour at noon to eat my sandwich and limber my fingers, I could not do more than a thousand a day. It was an experience. As I wrote my name, I tried to think how special each book would be to a particular library, to the children who would read it, but by the end of the third day I had to hold on to myself to keep from writing it wrong—Amos Yates did not look right, nor did Elizabeth Fortune.

"You've earned a treat," Bill said, so we combined a day in Boston, when he had an appointment with Dr. Barton, with a swan boat ride and luncheon at the Ritz.

After Bill's time, Dr. Barton asked to see me alone. I thought he wanted to give me some special word about Bill, but it was me. He didn't like the swelling on my throat and said I was to come down to the Hahnemann Hospital in Boston as soon as he could make the arrangements.

"But I can't. I have an important speech to give in Chicago in July."

He was firm. "I will explain to Bill." He did when we went out to the waiting room.

Bill was wonderful. He seemed to understand much more clearly than I what Dr. Barton was saying, what it might mean or not mean, and when we left the office I felt his courage becoming mine.

May, 1951

I was in the hospital four days and when I got back to Shieling it was with a bandaged neck and a voice like a whisper. Dr. Barton had told Bill and assured me that the tissue was benign and there was nothing to be concerned about. "Let your strength be your guide," he said to me.

So there I was, feeling like royalty as I sat in the garden and was waited on. The weakness I knew at first was beginning to go and every day strength came back to me like an incoming tide. But energy, where was it? I couldn't have written a page if I tried, but I could rest in the realization that the acceptance speech was written a month ago.

The garden never seemed more lovely, the birds more songful; perhaps because I was sitting in it, not working in it. The dogs cozied up to me. Nora brought cups of tea. Bill read aloud from his braille books. When I was by myself I had on my lap those typed pages, and I familiarized myself with them so that when the time came to give the speech it would roll from me as easily as talking.

June, 1951

Nora and I went to Boston and Dr. Barton checked the healing of the scar. He said there was no need to wear even a small bandage now. He was proud of his work. I know how he felt. I am proud of mine when I send a good-looking typescript off to an editor. Then Nora and I went shopping for the dress I would wear at the banquet on July 10. We found it—long, pale green, with the simplicity that is elegance. The neck is just slightly open, giving room for the gold-link necklace Bill gave me on our anniversary and which covers what is left of the scar.

July, 1951

There is always a train letter or a boat letter or a flight letter for the one leaving Shieling from those staying home. So when I tucked myself into my little roomette, with the wheels of the train purring through the darkness, I had two letters to read. Nora's was filled with joyous love and assurances that all would be well at home while I was away. She ended with those remindful words of Benjamin Whichcote's: "It is the chiefest of all Good Things for a Man to be Himself."

Bill's letter was quite long, written in soft pencil on his raised-line pad. It was not always easy to read, but I did not miss a word and I hugged his thoughts to my heart.

". . .You are on your way to the ALA and the Newbery Award. To many, this important event whereby you receive this high recognition will seem as if a new and shining light in the literary heavens had come into focal view. To those who really know you and who have seen you climbing, climbing up the steep trail, it seems more as if you had come to an altitude where the morning sun had found you and revealed you to the many who had not discerned you before. And what do they see? A young woman, youthful but mature, radiating health, strength, poise, modesty, joy, and a deep-lying inner oneness with her world and her Creator. They will not see the years of eager striving, listening, mastering of self and craft. They will see and feel the results. . .people may say you are going to Chicago to receive something. Actually you are going to give, to give more of yourself to more people than ever before. It is a part of your steady climb on the upward trail."

The two days before the program were filled with parties and people and bookstores and all sorts of lovely attentions, but Bill had made me promise to have some "do-nothing time" every day for myself, and I did. He also told me that on the afternoon of the banquet to go to the ballroom where it would be held, ask to see the microphone, and test it to be sure I would feel easy with it. I did. When I went up to my room to change, I thought of all that Miss Clements had told me about deep breathing to get richness into my voice, and those little exercises to limber lips and tongue. When it came time to meet Lillian and move into the evening, I felt ready and calm inside, and exactly right in my new dress.

It was a huge room, that ballroom of the Palmer House. There were twelve hundred people, librarians mostly, editors, publishers, and many who had to do with books in some way. It was all very festive, and people looked their best and happiest. The dinner was delicious, and it was pleasant to have conversation with the guests on either side of me at the head table.

The presentation of the medals and the speeches came after the dinner, and Katherine was first. Her words and her person brought ringing applause. Then Mr. Melcher spoke my name, and I took the few steps that brought me close to him and to the microphone. He said some very nice words when he put the medal in my hands. What could I say but "Thank you." There was applause, then silence, and that silence was my cue.

Standing before the microphone, I felt perfectly comfortable with it as it was in the same position that I had practiced with earlier in the day. I had my pages in a red leather folder, which I placed on the stand before me, but, except for an occasional dropping of my eyes to them, I looked out into all those friendly faces and spoke to them. The words were there, just as when I write on paper the words are there, and my voice seemed strong to me, and sure. Sometimes there was laughter and that gave me a chance to swallow and take a deep breath, and when I spoke of Amos, especially toward the end, there was something very deep. I could feel it coming back to me from that room filled with people.

Later, someone asked, "What do you do with a medal?"

There is no answer, for it is what a medal does to you. I see it as a trust, a symbol, of better work to be. I end these notes as I ended my speech: "And so I go on climbing."

Among the works by Elizabeth Yates

High Holiday

Quest in the Northland

Haven for the Brave

Under the Little Fir

The Journeyman (*formerly* Patterns on the Wall)

Mountain Born

Wind of Spring

Nearby

Once in the Year

Beloved Bondage

Guardian Heart

Amos Fortune, Free Man

Children of the Bible

Brave Interval

A Place for Peter

Hue and Cry

Prudence Crandall, Woman of Courage

Lady from Vermont

The Lighted Heart

The Next Fine Day

Someday You'll Write

Sam's Secret Journal

Howard Thurman, Portrait of a Practical Dreamer

Up the Golden Stair

Is There a Doctor in the Barn?

An Easter Story

With Pipe, Paddle and Song

On That Night

Sarah Whitcher's Story

Skeezer, Dog with a Mission

The Road Through Sandwich Notch

We, the People

A Book of Hours

Call It Zest

The Seventh One

Sound Friendships

Silver Lining

Books edited by Elizabeth Yates

Piskey Folk: A Book of Cornish Legends (1940 & 1996)

The Doll Who Came Alive (1942)

Joseph (1947)

The Christmas Story (1949)

The White Ring (1949)

Your Prayers and Mine (1953 & 1982)

Sir Gibbie (1963 & 1979)